RELIGIOUS EXPERIENCE

its nature, validity, forms, and problems

To my friend & colleague, [name]

With much appreciation,

[signature]

October 2021

by
The Very Reverend Principal
J. Ernest Davey, MA (Cantab) BD (Edin)

Honorary DD of St Andrews, Edinburgh, Belfast and Dublin Universities. Sometime Fellow of King's College, Cambridge. Professor of New Testament and Principal of Faculty, the Presbyterian College, Belfast.

Author, "Our Faith in God through Jesus Christ", "The Changing Vesture of the Faith", "Charles Davey DD, A Memoir", "The Story of a Hundred Years", etc

First paperback edition 2021

Book cover design by Irena Laskowska

ISBNs
Paperback: 978-1-80227-185-0
Hardback: 978-1-80227-187-4
eBook: 978-1-80227-186-7

www.lordalderdice.com

Contents

Foreword

A hundred years have passed since the young Professor J Ernest Davey delivered the 1921 Carey Lectures to members of the public, mostly Presbyterians, in the North of Ireland. After impressive academic achievements at the Universities of Cambridge and Edinburgh he had returned home to Ireland in 1917 to be ordained an assistant minister and appointed by the General Assembly as successor to Professor Heron in the Chair of Church History at Assembly's College in Belfast. He was soon in demand as a speaker and his lectures were published by popular demand. *The Church and The Gospel*, a pamphlet publication of the two lectures he had delivered for the opening and closing of the College's 1917/1918 academic year, was followed in 1922 by a book containing four public lectures under the title *Our Faith in God through Jesus Christ*. Then in 1923 the Carey Lectures that he had given two years previously were published as a volume entitled *The Changing Vesture of the Faith*.

These writings caused quite a stir. For some they were an indication of the exciting contribution this brilliant young theologian could make to the understanding of our Reformed Christian faith, but for others they represented a treacherous intrusion of liberal modernism, and it was not long before he was arraigned before the courts of the church on charges of heresy. He was acquitted and went on to have a very distinguished career at Assembly's College, where he became Principal, and then in 1953, the centenary year of the College, he was elected Moderator of the Presbyterian Church in Ireland by a huge majority, meeting just a few weeks later with Her Majesty, Queen Elizabeth and Prince Philip on their visit to Northern Ireland just after the coronation. Davey remained a very significant contributor to church and public life and was highly regarded, especially by more thoughtful and liberally minded figures across all faiths in Ireland and beyond, but after the trial he published relatively little of a theological nature beyond a few pamphlets, some articles, and a monograph on the Gospel of St John in 1958, shortly before his death in December 1960.

I returned to studying Davey's life some years ago because his heresy trial was a striking example of the struggle between theological liberalism and religious fundamentalism in a community under existential political threat. I was addressing such issues in my work on fundamentalism, radicalization, and terrorism in various parts of the world after the 9/11 attacks in the United States of America. When I read *The Changing Vesture of the Faith* I was profoundly impressed, as a psychoanalytical psychiatrist, by the fact that in the early part of the twentieth century this young Irishman, who was like myself a son of the Presbyterian manse, not only had a clear appreciation of the essential principles of the new science of psychoanalysis, but had adopted this approach in his own thinking and theology, and had taken it beyond the analysis of individuals and applied it to understanding the long-term evolution of faith communities, especially the Christian churches. I could not believe that such a brilliant thinker had not taken his ideas further during the next three decades as an academic at Assembly's College. It seemed to me that the trauma of the heresy trial must have discouraged him from publishing as much as he might otherwise have done, but surely his mind had remained active. I wondered if there was any unpublished work, perhaps some lecture notes, or private writings that could be found.

I was very fortunate because, Paul Gilmore, a good friend of the Davey family and a thoughtful researcher in his own right, was able to access for me a manuscript for a book which Davey had completed shortly before his death. Davey's colleague and successor the Rt Rev Principal, Dr J.L.M. Haire along with the Rev Robert Topping had arranged for some of the chapters of the book to be printed for private circulation, but the book as a whole had never been published. This was very exciting, and indeed as I read the manuscript, I was certain that it was exactly the kind of thing that I had hoped to trace. The quality of the old type-written script made its transcription for digital publication something of a challenge, but this volume now makes available to you, J Ernest Davey's last book-length contribution, *Religious Experience - its nature, validity, forms, and problems*. This was not only his last book, but as he makes clear in the Conclusion, he intended it as a statement of what he saw as 'religious truth' after a lifetime of thought and study as a theological teacher, and he hoped that others would read it and form their own judgement. I have sought to publish it as I found it in the original manuscript, including the list of additional reading at the end, without the modifications of current forms of publication.

I am most grateful to Paul Gilmore, and to the Davey family, for their support and for their agreement to let me publish this book and other works by J Ernest Davey.

I also want to recognize with much appreciation the encouragement given to me by Sir Ralph Waller, the former Principal of Harris Manchester College at the University of Oxford, and current Chairman of the Farmington Trust. The Trust awarded me a grant to make possible the research, transcription, and publication of this book and I am also grateful to Ms Lara Buchanan for her practical assistance in getting the book to publication. It is worth noting that it was the support of the Farmington Trust in the late 1960s that enabled Professor Sir Alistair Hardy to establish the Religious

Experience Research Unit at Manchester College, as it then was, and this led to a number of significant publications on the subject, so it is most gratifying to be able to acknowledge that half a century later the Farmington Trust is still giving support to enable a deepening of our understanding of Religious Experience.

For Ernest Davey it was not adopting the teaching of authorities, but personal religious experience, that gave real conviction in matters of faith, so it should be no surprise that his final contribution addresses the nature, validity, forms, and problems of religious experience. It is my hope that in bringing this valediction to publication you will be encouraged in what he would have called your 'venturing out in faith'.

John, Lord Alderdice FRCPsych
Senior Research Fellow
Harris Manchester College
University of Oxford OX1 3TD
July 2021

Introduction

The literature on the subject of religious psychology is already large; my one excuse for adding yet another volume to the existing number is that I was asked to do so by those who were in a better position than I to estimate the demand for such a book. My chief aim, in the study of religious experience which follows, is not to provide a rigorous and detailed treatment of the subject for advanced students, but for the sake of those who have no specialised knowledge of either theology or psychology, to present the modern psychological outlook upon religion in such a way that it may be seen to be fully congruous with the substantial truth of historical and experimental Christianity. I have long believed that the best defence of Christianity is a fair statement of it, and the following pages aim at such a statement in the domain of normal religious experience by way of description and explanation.

Thus, the present book has as its purpose a discussion, in terms, not of the textbooks, but of the ordinary language of the educated man, of the elements of personal religion and of the more or less obvious questions which they raise for the intelligent minds of the present day, especially in the light of recent investigations in history, philosophy, and psychology. And, in common with most recent writers on the subject, I would emphasise that my purpose is the study of the normal rather than the abnormal. The study of religious psychology, like that of medical psychology, though not quite so obviously, began its course with the investigation of the more abnormal types of experience - certainly the most arresting; but its study, like the study of psychology in general, has today passed in the main to the region of the normal in human experience and behaviour. It is the normal, then, which I wish for the most part to discuss - the ordinary religious dispositions and experiences of ordinary men - though references to the abnormal cannot be avoided. But, in any case, it is well to remember that "abnormal" may mean two very different things, (1) morbid and degenerate, or below the average, and (2) progressive and valuable beyond the average. Furthermore, I wish to deal with the whole, subject on human and natural not, a supernatural plane; not by way of depreciating what may seem supernormal in life, but as laying the only possible satisfactory foundation of a fair and useful study for the ordinary man either of the abnormally morbid or of the abnormally valuable in human religious experience.

Some of the readers of the present volume may recognise its relation to various conference addresses at Swanwick, Caerleon, Grindleford, Scarborough, Dublin, Belfast and elsewhere, addresses which served in part at least as preliminary studies for this book. A note on literature will be found at the end of the final chapter, and to books there mentioned, as to many others, old and new, I owe a great debt which I here acknowledge gratefully. To choose some names for special mention in this connection would often (though I have ventured to asterisk some dozen as important) be invidious and possibly misleading, since one's mental growth is so much by unconscious assimilation from many sources. Rather would say with Olive Schreiner - "To all the men and women without whom I could never know what I know or understand as I understand - 'Thanks'."

I might add here that in these studies I have dealt with many of the more important issues twice, once in a more general, and once in a more detailed form. I think this principle of re-presentation is of definite psychological value, but I have added these sentences to my introduction to make clear what might otherwise at times raise questionings.

BOOK I
THE NATURE OF
RELIGIOUS EXPERIENCE

CHAPTER I

The universal fact of religious experience

There is to-day, a very wide-spread and growing interest in religious experience as a subject with practical meaning and value, a newly awakened sensitiveness to its claims as a study of importance for the understanding of our life and our universe. Books on religious psychology succeed one another rapidly, classes in the subject are well attended; and few today would care to pose as experts in religion without some working knowledge of the material here available. This new interest in religious experience is part of the new psychological orientation of thought which has affected most spheres of scientific investigation. And, by the work of religious psychologists, we have already come to realise generally how narrow, and misleading, are the older views which gave the name of religious experience only to certain well-defined states of mind associated with well-defined sets of opinions. To-day we are coming to see that in some sense religious experience is a universal thing, and that most of our definitions in the domain of religion need to be recast. And as a universal phenomenon we see also that it must be treated as a normal thing in life, and from the standpoint of the normal, even though

3

the abnormal in its morbid or retrogressive, and in its progressive or creative forms, must also be studied with scrupulous care.

But there are many today - especially among the young - who, possessed of the newer outlook, and caught by the challenge of the great adventure of modern experimental thinking, are nevertheless losing much that is of importance to themselves, both mentally and practically, because they are in difficulties with the older phraseology of religious writers or organized groups, and so fail to comprehend the realities for which it once stood or even yet stands. Some honest seekers are "put off" by the seeming unreality of traditional religious claims and language; some, not finding in themselves the traditional forms of experience prized by their church or sect, come to think that this religion of the organised communions is all hypocrisy and humbug; others conclude that they themselves are non-religious types. And this problem has now reached an acute stage, for the men or women who think so can scarcely today avoid the conclusion, as they look around them, that if they are non-religious so too are the majority of their fellowmen, which observation leads naturally to the conclusion that the religious type is abnormal, and either an exclusive spiritual aristocracy or a morbid by-product of human evolution.

We all recognize this conflict today between the organised church and the man in the street, but it is probable that it rests in part upon a real failure of spiritual adaptation in the churches, and in still larger measure upon a misunderstanding of the language of the churches, archaic as it is in feel, and often out of touch with the living vocabulary of the ordinary man or woman. The churches are still largely under the control of the old, while it is the young who are most susceptible to the extraordinary revolution of thought which is proceeding so rapidly today. The language of the Church is often foreign to the young mind, because it is not the language of either classroom or street, not the language of the newspaper, or the stage, or the modern novel. Thus, the supreme tragedy of the church today is that it is being cut off from its natural supply of young life and energy and idealism, not by realities, but by words. There are few if any intrinsic differences of experience involved, and the differences which can be found, in human nature, of temperament and development are to be found almost as much within as without the churches. It is vocabulary and vagueness of thinking which stand between the supposedly religious and non-religious types. And if only the universality of the experiences which are fundamental to religion can be truly appreciated, we may then expect some real attempt to mediate between the two divergent points of view with their different vocabularies. For example, the difference between "ecstasy" and "thrill" is almost entirely one of words, yet "ecstasy" is a word of the churches and "thrill" of the playing field or the cinema. All human experience is partial, and its communication limited by use and wont and the supply of words lying to hand; but in the fundamental experiences of religion, while there are stages of development and differences of intensity and association and proportion and temperament, there is no real antagonism as between different types, if only these experiences can be expressed in a common language and in terms of real life. Differences in life there are, but difference, properly appreciated, does not divide but binds together; for differences are the cement of unity, and stand for the ideal truth that as social animals we complement one another and so contribute our individual riches to the common social organism to which we belong,

I wish, then, to begin my examination of religious experience by denying this confusion of thought and vocabulary, and by making the definite assertion that religious experience is in some degree a universal thing. Religion can be treated from two standpoints, the social or objective, and the individual or subjective. The social aspect is more obvious as we go backwards in time; the individual, with his cognizance of personal experience, is of more recent development.

Historically viewed, at least, religion appears as a practically universal phenomenon; professedly non-religious types have almost no place, comparatively considered, in human history. In its origins and early development religion appears as an organised social activity; it has reference mainly to social or group values, it lends its sanctions and authority to those customs and taboos, those laws, and moral systems, which have had social meaning and utility. And even where religion so-called has been absent in group or individual life, its place has always been filled by some philosophic or scientific or ethical substitute, which is but the same thing in other terms. It is therefore with considerable reason that Professor Ames has defined religion as consisting in the consciousness and conservation of the highest social values, a definition which, fairly interpreted, includes even individual religion, since man is unmistakably a social animal. Such a view of religion immediately sets it upon the plane of the normal and universal, and all the great religious conceptions such as sin and love and God are susceptible of a social interpretation, and indeed must find one to-day. But on its social side religion has in the past seemed to consist mainly, though not wholly, of external things, rites and formulae, conventions, and modes of behaviour.

What then of individual religious experience, the subjective side of the question with which I am primarily concerned? Is there such a thing? And is it universal? If man be truly a social animal, as both historical and psychological studies seem to prove, it is natural to assume that on its subjective individual side religion will also be social and fundamentally universal in character, and concerned with social values and qualities, whether these values be considered in the abstract or concretely viewed as means to the life of the immediate social group, or personified as Humanity, or integrated as "God".

With the development of life from collectivist to individualist forms there has come a progressively greater differentiation of individuals, a greater self-consciousness, and a greater growth of personal religion with its private forms and experiences. And the existence of such individual or subjective experience, as a more or less universal fact, must I think be admitted today after the careful investigations of recent years, however it may be accounted for or evaluated. But personal religion does not seem to belong to a different order of things from the rest of the life of man. Rather it is the seeing of life and its needs from a certain angle, with which I shall be concerned later; but fundamentally it is a psychological phenomenon, varying in form, and degree with the individual, found in normal and abnormal forms, yet a universal fact in some measure; and it has to do primarily with the social relations of man, i.e., the relation between the self and its environment of human society, its environment of the universe of time and space, of truth and value, and its environment of God or the ultimate life and reality of our being. Religion is the most ultimate, the most real and the most compelling form in which we conceive the social or universe relationships and obligations of our lives; and in the case of those who may be called non-religious it is only necessary to invert the form of the sentence; the most ultimate, real, and compelling form in which they conceive their social or universe relationships and obligations is their true religion.

Universal religious experience will then consist of such experiences, emotional and otherwise, as are involved in this process of perceiving and maintaining such ultimate relationships, and especially such as are involved in the realisation of the principles and values, ideals and aspirations which are bound up with it, the deepest life of men. Man has always a conscious relation to something greater than himself, with its own peculiar pleasures and pains, its own relatively ultimate demands, and purposes; and that something at its highest and best is the object of such religion as he possesses. Here then is a universal description of religion which seems to be in harmony with the results of historical and psychological investigation on both the individual and social sides of the question.

Men have fought for long over the definition of religion, and it is not my wish to add a new definition to a list already so long; for the essence of a definition is that it shall be complete and comprehensive, and such a claim would, I think, be folly at this stage. But the above point of view seems to me to be at least a fair and true description of religion as a universal fact, both as it has been in the past and as it is today. And now with the purpose of establishing on the basis of facts my claim that religion is a universal thing, I wish to fasten upon certain elements of human experience, which we all recognise as fundamental in religion and which are common to man, and from this absolutely human starting point to develop my view of religion as being normal to man as man, ie as a universal and healthy phenomenon. I would choose for consideration here, then, four such elements, as examples and proofs of my contention, the experimental elements of revelation, worship, aspiration, and achievement. Personal religion by common consent has to do with the ideal or purposive experiences of the mental or inner life and to them belong these four.

The fundamental fact in the experience of revelation is that something within us responds to something coming from without, in such a way that we know we are in touch with reality by an accompanying sense of satisfaction, unity, or harmony. For example, the moral beauty of Jesus Christ requires no proof; we recognise it of necessity. The divine within us responds to the divine from without; that is, revelation is the conscious recognition of what in some sense is known already but so far latent or potential only. As for worship, we react to the stimulus of a noble action, a beautiful picture, a vision of truth, by an instinctive homage; we feel admiration, we thrill. The doctor's thrill over his discovery of a new cure for some human plague; the music lover's thrill over the beauty of a Beethoven string quartet, the universal thrill of moral triumph as we read of the death of Sydney Carton in fiction or Captain Oates in living fact - what are these but worship, our response to a divine revelation, our homage to God? The devotion of man or woman to science or to art, or to the figure of the Christ, is at bottom one and the same experience. We glory for example, in the stories of human heroism, even if they are fiction, because we find in them God, our own best thoughts and values, our own highest vision. This is perhaps the fundamental element in all specifically personal religion - the intuition or awareness of reality both known and felt. Where this is awakened or enhanced in us by some stimulus from without, which reveals to us our own best selves, there we have revelation, and our instinctive response is worship or homage to reality.

Following upon the experiences of revelation and worship we come to that of aspiration. That which has been seen and loved, kindles in us desire and longing; by revelation and worship our ideals are released within us; we aspire after the vision we have glimpsed. For example, we desire to become that which we have admired in the characters of others. Even if practical difficulties, or fear, or laziness, or other obstacles come in our way and fall back or fail, we do not cease to desire; we aspire, even if we do not accomplish our aspiration. The criminal instinctively honours nobility of life even if he has his reasons against an immediate acceptance of it for himself; the brave act of the hero, in the novel which he reads, will make his breast swell with the same unforced human emotion as it does that of his kindlier or more law-abiding fellowman, even though he may feel that higher path to be shut to his own feet or for the moment inexpedient to pursue.

The tragedy of our Christianity is that our aspiration so rarely, and in such small measure, becomes achievement. When we come to action we are frightened out of our ideals by the world as we know it. We should not dare to call Christ a fool, at least not many of us, yet we act as though He were - a well-meaning fool a splendid fool, but a fool - or we attain the same result, some of us, by calling him God and not man, and therefore no true example for us; so, we put Him up on a shelf labelled 'divine' and feel no obligation to imitate Him. For revelation, worship, and aspiration are not enough; there is a practical creative element in life which must function, or we are worse off than before our wakening; since we are now no longer animals, content with the present moment; but men and women with a vision which we dare not accomplish and which reproaches us continually with our failure. The emotional and intellectual factors in life matter greatly, but with these alone there is something still lacking to a true life; there must come the venture of achievement. This element of achievement is the crown and satisfaction of religious experience; it stands for action, the putting of the physical in line with the emotional and intellectual factors in the personality; and so, achievement means harmony and progress.

True achievement always costs something, but it brings with it the chief satisfaction of life, that self-respect, that sense of blessing, which is life's true coronation, the feeling of having done something worthwhile of having lived not in vain. Feeling and thought tend to issue in action; if they do not - and they can be held up - then we have morbidity, whether of the soul or of society; for, to be healthy, a harmony must be achieved between desire, thought and action. To fail in achievement is to fail utterly - I speak by way of generalisation - for revelation and aspiration are experiences which come to us by a necessity of our natures; they are not so much ourselves as God in us urging us towards achievement. If they issue in nothing, the whole process has been wasted and life in so far has been in vain. Christ not only preached the Sermon on the Mount; He lived it. True achievement means creation, it is the bringing to birth of something new which without us, must remain unborn. And there is no thrill in life like the satisfaction of achievement according to the will of God or the urge of the highest we know, the sense of co-operating with God and of having pleased Him. Life in a struggle of creative experience, tremendous and desperate for us all, however we may hide it from others; for in us a dynamic thing is being born in travail. The problems are real, the cost is real, the achievement can and must be real. The very height of religious experience is not the mystic ecstasy but the sense of achievement, the sense of the triumph of God in us. Gethsemane was the place of venture, a venture consummated on Calvary; but on the Cross, with the great last shout "It is finished", we have the glory of the supreme human achievement. For God needs man; life is not merely passive, the receiving of the gifts of God, nor is it a mere play written by God and acted by men; it is an active reality, the making of new things, even as God Himself makes all things new.

In achievement we reach that which man in some real sense contributes to God. He gifts us revelation and the capacity to admire and love that which is akin to our own true nature, and in such ways, he kindles into flame the desires He has implanted within us, and we aspire by a necessity of our own being, whether we shirk the battle or not; but in achievement, though He is still working in us, yet man too is independently cooperating. And if there be present elements of will in the other two factors, in thought and feeling, a will to believe or to desire, as some claim, these are still achievement. Life's only real satisfaction in in throwing the weight of one's whole personality upon one's faith, that is, upon the joint experience of revelation, worship, and aspiration which is challenging us to action. There is more satisfaction in courageous failure than in a timid safety; there is even more genuine satisfaction in straightforward sin than in a jelly-fish piety of fear; and such is even the judgment of God as recorded by the seer in the epistle to the church of Laodicea, "I would thou wert cold or hot." This is not an argument for sin, but it is an argument against futility and cowardice, against a static or mean level of living. Of course, we shall be afraid; but our call is to conquer fear by tasting it, and to triumph over it with a faith and a power stronger than fear.

These four elements, at any rate, of which I have been speaking - revelation, worship, aspiration, and achievement - are universal elements of human experience; and in them is much of the life of religion. We can see the universality and the broad human significance of these distinctively religious experiences; it is along such lines that we can find a view of personal religion which like Ames's social view of religion on its corporate side, will fit theist, agnostic, and atheist alike, and so give us common ground with all men for a mutual understanding of religion, and a reasonable basis for the commendation of such religious forms and beliefs as have brought to ourselves vision, desire and power, or revelation, aspiration, and achievement. If Christianity truly means these things to any of us, then it has a real significance for all men, if only we can translate our vital experience into a language human enough and living enough to convey to others the good news which we have learnt in our own lives to appreciate. I am firmly convinced that what is true for anyone is of some moment for all; and if our religious experience is of real practical value to us, then it is for us to see that it is expressed, not in the language of the churches, but in the language of ordinary human life and intercourse, that what is true for some may become, so far as it can be, available for all. It is for this reason in particular that I am seeking to stress the normal and commonplace and human, rather than the abnormal, the ecstatic and the divine, as the true line for a fruitful discussion of such a universally momentous thing as personal religious experience.

Again, there is perhaps no experience which has been more prominent in the discussion of religious psychology than that of conversion, yet here once more we are dealing, not with a specifically Christian or even specifically religious phenomenon in any restricted sense, but with a more or less common human experience, differing in degree and form in the individuals who respond, but at bottom consisting in an ethical readjustment of personality, which is possible at almost any age, but which is predominantly associated with adolescence. In some degree and in some form, conversion has its counterpart or opportunity (whether accepted or not), in every normal life, and the process of adjustment may show a supreme crisis, or its crises, or new conversions, may, as is perhaps more usual, continue through the greater part of a normal and healthy life. Here again we are dealing with broad human, not with specifically "religious" phenomena.

It is so again with the experiences of ecstasy which, in the form of felt union or communion with God, have often been claimed as uniquely religious. Not only is ecstasy found in considerable measure in such ordinary spheres of life as those of music or sex, but even the theist's sense of God can be paralleled by the atheist's sense of nature. I have personally heard atheists and "naturalists" lay claim to a nature sense - a sense of conscious kinship in and through nature with ultimate reality as they know it, or of "belonging here" (the fundamental meaning of 'sonship') - in no way radically different from the Christian mystic's sense of God, save in the degree, for example, of moral content; though even moral content has, to my own knowledge, been definitely claimed for this, sense of nature (cf Wells, First and Last Things). Here once more we are dealing with facts of experience belonging to humanity at large rather than to any fixed circles of organised religion.

Yet again, if religion be studied historically and genetically, it will be found in its primitive expressions to have definite relation to such essential human interests as food and sex. Primitive taboos, totem worship, and the actual form and content of primitive religious rites and myths show clearly that organised religion is from the beginning concerned with such normal human interests as occupational activities and the conservation of the race or group, as any textbook on comparative religion will make plain. Here in one more instance, we see the universality and broadly human interest and meaning of religion. If the phenomena in question could only be translated into a common language for all types of men, we should soon see the universal meaning and bearing of even the most obscure points in any form of religious development, whether in doctrine, rite, or institution. The chief difficulty is always this of the translation from the categories of religion in some narrow sense into the universal human categories of everyday life. And as with religion on its social side, so (as in the cases enumerated earlier) is it with religion on its individual side as personal religious experience. Even personal experience is social, as being the experience of a social being's relationships with his environment, with other human beings, with other than his own, with the universe, ultimate principles or values, or, in ordinary parlance, with man and God. I do not personally believe that there is any specifically religious experience *per se*; all such experiences belong to life in some degree as found in the so-called non-religious types; but there is a specifically religious sentiment, or point of view, or angle of vision - a conceptual outlook - just as there is an aesthetic or an intellectual or an economic, and its chief marks are unity or integration, personality or an organic social life and outlook, and practical aims. It is concerned with viewing life and the universe as a whole and with finding wholeness or health of spirit or of society; it is concerned with the social relationships in which self-conscious personality coheres and grows, especially with the soul and ultimate realities and their relations; and its aim is not to feel or to know, but to do and to be - in it power has been found and is still sought. And this ultimate religious complex of Integration, Social Personality, and Practical Power is most clearly stated and grasped in the conception and experience of 'God'.

Having thus attempted to show the universality of the elements and material of religious experience in the foregoing examples, let me turn back to the more general aspects of my subject. Religion can be approached from the objective or subjective side, from the standpoint of behaviour or from that of experience, from the standpoint of the community as organised for religious ends or from that of the individual experiencing the demands and sensations of the religious sentiment. But the two side meet at the foundation of things because man is a social animal and can only find satisfaction in the social development of personality. Fundamentally personality is a social entity, and only in unselfishness is self-realisation to be found. Thus the soul and society, the two foci of religious thinking, are in an essential relation of inter-dependence, and social progress is bound up with the individual as the cause of variation and advance, as the necessary contributor to the common heritage; and thus the highest self-interest is the most altruistic. The whole life of religion is to be found in the purpose of integration or unity, for religion is the soul of the process of making greater and ever greater wholes. In society this integration has shown itself in the creation of increasingly large and complicated units, the family, the clan, the tribe, the nation, the empire, the human race, and religion has been the soul of the movement - in Christian terms it is now expressed as the fatherhood of God and the brotherhood of Man. In the soul of man this integration shows itself in the struggle after peace, harmony, sanity and satisfaction, or the resolution of the stresses of the mind; in Christian terms it is expressed as atonement, forgiveness, peace, and power. The individual life influences the social process by variation, experiment, and the contributions of achievement; the social life influences the individual process chiefly through, the herd instinct, the fact and building of community and also, in a sense, by sex.

In social psychology, or the science of the relations of a man and his community, we recognise today three great universal complexes or general innate tendencies bound up respectively with the ego, the herd and sex. All three enter in a man's religion. The sex instinct provides the creative impulse after beauty and self-reproduction of self-expression. The herd instinct provides suggestion and conscience and codes of moral sanctions. The ego complex grows more powerful with the years, and in individual religion or ethics it is the dominant factor, expressing itself in the conception of the self and the strong sentiment of self-regard, viewed either as self-protection or as self-respect. These three complexes furnish the raw material of most of the religious experience and conflict; our necessary adjustments to all three as we grow in years or as the race progresses, are the chief elements in the history of religion. The underlying fact in religious experience is the fact of conflict and of necessary readjustment as we grow and as the race grows. This adjustment is twofold; it is an adjustment to an objective social order or environment without; and it is an adjustment to an inner subjective world of instincts and values and conceptions. In religious experience this is chiefly conceived of as a fight between two selves, the individualistic and the social, between desires and conceptions, between our creative impulses and the objective system of our actual life. Both the individual soul and the social system inevitably seek increasing integration, and the note of *unity* is characteristic of religious activity and experience in all their true forms, thus finding in "God" the word which embodies most perfectly the principle of integration, and so a necessity, in some sense or measure, of the best thought about life. For religion has to do with the "seeing of life, steadily and as a whole." It is a felt universe relationship.

Life may be departmentalised by special scientific studies which yield us knowledge. But religion is not knowledge but wisdom; it has to do with attitudes rather than facts. Knowledge is a help in religion as elsewhere; but where knowledge fails us, as so often, we have still our adjustments to make to life, our integrating universe relationship to maintain as best we can. There is a healthy universe attitude - an attitude making for peace and harmony of soul and of society - and the story of its discovery and growth is the story of religion; and its highest point for us is marked by the spirit of

Jesus Christ, that spirit which created the Christian church, and which has laid its spell upon most of the serious, thought of our day, and that in increasing measure. Thus, the aim of religion is practical, not opinions but life more abundant. From the days of magic, man's aim in religion has been to feel at home in the world and to find peace, freedom satisfaction and power. So, religion has always been a conscious, progressive and (as Mr Lowes Dickinson says) a passionate relationship of the self to a more, a greater, to the not-self, to the universe, to God. Into this relation come all the elements of human nature, material and mental, such as food, occupation, sex, the herd, or group to which one belongs, curiosity, wonder, affection, hopes, fears and the like; and religious experience is the experience of realising, facing and co-ordinating, more or less satisfactorily, these social and individual hungers, ideals, forces, and conceptions. No normal man can wholly escape the religious experience of the conscious adjustment and attempted unification of life, though not all will call it religion. But a dislike of the word does not cancel the fact that all men have a religion and a religious experience of their own.

Whether we deal with primitive or with developed religious phenomena, we find them grouped round the same fundamental elements, but, as religion, develops individually and socially, so its forms express a growing complexity and show ever greater sublimations, as well as satisfaction of the instinctive urges of life. But at every point religion has a universal human significance, as we see in its expression, such as the creative hungers of sex, or the hunting impulse seeking food or victory, or the bracing challenges of self-respect, or the sense of social obligation.

Ethical development may enlarge and ennoble the forms of the activity; thus, the food instinct now covers, intellectual and emotional as well as physical food - food for mind and spirit as well as body. There is a bread of earth or of heaven for each hunger. And so, with the other elements of life. By religion, an ever higher manhood is being created, richer, more sensitive, more integrated, more social. And so, religion appears as the creative emergence in human history of the divine and progressive activity of the spirit of man. No man can stand outside the process; in some form and measure he is religious by an inevitability of his nature. But at every point, if truly appreciated, religion will be seen to be, not the possession of certain circles of men nor an experience of special moments of ecstasy or significance, but a universal normal fact of human life, a central and necessary activity of every sane human spirit.

CHAPTER II

The specific character of religious experience

The claim used to be made that religion was a thing apart, a department of the life of man with a special religious faculty of its own, associated with its own peculiar circle of experiences and facts, a department as distinct as that of food or sex or politics. This claim is seldom met with now among those who have studied the subject seriously since psychological research has restated the whole problem and has abolished the older faculty psychology. But if religious experience is not in its material different from other experiences, what is it, and wherein does it differ from the other departments of human life? The answer to these questions will involve, in particular, an enlarged treatment of the conception of the integration or unification of life, which I mentioned above as the chief characteristic of religion, when it is treated as distinct from other human activities.

Religion is not a part of life so much as an attitude towards all life. Apart from that characteristic, religion is mental medicine, or it is ethics, or education, or sociology, or philosophy or some other branch of pure or applied science, and its material belongs to these various branches of science or knowledge. These departmental studies belong to the *science* or knowledge of life, but religion is the *art* of life, a practical unifying thing. And theology is but the attempted explanation and systematisation of religion, the theory of the art of life. That is, there is not specifically religious faculty or experience except in two related respects, that religion is the seeing of life as a whole, a unity, or attempting so to see it, and it is the practical integration of life which follows, and which is the aim of all serious religion. The other elements which I have mentioned as characteristic of religion are also found elsewhere, but in this note of unity or integration religion has no rival, except where philosophers or scientists have developed philosophy or science as a substitute for religion i.e., have made a religion out of philosophy or science. The idea of God in particular stands for the unity of human life or experience, and of human values; religion is the relating of oneself to the All, i.e., of the soul to its ultimate Society, the universe of body, mind and spirit. That is the only unique characteristic that we can find today find in religious experience, viz., that it attempts to view and to keep in touch with life, as a whole. And remembering the practical interests of religion, we see, as I have said above, that it is not a science, but an art, the art of life. True worship includes all life, and nothing really is secular, all is sacred.

Religion is thus the seeing of all life against the background of God, or reality; and the two great laws of religion as stated by Christ are to love God with all your powers, and your neighbour as yourself, or, in modern phraseology, "Love reality more than yourself and every human being as much." So, religion is seen to be an attitude to life which attempts at every point to omit or leave out nothing, at every point to think and act, not for oneself, but for the whole universe. Thus, there are many philosophies and theologies possible as attempted explanations of life, but only one real religion - the religion of reality, so far as individually or socially we are able to visualise or find contact with reality. The real growth of religion is the total growth of man's experience of reality as it is fused into some sort of unity in thought and behaviour. The true test of a religion thus is reality, the measure, that is, in which it sees the truth, and, in the pregnant Johannine phrase, is able to "do the truth."

The almost universal symbol for this ultimate reality of life has been the word "God", and every individual human experience has its own peculiar symbol or conception of God as a fact, though some may deny the actual word in question, and others may make use of it in very absurd ways. But there is a fundamental reality in life to which a man consciously adjusts himself, however he may name it, whether "nature," or "truth," or the "not-self," or "the "unseen" or "Providence" or "the Father," or whatever form of words he may fancy as expressing his own universe sense. Perhaps the most specifically religious experience is that - call it "awe" or "humility" or what you will - of getting a universe perspective in relation to one's life, the kind of thing which the sublimity of nature, in the great mountains or in the restless sea, or loneliness under a night of stars, or a conviction of sin, or a vision of love ineffable, may bring with them. But one must be careful to distinguish between the experience and the formulation of it in positives and negatives. Of course, religion cannot rest satisfied with God as a name, a term, an inference; there must be achievement as well as a theory built upon feeling and thought. Our thought of God or reality must be tested in life, and religious experience has always grown in power and scope by such testing or venturing upon faith; and somewhere there must be *experience of God* as well as *thought about* Him.

Our own real faith is simply the best theory of life we have reached; it will remain a theory if we do not risk ourselves upon it but cling instead to the opinions and achievements of others. And how many there are whose religious faith is thus parasitic! It was Christ's life and death which tested and proved His faith. If we believe in a personal God, for example, then we must be venturing our life upon that belief, and, like Christ, committing ourselves continually to a love, intelligence, and power greater than our own. Indeed, it would be a greater service to mankind to disprove by venture the existence of a personal God, if it were not true, than to preach it and yet refuse to venture upon it; for that, at least, would be an achievement of sorts. Of course, as I have said before, our experience of reality or God is to be distinguished carefully from our theory or interpretation of that experience. We have all substantially the same elements of experience - though with individual variations - we have all substantially the same values which we regard as ultimate, and the same kinds of emotions and thoughts as nature reacts to our efforts or we to nature's stimuli. In these we find our experimental basis for a doctrine of God, and to these we add what we have learned from others whom we admire or value, and especially, as Christians, from Jesus Christ. But sooner or later we are impelled to recognise that we must have more than knowledge about God, we must have knowledge of God. In our values we find something of this and in venture and achievement we shall find still more; but at all times it behoves us to be humble with regard to the theology of others, and simply to do the best with our own lives, believing that there are varieties of types and of experience in religion as in all life. Much in the universe we may be able only to apprehend,, not to comprehend, but, if our apprehension be true, it must stand the ordinary tests of honest life.

I have attempted above briefly to discriminate with care between theory and reality, between experience and its interpretation; to emphasise the substantial similarity of all human experience, and the fact that the greater part of our problems and differences arises from language, ie from differences of definition or explanation; and further, to show the ways in which our mental conceptions become systematised in the religious sentiment. Is there, then, no essential place for theory or definition, no real room for doctrine and forms of words and a definite vocabulary of terms? As surely as man is a thinking animal, there must be. To think we must define. Dangerous as it is, definition is essential both to power and to progress. The more or less concrete conception of "God the Father" for example, is much more powerful and effective in life than such abstractions as spirit, ultimate reality, the not-self and the like. Human civilisation and progress rest largely upon language and writing, i.e., means of recording, defining, systematising, and communicating experience. Definition gives man's reflections upon experience a cutting edge for practical purposes. Yet to define we must kill or stop a thing, where life is moving, and isolate it, where all life is essentially bound together and inter-related. Thus, the danger of definition is in its artificiality and its limitation, but its value is more obvious than its danger, as the progress of modern scientific research has shown. There is risk everywhere, theory and definition are quite essential to all our life; and in that necessity of accurate and systematised thought we have the apologetic of theology and of doctrine even in its crudest and most repellent phases. For there is a great danger of a kind of good-matured blurring of all distinctions today in the reaction against dogmatism, and it is well for us to remember the necessity and value of ordered thought, in spite of all the limitations which definition and human system impose upon us in an imperfect world. Whatever the defects of their presence, their absence would be definitely worse. If we would progress, we must think and think hard; we must define, criticise, and systematise all the time. Therefore, we cannot in religion get rid of theology, however much we may rebel against its past or present evils or defects.

But theology is not life, for definitions are dead things, even though they may serve life. And theologies may differ greatly where the religions in question are not very different, because the opposed thinkers, for all their similarity of experience, have begun from different standpoints and have worked with different vocabularies. The points I have really been seeking to emphasise are the universality of religious experience, among men of all sorts and conditions, in its essential or fundamental elements, and the peculiar function and characteristic of religious experience as consisting in the unification or integration of the life of man in his adjustments to the physical, mental and spiritual universe, in relation to which he lives his life. Thus, we are sooner or later driven to the use of some symbol which shall represent this universality and unity of experience, this sense of life as a whole; and it is here that the word "God" finds its chief argument and apologetic. We must use it, or some other word or phrase synonymous with it, if we are to state religion adequately, concisely, and effectively. The conception of an ultimate unity of life, for which the idea of God mainly stands, is one which is common to all human thinking about life. Our attempts to think really involve the assumption. The ordinary scientist works upon the assumption of the uniformity of nature; the ordinary philosopher works on the assumption of the rationality of all life, i.e., that all life is capable of being understood by us and that we and it are akin, and part of one great unity. All men assume a fundamental unity or commensurability in thought and action, in part as a fact justified by experience, in part as a faith unverified as yet, but probable and mentally satisfying. For this unity of life, as known or believed in, the most concise and comprehensive symbol is the word "God". And in its ultimate meaning that is what God stands for - LIFE.

There may be parts of life that may seem incommensurable to us, such as the kindlier ideals of man and the cruelties of physical nature: or body and mind. But as in human behaviour, body, and mind, however different, seem to interact or find a common ground or unity beyond our thought, so it is not unnatural to assume that the so far un-synthesised elements of our lives have the same basic kind of unity as we find more and more in the study of the world of science or psychology. No science or philosophy or theology can be built, on the denial of the unity of experience; it is an axiom of sanity and progress, even if at times it passes from being a fact to being a faith. Man may use various names for this unity, but most thinkers are turning, in spite of anti-God movements, to the old simple word, "God", though they interpret, it as they may think best. But if the idea of God is to be recognised as more than an inference, it must have more than the mediated elements of thought about it; it must have become in some measure an experience. And till God becomes an experience religion has little cutting edge. For the art of living cannot rest in God as an inference; there must be testing, achievement, proof in relation to the idea, or it will tend to die as an unverified and fantastic product of the imagination. But to this logical inference and this practical testing the best religious life has always been able to add immediate experience, in which the idea of God becomes a matter of direct feeling and definite conviction. The mystics have so felt God; and their experiences, like all genuine human experience, have a social as well as an individual value; and in every human soul there is some element of mysticism, some immediate perception of values and the meaning of life and the significance of the individual, some God-sense of the unity and worthwhileness of life, intermittent or vague as this element may be.

We may begin with faith as the best hypotheses of life open to us, and proceed to test it; but some day, be it early or late, we reach convictions and the feeling or vision of reality, perhaps even rich ecstasies of self-completion. Most men and women seem to have such points or periods, long or short, frequent, or occasional, vague, or clear. They may come in the realm of truth, or of beauty, or of goodness. They may never come in any very definite way, for temperaments differ; indeed, as social beings we are members of one another with our own peculiar work and limitations and contributions, and only in social contacts perhaps may we find or come to believe in that which individually we lack, perhaps, by some constitutional disposition or defect. But in some sense or measure the experience of God in conviction and vision, in the thrills of goodness, truth and beauty, in the sense of the unity and significance of life, is found in every normal life - at least I have never known such life without it. The measure of conscious experience of ultimate reality differs greatly, but it is well to remember the distinction earlier drawn between words and realities. Starting from substantially the same experimental basis in life, we build our interpretations of life and its valuable experiences very differently according to environment, education, opportunity and the actual course of our lives, according to prejudice and the particular cast of our thinking or desiring. To our preconceptions we add what we learn, what we admire, and our own best moments at least; and so we reach some kind of faith for practical life. But it is well that we should be humble in our judgments upon the faiths and theologies of others who have passed by a different road, who are perhaps doing the best they can in their circumstances with their own material; whose views may perhaps be truer than we think, especially if we can translate them into terms of our own thinking.

The all-important word "God" then stands for the unity of our complex life, inward and outward, physical, and mental, for the unity of our powers, desires, values, ideals, conceptions and interpretations of life. Thus, it is the symbol of unity, of worth, of power, of meaning, of purpose. The atheist does not deny God, but only a definition of Him which he dislikes; for nothing can really be denied till it has been defined. All men have some corresponding conception and experience, for it is essential if life is to have meaning and purpose, or mental life, health and usefulness; the striving after the integration of experience is an urge from which no human mind can escape; and for life as so integrated, and so far as it is so, there must be some mental encounter, or life as a whole tends to be meaningless and purposeless, and thus the mind disassociated, with all that that means of futility and mental ill-health. Certainly, in as much as the integration of mind and life is an essential part of our conflict and experience in life, the onus of proof is upon those who would deny the kinship, coherence and unity of life, and the consubstantiality of God (or the centre and totality of the universe) and man, not upon those who assume it. Unfortunately, however, just as the Union Jack has often been regarded as a party flag in Ireland or South Africa, so the word "God" has become a party flag of the Church, above all in communistic states. But it is realities and not words which really matter.

A good many years ago in Germany I came across a book dealing with the industrial problems of the day entitled "Die Arbeiterfrage" which consisted largely of an analysis of the answers to a very complete questionnaire on all related matters, sent out by a committee to various types of workers, especially miners, textile workers and engineers. In the section on religion the question "Do you believe in a God" was answered in the negative by over two thirds of those who sent in answers; and the further question "If not, why not?" mostly by some reference to the cruelties and unhappiness of life. But in a later section on Ethics, one question which had reference to the German's love of nature and especially of the woods, inquired whether, when they were lying on Sundays amid the beauties of nature in the Wald, they were conscious of the stirring of ethical forces in their minds as they looked around them. And some two thirds of those who answered this, answered it in the affirmative. Probably most of those who answered the two questions were the same persons; that is, owing to the miseries of life they denied God, i.e., a particular conception of God, gathered from the imperfect teaching of the churches, no doubt; but in the beauty of nature they, found again what they had lost, inspiration and power for better life. It is a case of the denial of a word and the assertion of the reality for which it should stand, in this case the moral quality of human experience. And what really matters in the problem is the experience, as here of uplift, power, and worthwhileness in life. For religion is not an attitude to a concept "God," but to life; and the word or concept is only useful as a means to life.

Further the word "God" in spite of atheists and agnostics, is probably the best term at present available to us to denote this essential element of human life. This relation of man to the universe has two main divisions, his relation to the seen, and to the unseen, to persons and principles, to God and man, as we say; and it was so that Christ defined the true law, to love God more than self and others as much, i.e., surrender to the whole and unselfishness towards the parts, so that each can live for and contribute most perfectly to the whole in which and for which they all exist.

It is from the completest possible evaluation and integration of experience, in which we are determined to omit nothing of value that we come to think of God as personal. We naturally infer that what is highest in us belongs to the more valuable elements in God, our source; that He is the true Personality of which men are, as it were, imperfect adumbrations; and, living on this faith, we find in God in practical life, as we test out our faith, the satisfaction and completion of all that is truly personal within us. I use the word "personal" of course as covering the higher elements in our natures, not as implying that which separates man from man, which is rather individuality. Individuality means separation, but personality stands for the integrating elements of man as a social being; not indeed for likeness or uniformity, but for difference only as it cements unity, i.e., as the different functions of the members of one body make these members coessential to their true life and unity. By raising the barriers between us and others we may grow in individuality or separation, but it is by lowering those barriers, and giving and receiving freely as social beings, that we grow in personality, and so more upwards into more perfect union with God and into more complete integration both of the soul and of society.

By integration or unity social beings become nobler, and not less but more personal; one's personality is not diminished but increased by closer contacts with other men and by more adequate contribution to one another as members of one body. And that one body is, in its ultimate being, God. As water will not rise above its own level, so the highest things in us presuppose God as their origin. And as God is the source, so He is the way and the goal of our true life; God is the power and the meaning of life, as He is the focus and totality of life. We may conceive him as possessing both body and mind, both physical and mental attributes; and certainly, no definition of God which is not complex can be adequate to account for our complex experience of life. But here, in the word "God," we have an adequate means of visualising and interpreting practically the facts and demands and differentiated unity of life. As integration is the end of our striving in all spheres, so God is the one adequate and concise and effective symbol of the meaning of life which is available to us; and within the meaning of that word we must find place for the lowliest as, for the highest elements in our experiences, for personality as well as for the impersonal elements of our physical life. And Christ's description of God as Father gives us a concrete expression of the higher elements in that conception; yet here the nature God of the early Hebrews is one with the personal God of Jesus. Christianity, in line with the Old and New Testament evolution of the word, affirms, in God the unity of the physical, intellectual, aesthetic, ethical and social worlds; and only in such a conception can we - who are physical, intellectual, aesthetic, ethical and social beings - find rest and that integration of our experience which we seek by the urge of, and as the goal of religion. And in the doctrine of the Trinity, Christianity has adopted a statement of a complex unity such as alone seems adequate to the facts of our experience.

Of these matters I hope to say more at a later stage, but it is sufficient here to emphasize that the definition of God as personal is a necessity of the religious instinct facing all the facts; and the denial of the word "God" has usually been due to nothing except a confusion of thought, which has identified personality with that individuality that separates man from man, ie with division, not unity. Super-personal God may be, but not impersonal, though the impersonal finds itself within the circle of His life as the carbon and salts of our bodies are within the circle of ours; but in Him, we may at least affirm, the values of personality, or the highest values of our natures, cohere and are conserved. And religious experience on its emotional and practical side corroborates this faith by showing that our personal lives are consciously satisfied, completed and energised by something or someone who is akin to us but more, what Williams James has called "a more of the same quality." This is the more or less uniform experience and teaching of living and articulate religion, when fairly analysed, both today and, in its own measure, at all points in man's upward climb.

The elements that enter into this universe experience which we call religious experience, and which we visualise concisely under the phrase "communion with God" are first and foremost integration or the perception and finding of a larger unity in life. Religion means the integration of the mind or soul in peace and sanity and power, so that it may function at its best without morbidity or a cancerous self-centredness. In other words, true Christianity is a statement of the laws of health for mind as well as for body, and medicine is its natural ally. Religion also means the integration of society in peace and prosperity and well-being, as man, the social animal, functions aright as part of the society he has perceived and serves. To these integrations, for all we know, there may be no end, but religion is primarily concerned with what is, at the moment, the next step in what may be an eternal process. Again, religion stands definitely for the experience of significance. One might even universalise the doctrines of the evolution of Israel or of the Messiahship of Jesus by saying that the one stands for the divine significance of a people or society, the other for the significance of the individual soul. It is not religion but physical science which paralyses or terrifies men with a sense of their insignificance. Religion has always stood for the significance of man, though realised in awe and humility; for the doctrine of the kinship of God and man and the meaning of human life as being a thing of concern to God. If the stars give one the sense of insignificance, it is by a physical or quantitative shock; the true religious reaction is that of the eighth Psalm: "What is man that Thou art mindful of him?" The writer knows of God's concern with man, and the stars only wake him to a humbler wonder which does not destroy significance, but leads to worship, to the thrill of God realised anew with amazement. True religion does not beget self-importance; religious significance is humble not proud. Life has meaning, but it is not a selfish meaning.

Yet again, religion in its higher developments, and in measure all through, stands for love, the social passion and attitude, and the only possible way by which conscious and free beings can, out of multiplicity, be integrated in one. Love for the Christian is one of the deepest names of God. In 1 John, twice the identification is made; God is Love; but the same basic fact is clearly implied in Scripture, in Luke 15, in John 3:16, in Romans 8:35-39, in 1 Corinthians 13, and in the book of Hosea. The two great commandments according to Christ are (1) to love God with all we are and have, i.e., more than we love ourselves (for we all have things in ourselves we do not love), and (2) to love our neighbour as ourselves. Christ assumes that we love ourselves; this innate and passionate concern for the life which is ours, and which matters to God, is an element set within us by God making for the care, preservation and development of His child: and thus, self-love is not only not wrong, except where it becomes selfish or self-centred by refusing such love to others but is actually the basis and power of love in our nature our spiritual dynamo. Thus, that we should extend to others the same love as we have for ourselves - or what we call altruism - is no dream, no unreal ideal, but an activity natural to man as a member of a society, and one rooted actually and dynamically in the fact that love is already there in control in a man's concern for himself, i.e. in his self-regard, making both for self-protection, on the lower level, and for self-respect on the higher, and for a concern about all men which is an extension of the self to and in others as brethren. So, Christ's demand (taken from Leviticus 19:18) is that we should extend to others the same concern that we find set in us by God for ourselves. Its source is God, and in a healthy social life it goes forth first in a love of God, i.e., of principles, values, and life generally, and also in love of men as our neighbours. The craving of love - to love and to be loved - is perhaps, with the possible exception of the craving for beauty, the most powerful impulse in life; from self-protection up to altruism it underlies all our living; but if it is to be kept sane and healthy it must not be selfish. Love is a mutual giving and receiving, it integrates life; and many others of our deepest impulses are akin to it, such as joy and honesty, humility, and pride. True pride is a positive and valuable thing, for example, pride in good work well done, which is really the joy of contribution to the whole of which we are a part and so a sense of the blessing of God. Though selfish pride can be one of the worst of sins.

Finally, there is one other emotion imperatively calling here for mention - probably of universal presence among human beings, whatever their conscious relation to a creed, positive or negative - which is bound up with the religious sense or experience, viz. the feeling of awe. Modern psychological studies of religion uniformly lay some emphasis upon this element in religion as it is witnessed to or represented in the terms and forms of the "holy" or the "sacred"

- irrational or aesthetic constituents of consciousness which are associated with the sense of mystery or reverence - though its strength seems to be particularly in the domain of the unconscious mind. The relevant and useful adjective "numinous" has here been coined by Rudolf Otto in his well-known book upon the "holy," and the unity or complex of ideas that cluster round the topic was largely introduced into theology by him; but the roots of the matter lay partly, 1) in the modern psychology of the unconscious mind with its emphasis upon the non-logical or feeling element of religion described variously by the adjectives "sacred", "holy" (and now "numinous") and associated especially with the sense of awe, i.e. a feeling that is not in itself fear, even if some tone of fear may cohere with it, but something beautiful, constraining, mysterious and noble, though it is also associated in measure with danger and apprehension; and partly, 2) in the more theological treatment of religion by Schleiermacher as based upon feeling, and especially the feeling of dependence.

I have referred, and shall at times refer, to this type of feeling at various points in this book, as, for example, in the discussion of man's sense of nature and of his felt significance on earth in spite of, or along with, his seeming logical insignificance. This feeling of creature-hood and of apprehension (Paul's "fear and trembling"), yet of belonging here and enjoying the world as akin to it, enters into religion at every stage, lower and higher; but it is chiefly relevant, in our discussion, in relation to mysticism, less or greater, and to sin and conscience.

Awe is a feeling tone associated with practically everything in the circle of religion and largely responsible for much of man's shyness or embarrassment in thinking or talking about it; but, as being in quality non-intellectual and in part subconscious, it is difficult to analyse or discuss concretely; and I have nothing to add here on the topic which is my own except in the few places where I have considered the complex, somewhat vague, yet related elements of mystery, dependence, significance, goodness and the aesthetic. So, I merely call attention here to the value and illumination of this somewhat fugitive element found in the analysis of religious experience; and I would note in particular that this area of our study has to do largely with the felt "otherness" of God, with the religious recognition that He is "God and not man" (Hosea 11:9). Otto's book (The Idea of the Holy, in its English translation) has influenced many writers since it was written, but in itself it borrows from the psychologists who preceded him; and little has been added since he wrote to his statement of this aspect of religion, for we have here a subjective element or atmosphere springing out of the unconscious mind and as little analysable as beauty, with which it has contacts, as it has with much of the aesthetic or non-rational features of our consciousness and especially of our felt universe perspective, which is bound up with the microcosm within us.

It is important, indeed, to recognise the existence and influence of this element of awe, but I have little to offer readers in the way of an individual construction of it, except what I have set down at various points in the book in speaking of man's immediate sense of God, his mixed experience of insignificance and significance, his appreciation of the beauty of mystery and the mystery of beauty, and of his creaturely sense of dependence, poignant yet comforting - all of them associated with those experiences of man which we call religious. There I must leave this remarkable foundation element or accompanying feeling tone of the religious sense.

There are indeed many other emotions to be observed at work in religious experience, for all the emotions of human life are the material which may be used in it; but the emotions calling for attention here are those which have to do with unification and the victory of the better. With social and anti-social behaviour, or with the conflict between good and evil, between the past and the future, between God and the Devil, between the tendencies of religious life and religious death in their most urgent forms. The realisation and quest of integration, unity, purpose, God, and our relations to these conceptions or urges are the specific material of the religious life and of religious experience; and they cohere in a focal mutual relation; centrally one of man with God, and circumferentially one of man with man.

CHAPTER III

The varieties of religious experience

So far, I have attempted to deal with the fact of religious experience, its universality, and its characteristic unification of life. I turn now to the complementary consideration of its variety. By many people, even yet, religious experience is regarded as a more or less standard and definite thing to be reproduced in each believer according to some authoritative pattern. This idea is perhaps due in part to a desire for certainty, that has led to rigidity and a precise formulation of all the supposedly essential elements in religion, but it has been enhanced both by the historical tendency of groups towards a uniform religious ceremonial and custom, i.e. by the similarity of the external side of religion, and by the fact that, in the Christian and especially in the Protestant tradition, a certain type of experience has been found in most of the historical figures who are regarded as standard or important. The similarity of religious experience in the three all-important names in the development of evangelical Protestantism, viz, Paul, Augustine, and Luther, has tended in Protestant countries to standardise as normal and requisite their religious experiences of conviction of sin, sudden conversion, and human pessimism, with their emphases upon spectacular grace, dependence, human corruption, fore-ordination, and mystical moments of vivid God-consciousness. But a historical examination of the forms and psychology of religion, both on its collective and its individual sides, will soon correct for us this view of the substantial similarity of religious experience.

The study of the growth of religion in society or in the individual is a study of the realisation and publication of half-truths, or rather partial truths. The religious outlook of every stage has been corrected and improved at following stages, and men normally tend to regard past expressions of religion on the whole as wrong and untrue and to regard their own as true and right; forgetting that the future will class their own views also as untrue. If one is to class as falsehood all the imperfect reasoning of the past, because in formal logic it is no longer possible to stand over it, and to regard as true only what is syllogistically sound, then truth is beyond us, for our own syllogisms are being continually exposed as based on false premises and faulty definitions or uses of terms. The only alternative, to this classing of all human thought as false, is to admit that all our truth is partial, and that progress is by the increase in the ratio of true over untrue in the complex judgments which form our so-called knowledge. This acceptance of the conception of partial truths is the only one which is fair to that organic and kinetic development which we see on all hands to be the fundamental fact of our experience on every plane. In such ways has religion developed from taboo and totemism, through fetishism, shamanism, animism, polytheism, monolatry, ethical monotheism up to the highest social demands and experiences of the modern Christian consciousness.

And on its individual side experience has kept pace with the more social development, through legalism, rationalism, and mysticism in various forms and stages to the comparatively reasonable and social religious enthusiasm of the present-day Christian reformer. Men have, like societies, grown, in religion as in all else, at different rates and along different lines and the partial truths of past religion or of present-day religion show a great diversity in development, in degree of perception and in geographical distribution. For the almost necessary corollary of partial truth is diversity. Partial truth means the, seeing of truth from a certain angle, which only gives us an incomplete vision of the object. But the history of man is a history of vision from many angles and the diversity of personalities makes this difference in angle of vision inevitable. And differentiation is proceeding at least as rapidly as integration in the human species. Hence in individual experience we are dealing with the partial perception and appropriation of life's realities from very varying standpoints; and the study of religious experience has emphasised variety as surely as universality. Whether we approach religion from the standpoint of society or of the individual matters little, for religion at bottom is the relation of these two elements, the individual and society, which at its completest, is the relation of the soul and God. The relation of the microcosm to the macrocosm is the deepest meaning of religion, though historically it has been developed in a group life which only very partially represents the values of the macrocosm or universe at large.

A universal definition of religion is only possible along the lines of historical research, i.e., by a genetic investigation and analysis of what religion has been; and it is in this study that we come to see the essential relation between religion and immediate, and (later) ultimate, social values. This study will not perhaps give us a definition of religion at its very highest, but it makes clear its essentials and gives us a direction or plotted curve from which we can argue the higher and future meaning of religion as consisting in a universe perspective and service. Along this line, then, religious experience ought to be the experience of those emotions and visions which foster and stand for the highest social values, in particular the emotion of love genetically derived from sex and parenthood and the herd, but sublimated and extended progressively towards the universe; it should be an experience of all the motives which urge towards these higher social values, and of conflict with all the obstacles which deter from them, and of relative achievement in the process. If then religion consists in the relation between the actual individual and his actual universe environment, and so all the feelings and thoughts which concern that relationship, it must be at every point a matter of urgency to keep in touch with reality. For religion is not a figment of the mind, but the essential of social development and stability. Viewed in this way then, religion, as already pointed out, is an attitude to all life rather than a part of life. Therefore, it is true in a very real sense to say that all life, so far as it can be appreciated by men at all, can be religious experience; and the varieties of religious experience are as clear and as many as the varieties of life and temperament. But certain dispositions and states of mind are necessarily more "religious" than others because more immediately and vitally associated with the religious outlook and aim. All parts of life are sacred, but not all are equally religious (sex for example is more sacred than sneezing, pace A. S. Neill); some are political or economic or aesthetic rather than religious in their more immediate meaning, for all these categories cover parts of life, but from different standpoints. So, though all life is religious experience in essence or potentiality, yet, when life is viewed relatively, it seems true to say that in all of us the more important elements of conscious religion are intermittent. Attention can only be given to one thing at a time; hence the religious angle of vision only receives a partial and intermittent attention. We do not live on one level in religious or any other form of experience; speaking in general terms, our religious experience is discontinuous, as a friend of mine once put it, "We have our great religious experiences, our great moments of revelation, of aspiration, of achievement; and a successful religious life will keep in touch with the great moments of religious history, social and individual, with Jesus Christ and the great saints of the world, and the achievements and thoughts of outstanding figures or groups of men. The religious problem is like the so-called "social problem" - to raise the average level, of individual life to the ideal or perfectly satisfying level, and formation now of mental habits which will keep us in touch with the best of the past till we have found better. For true religion means living up to the best we have got. It is particularly the moments of revelation or vision which matter in our mental life, for there we find God at His most immediate in our experience; though all vital past experience matters as the food of the spirit of man.

And, as we recognise the intermittence of religious experience, so we must recognize its varying levels both among men generally i.e., in the race, and within the bounds of the individual consciousness. Some, men are progressive, some ordinary, some retrogressive or reactionary in religion as in other things; and in our own personal experience we have fluctuations, especially of the emotions which accompany or initiate the other mental processes. In the epistles of St Paul, for example, we can see very clearly the fluctuation of emotion from the optimism and certainty of faith to depression and a kind of pessimism, from "I know whom I have believed and am persuaded" to "lest, when I have preached to others I myself should fail" and so forth. Even in the experience of Christ as recorded in our Gospels something of the same human fluctuation of mood and faith may be seen. And just as evident are the progressive levels of growth and attainment found in the religious history of all kinds of men, of which I shall have more to say later; suffice it here to observe that there are stages in religious growth alike in childhood, in adolescence, and in full manhood, stages which in childhood and adolescence have a more or less fixed order, but which in later life are not so easy to arrange in any definite scheme of development. But practical, authoritarian, mystical, and intellectual elements are all found in each individual's religious experience in varying proportions and in varying stages of development.

No experience has been more used to point the lesson of variety than the experience of conversion with its great differences of form, intensity, and content. The experience of conversion is the prerogative of no one form of organised religion, and certainly it is not a peculiarly Christian phenomenon. The classical instances of Paul and Augustine can be paralleled in the remarkable case of the Mohammedan saint and scholar Algazel or in the pagan philosopher, Dio Chrysostom. But the study of the conversion experience in the work of Starbuck, Coe, James, and their successors has certainly shown an extraordinary diversity in this outstanding and crucial experience of personal religion. I would refer the reader here to the later section on Conversion. The study of mysticism has yielded the same result of variety; indeed, it is true to say that the systematic study of religious psychology began with the fact of variety and the study of the abnormal, rather than with the unity and universality of the phenomena and with that study of the normal, to which we have come in the present generation. The diversity of religious experience as corresponding to diversity of human temperament has been one of the axioms of the recent work on the subject; and if we press the study far enough, we shall no doubt find that the varieties are as many as the personalities involved, for in some measure every man, certainly every vital man, has his own approach to and appreciation of reality. Indeed, it is interesting to note in this connection that there are nearly as many definitions of the word "religion" as there are writers upon it. Much of the real diversity in question has been obscured by words and by the attempt to standardise certain forms of experience, which latter attempt has led men often to keep their own counsel when the required form failed to reproduce itself in them. The new emphasis on reality and spontaneity has taught men greater candour and released them from cant and so is increasing every day our knowledge of human and therefore of religious, diversity of experience; and I do not think it is necessary for me to labour further a point which is today so obvious. (The classical work on the subject is of course William James "The Varieties of Religious Experience".)

But, let me say, again, it is important that we should cling, in all these questions, to the realities of life and of religion, and not be "put off" by words. Many today are made, or allow themselves to be made, to stumble over words like "saved", "grace", "sin," "justification," "saint" and the like. These words have had their values - real values - as theological counters in past thinking; some of them still have such value; and most of them at bottom can and do mean more - something more broadly human - than the scholastic theologians, who have used and pigeon-holed them, have usually allowed. I verily believe that we could find points of contact with all these words and with every type of religious experience and its verbal expression, if only we could visualise their actual content, their inner meaning, in terms of *real* experience and not merely in the forms of ancient definitions. I think it is well to remember this fact - that even the most pious or obscurantist of people are at bottom like ourselves, and that their experiences have a real value for us all, whether they can define or express them to our satisfaction or not. If the mental states involved could be translated into the speech in which we describe our own mental states, we should find real value in them and genuine points of contact with them in our own experiences of life. Let us not then be turned aside by words, nor, again, by philosophical difficulties of definition and comprehension; for, the greater the realities in question, the greater the difficulties of thought in relation to them, since life is in fact not lived on the static plans of human logic, but on the kinetic plane of human energy, desire and movement. It is always difficult to define; and the more living a thing is the less definable it is, because life is in flux continually and is so infinite in potentiality, while to define means to take life as at rest and there limit it by our senses and understanding. Life is greater than thought, and religion is greater than the philosophy or theology, whether of theist or atheist, pantheist or agnostic.

To recur to some of the more important points I have been making in this chapter, that I may enlarge upon them, differences in religious outlook and theology are inevitable at present, as our theories, doctrines, and definition, necessary as they are, are still but tentative; often poor and always provisional. There is ground for great differences in theology, and even in religious experience the real differences that are to be found in the instinctive and emotional and intellectual make up of individuals, result in great differences in religious types and experiences. Standardisation of experiences, however explicable on the basis of the desire for authority and certainty, the prestige of great names and the tendency of similar conditions to produce similar results in group environments, breaks down in fact, and in a rigid form is nothing less that ridiculous. Human experience moves between fundamentally opposite poles with innumerable variations, as the individual approximates to one or other. These poles have different names on different levels, but they can be recognized in such contrasted terms as stable and unstable, extrovert and introvert, masculine and feminine, active and passive, and the like, which may be applied also to types of religious experience in estimating them comparatively as psychological phenomena. Thus, in conversion we have a great variety of types representing different psychological mixtures of personality. We recognize two main types, a more normal and a more abnormal, or adjustment by a continuous process without clear crisis, and adjustment by crisis. The ethical adjustments of life *must* be made because life in both subject and environment is moving, but there are certain periods of greater stress than others. It is usual to employ the word conversion of the adjustment by crisis, of which, again, there are two main types, with a great variety of sub-types, and adjustment through a crisis passed by active effort, and adjustment through a crisis passed by a passive relaxation of effort (cf Baudouin) both operating according to psychological laws or necessities of nature, yet very different.

The more normal adjustment without any outstanding crisis also has its stages of development. Modern Sunday school methods till recently recognized three stages in the pre-adult period which were provided for in the graded school by primary, junior, and senior departments. These have more recently been increased to five i.e., five periods of growth from the infant class to the bible class, and beyond these at either end we have the baby stage and adult state – and the number tends to grow.

Any good recent handbook on religious psychology will give the main facts of the conversion experience and of normal development, and I hope to touch upon them in a later chapter. Let me however mention here the fact that the chief religious adjustment is associated with adolescence, and this the usual time for conversion in one or two or more crises. Thus, adolescence for all is the most startling period of religious experience and probably the most important formatively i.e., between nine and (perhaps as a limit) twenty-five. Here the varieties of religious experience are very obvious and have a very definite physiological background or setting; but all through life the varieties of experience and of type reflect themselves in the religious as in other spheres. Thus, we find various levels or stages of religious development such as legalist, rationalist, mystic; or various innate characteristics such as optimism or pessimism, hypersensitiveness or a more superficial healthy mindedness, differences in depth or breadth of outlook, in the pain or pleasure of living and feeling and thinking and so forth. All through history and experience we find truth, some truth, on every side of every real question, for nothing is living without some cause behind it and some life-energy in it; we find truth in orthodox and heretic, in collectivist and individualist, in every living type of religious or "non-religious" life; for life's antinomies and paradoxes are beyond our power to resolve, and no one life can taste all possible religious experience even of a fully genuine kind. We are social beings; our experiences are given us, not for ourselves alone, but even more for society. The experiences which others have had, and which we have never had, may be as important even to us as our own, in so far as they serve the social organism in the life of which we share as members. As a friend of mine once said to those who claimed mystical raptures. "If you have these raptures, remember they have a social meaning and value. They are not given you merely for yourselves but for the sake of all. Your business is to contribute what you have and make the most of your life for the sake of the whole Kingdom of God." There is no doubt that a conviction or faith such as Jesus had, or Paul, or Francis, can lift and energise men and women who can share it only in the most shadowy way. No man liveth to himself; and society means mutual giving and receiving, as God has dealt unto us severally His gifts and His wisdom.

The varieties of human nature in religion, of which I have spoken, can affect every part and expression of one's religious life, such as one's sense and thought of God, one's understanding of the meaning and need of prayer, one's relation to the social life in state, or church, or world, and to ultimate principles or values. There is unity and there is diversity at every point, and no man has more than a partial grasp of truth. The legalist may find the centre of life in the herd and its code, the rationalist in criticism and logical analysis and synthesis, the mystic in direct feeling of what he regards as ultimate reality. The religions of the typical artist, the typical philosopher and the typical social reformer are probably very different both in form and in substance, though they have a common human basis.

The life of religion is in the relation of the universe within, to the universe without, of microcosm to macrocosm. And the more truly personal the individual becomes, the more he is one with others, and yet the less he is like them, for, as I said earlier, differentiation is proceeding in human evolution as fast as assimilation, and integration does not seem to suffer but to benefit by this growing complexity and richness of the life that is being unified both in the healthy soul and in the healthy society - there we touch the doctrine and the problem of the Holy Spirit. The tendency of Protestantism to variation will probably proceed in some sense till every man is his own sect, and yet the true Catholic ideal of unity (which is not uniformity) will be realised, not in spite of, but through that differentiation which is the cement of our true unity. Our true harmony with others in the integrated social organism will be gained, not by likeness, but, as in the notes of a chord, by difference.

Owing to the nature of mental attention, religious experience is necessarily intermittent and discontinuous, varying, moreover, where present, in level, in the proportion of its integration, and in actual personal content, according to moods, and needs and environment; and at bottom each individual has his or her own peculiar relation to the universe. The modern physical and psychological theory of relativity has stressed this peculiar status of each individual consciousness as a real focus of the universe, and, for the individual experience, the most important. The variation of experience even in one individual are great, and the richer the personality the greater the variations; for a rich personality is really many people in one; and progress in personality is by the combined and complex growth of both differentiation and integration as representing two poles of the experience of self-development. Typical religious experiences like conversion or ecstasy differ enormously, from individual to individual, in form, intensity, content and results. I have said that religious psychology began with the study of the abnormal and later proceeded to the normal, but the terms are but relative; for each one of us is in measure disassociated and abnormal, both pathologically and more healthily, and also in measure integrated and normal.

Every individual experience is the focus of both morbid and healthy influences, and the more sensitive and creative the soul, the more cataclysmic its adjustments may have to be in the light of our present morbidities and unintegrated consciousness. But, even apart from the morbid in us, each soul is different, and norms are but generalisations. There are twelve gates to the celestial city; there are many ways to God probably as many really as there are souls, for our experience of God remains at points an absolutely unshared and isolated experience; in our ultimate life we are all lonely souls. So, to be truly original does not mean to be eccentric but to be yourself - as spontaneous or natural as possible. To be reborn or begotten from above into a new childlike integration or spontaneity of life, that is true satisfaction and that is true originality. For sincerity, not only in thought and action, but in feeling, is the basis of the true or best life. Therefore, let us keep to realities and to positives in honesty and humility, not denying the experiences of others but nurturing our own, not shying at words like saved, grace, sin, conversion, justification and the like, which have been real counters of thought with a past or present value, but seeking to find our own best vocabulary and our own vital experience of life. Movement is still beyond our analysis or definition and, as life is organic movement or growth, it too is beyond our power adequately to confine within the boundaries of definitions.

Thought, therefore, is difficult; we need a new philosophy and psychology and science of movement and of mind; and, till we can pass from our present static and materialist vocabulary to one of kinetic or organic meaning, we shall have great difficulties in expressing, religion or the relations of life to LIFE; but let us not be side-tracked by difficulties or by theologies. Theology is necessary, but religion is more than theology, for religion is life. And whatever our theological outlook, the main facts of the religious experience stand firm; the universality of a social or universe perspective and activity of the human mind, with its characteristic tendency to the unification or integration of life in its individual and its social aspects; the great variety of types of that experience and the reality in some sense for every conscience of a universe or super-self meaning and demand in life denoted by the word "God", or by some less effective synonym; and the reality of the moral conflict and of the visions and aspirations and achievements which make up the true life of religion in every soul.

Before I leave this first section of the present volume, in which I have discussed the fact and nature and varieties of religious experience, and pass to a discussion of the problems of its validity in terms of the modern outlook and the challenge of some psychologists or scientists, let me speak for a few moments more specifically of the Christian experience, with which most of us are specially concerned. Christian experience is religious experience in its highest and broadest sense, but with a special relation to Jesus Christ, and to the specific spirit and experience of which He was the creator, and which has come to us through the society and records of the Christian church - the experience of sonship and power, of progress and love, through faith in God as revealed in Jesus. Christ is at the centre of the Christian outlook because we believe that in Him, we have the supreme revelation of God, a divine humanity which makes Him for us both the focal life and the creative life of human history. And the general experience of His influence today upon all sorts and conditions of men, amid all sorts of traditions and prejudices, supports strongly that view of Christ as the divine man and of His life as the supreme creative moment of human evolution Godward (2 Peter 1: 4). This Christian experience of finding and following the meaning of life as given in Jesus of Nazareth contains the primary and universal elements of religion, of which, I have spoken earlier, yet not as a vague complex but as a definite and concrete system; and these primary elements, together with the later and more developed forms of religious life and experience derived historically from the conscious growth of the religious sentiment in the Church (under the leading of the Holy Spirit) in more and more conceptual shapes, are all taken up, interpreted, co-ordinated and integrated by the fact of Christ, the experience of His followers and the grace of God, into a fairly definite and coherent system of values, beliefs and conduct, not final, however, but progressive; not the forms but the Spirit only is final. The churches differ about many things, but the fundamental Christian beliefs seem more or less clear and agreed, as the World Conferences of Lausanne, Edinburgh, Amsterdam and Evanston have made evident in a very remarkable way.

The characteristic integration of life by religion with its sense and inference that all things, seen and unseen, are One Life akin to our own, a life with a soul and a body of its own – or transcendent and immanent; God in all and God as the ALL - a life from which we come (i.e., our Father) and by which we grow and are measured (our Life and our Judge) is gathered up, as for most of the higher religions, in the term "God"; but the Christian faith finds the highest revelation and the historic norm of the divine in Jesus Christ, in His experience, His life, His person, His teaching, His death, His victory over death, and His growing spiritual reign in the hearts of men. In God, as revealed in Jesus, we Christians believe and claim that we have found a greater self, a Father of Whom we are children, and in and through Whom we find peace and satisfaction and power, and a harmony of life in all its functions of feeling and thought and will; a universal spirit and gospel with the promise and demand of a universal society, and so an integration together of the soul of man and of human society as being mutually necessary elements in the consummation of a divine purpose concerned with what we call personality and the kingdom of God. Thus for us God is the highest conceivable, the most completely integrated life, higher by far than we can conceive (though in our religious experience we may at times apprehend it where we cannot comprehend), a real, not an imaginary, life, in and behind ours, a genuine basis and means and end of our lives, a real treasury of individual and social values and of power to achieve them, a personal, wise, loving and in some real sense almighty being, whom we call Father, the Father of Jesus Christ and our Father. His character and purposes, in their operation in history, is our Gospel, especially its highest operation in and through the facts and spirit and fruits of the earthly ministry of Jesus. This is our faith and our experience, however fragmentary, as Christians. Is it valid? To this question of validity and the challenges of some recent writers, critical of Christian claim, I now turn.

BOOK II

THE VALIDITY OF RELIGIOUS EXPERIENCE

CHAPTER IV

The charge of subjectivity

A generation ago the great problem which challenged Christian theology was the problem of biology, just as earlier it had been that of geology, or earlier still that of astronomy. But these earlier challenges have for the most part ceased to excite us, and the supposed conflicts involved have been brought to a peaceful conclusion; and today the chief problem of theology and the chief parent of serious religious doubts is to be found in the study of psychology. Perhaps no such vital attack upon religion has been delivered as that of some modern psychologists with their pathological and delusion theories of religious experience and of the material of organised religion. The attack is vital because it is an attack on the very core of present-day religion - its foundation in personal experience or mental states - but, for all that, I cannot myself believe that it is any more dangerous than the earlier attacks, because the essence of the meaning of religion, to one who studies it historically, seems to be something beyond the power of any new discovery to do more than modify in interpretative expression and quite beyond its power to destroy. Religion is life itself, on the side of its higher social meanings; and no increase of knowledge can harm, or do anything but strengthen, these primary and universal elements of man's universe thought and behaviour.

I am among those who believe that modern psychological research is one of the greatest allies religion has ever had or ever will have; but at the moment, in the persons of certain recognised experts, it has seemed to challenge our religious philosophy seriously upon the question of the validity of religious experience. Even if it could be shown, however, that religious experience was all subjective in its content and had no objective counterpart which thought could certainly establish, I do not think we should be driven back to anything more serious than the old controversy between idealism and realism, between the subjective and the objective treatment of experience, i.e., if the subjective is all, then the subjective must have different degrees of what we may call relative objectivity, and religion will be found to be as objective as any rival. Suppose we are our own God, we are also our own devil, and the very real fact of religious experience, in the conflict between the higher and the lower within us, still remains.

In some sense everyone acknowledges a not-self with whom the self has relations; and, as the essence of religion is in these relations and the impelling or accompanying emotions, psychological criticism can do no more in relation to religious experience than to test its present definitions and, where necessary, restate, them; it cannot deny nor explain away the fundamental elements of our experience of the universe, of values, and of social relations, nor the various emotional and mental states associated with them, such as love, or awe, or satisfaction. When psychology has done its worst, or its best, there are two tests of objectivity which remain to us, i.e., tests which demonstrate our personal experience to be no mere individual fantasy, no mere subjective delusion. The first of these tests is, "Is my experience shared substantially by others?" and the second, "Does it work?" And true religion will win the day, after it has been reasonably analysed, modified, and enriched by modern psychology, simply because it can answer both questions, in a real measure, in the affirmative. For, speaking generally, religion has been a universal experience, with minor differences but greater agreements; and it has worked and does work. I have limited myself to these practical tests as being obviously important; but those who wish a reasoned apologetic against the subjective challenge will do well to read carefully Canon Balmforth's volume entitled "Is Religious Experience an Illusion?" There is a great deal that could be said here by way of showing the inherent reasonableness and strength of the religious defence and the inconsistency and superficiality of the psychological attack; but my aim is not to duplicate Mr Balmforth's work, to which I would refer readers for a psychological discussion of the whole question, but to supplement it from the more practical standpoint.

The two arguments I have used; that religious experience has some measure of universality, of corroboration in others, and that it has worked and works, do not carry us logically to the perfect demonstration we crave; but then, in the higher reaches of life, and above all in religion, the primary interest of man as concerned with the fundamental sanctions of life and society, such irrefragable proof is nowhere to be found; but they do carry us as far as we need to be carried. The first proves that our experience is no mere individual fantasy, no isolated dream, but is shared by others. If it is a delusion, it is a corporate or racial delusion and most of the psychological critics of religion will admit, at least, that for the past it was a necessary delusion with real values. Their assumption, that its value has suddenly ceased to be, savours rather of egoism than of a reasonable perspective. This corroboration of individual experience by others undoubtedly gives it some sort of objectivity; the religious sentiment in question may be wrong, based on false premises, a collective misconception, a vicious product of uninformed mass suggestion, or a misunderstanding of actual experiences which really mean something quite different; but it is no mere isolated mistake, no mere fantastic dream of a morbid or uncontrolled individual imagination. To call it universal does not indeed take it completely out of the category of the subjective, but it gives it a relative objectivity compared with purely individual thinking. It may still be wrong, unfounded and inconsistent with reality, but, if so, it is a mass mistake, a collective error, and therefore the presumption is strong that it contains some truth within it, by which it has established its obvious hold, upon the great body of mankind, who cannot be unconscious of the actions and reactions of their religious sentiment in contact with the real facts of life, and who therefore will not be disposed to cling to something which has no point of contact with real life. For at the very lowest the religious experience has in it, on the admission of the psychologists themselves, the material of human dreams and aspirations, human wishes, and fears; and here at least one is in contact with the emotional realities of life and with the creative elements of personality. Even if religion be a dream, it is a dream which has been coming true and so proving itself more than *baseless* dream, indeed a prophecy or vision of life's potentialities based upon some vision or understanding of the actual laws of life, and therefore in a real sense objective or corresponding to reality. If we find a certain experience reproduced in a number of individuals it may be a collective delusion, or it may be true. How are we to distinguish which it is? The only final test is the test of practice. How does life react to it? Does it work and so prove itself in line with life's fabric and laws? Or does it fail and so show itself an unfounded and idle dream? And this test applied to individual experience has shown very clearly that it has worked, speaking generally. There have been failures, no doubt, due to many causes, as there have been scientific failures; but, broadly speaking, the path of religion has been one of success and steady advance; and even its critics to-day will admit that it has served mankind in the past, though they may happen to have come personally to the conclusion that, with the coning of the modern scientific outlook, its day is over. Of course, there is an element of truth in this claim, for each age with its new wine needs new bottles, and in its older forms, religion is as dead today as language in its older forms; but in its essence religion is no more dead than language.

Of course, the thorough-going sceptic may declare that nothing is objective, that all experience is just a stream of consciousness and that nothing beyond consciousness can be proved; but this is purely a matter of definition, for in this case and on this view, what we call "objectivity" is implied as a category of the subjective, and the relative differences remain. Solipsism may be a logical view, but none the less it is an insane or absurd one even in religion. I do not really believe that any psychology can touch the reality of a religion which can show, not only revelation and inspiration, but achievement and substantial agreement among the individuals who hold it. The true tests of life are always practical. In the first days of the church the miracle of Christ, His victory over death, and His spiritual power in the hearts of men, provided the, tests of His teaching and outlook, and so turned the church into a militant and living organisation. It is as life reacts to us according to our faith that we know our faith is justified. It is very interesting to see to-day the new appreciation of the old religious demand for faith, in psychotherapy and the study of psychology; in former days the demand for faith, never the demand of an isolated individual, might have been regarded as part of a corporate delusion; today it is seen to be true to psychological laws, i.e., we see here manifested, what is so common in religion as historically known, viz intuitive and anticipatory understanding of laws of life not yet investigated or systematised, a wisdom which needs to be turned into knowledge by thought and practice. Psychologists have done rather more to rehabilitate religion as something practically true than to destroy it; and it is very interesting to find the common admission of psychotherapists that suggestion based on or reinforced by religion is much more powerful than suggestion employed in purely scientific ways and associations. In reply to the psychological critic religion can point triumphantly both to a modified universality of religious experience and to the corroboration of that experience in practical ways. Religious experience is therefore as objective as anything can be, as objective as life at any point; it awakens response in other minds than its subject's and it elicits response from nature, i.e., from its material and mental environment.

There is an unfortunate tendency today for some psychologists to go outside of their province by such *obiter dicta* as that "religion is but infantile regression"; the tone of that statement implying of course that religion is therefore at fault. Now this is not science but personal prejudice. Science describes and classifies; it does not prove nor blame nor even explain. Explanation is the function of philosophy or theology. The true function of psychology, like any science, is to describe and clarify its own peculiar phenomena, in this case the functioning of the mind; not to attack moral judgments nor to see life as a whole. Science is specialised, not universal, in its true emphasis and scope. Now in religion, or the universe relations of man, infantile feelings and actions simply stand for the relation of creature-hood or dependence, which is true both historically and experimentally, i.e., they stand for the universe sense of man, which Schleiermacher declared to be the essence of religion, and are obviously true as tested in fact. The universe is in some sense a father even for the most dogmatic of atheists; he has come from it and owes it everything he either has or gains; and so to stigmatise religion as infantile in part is no slur, but one of the sober facts of life stated in rather an offensive way. It would be serious if it could be shown that religion was nothing else than infantile, but that is not true; and every reasoned and courageous venture of religious faith disproves it shows that it has its adult as well as its child meanings. The main question of the validity of religious experience is the question of "God" - does the word "God" stand for a real experience which has objective as well as subjective value, or at least (dropping the words subjective and objective for the moment) is there a real experience of God and has it real value, i.e., value of a kind which gives life meaning and direction; is it an experience that stands the ordinary tests of life in the interaction of subject and environment? In other words, does the idea or experience of God affect life practically, does it work, and does it enrich and maintain and advance life? Such are the questions I have been already seeking to answer, and to the two questions I asked above as tests of objective or real worth (Is it corroborated? and Does it work?) one might fairly add this more general question: "Is religious experience any less real than any other important category of human experience in life." For example, is it any less real than the experience of music, or of the beauty of nature, or than the experiences found in reading great literature? Scientific and technical studies of course, belong to a different level, and I do not consider them at this point, as they are specialised studies of portions of life, not truly experiences at all in the sense in which I have used the word. I think the answer is that religion is not less, but more, real than these, more central, more controlling, and more valuable for life as a whole.

In discussing these questions, I am chiefly concerned with the Christian experience of God as a most definite and developed form of the religious experience, believing that, if the greater and more definite experience be conceded, the lesser and vaguer experiences of religion in its more elementary and primitive forms must *a fortiori* be conceded. I shall not deal here with the metaphysical question of the doctrine of God and the arguments for the existence of a God - any good handbook of Christian theology or metaphysics will be found to deal with them - but I wish to confine itself to the psychological aspect of the problem. My subject is the psychology of religion, the experience and not the forms of the belief, except in so far as they are symbols of experience; that is, in referring to God I am concerned with the sense of God, of ultimate reality and ultimate unity, of our

kinship with an unseen and greater life in and behind our world of
sense experience; I am concerned with the experimental, not the
dogmatic side of religion, with God as a felt presence, a power, a
felt unity of ultimate meanings and immediate values. Religion is
life on the side of its higher meanings, and to the validity of the
fundamental or primary elements in religion no serious challenge can
be entertained; one might as well challenge the validity of our seeing
a tree green or a rose red - these things may be challenged, but not
with common sense. Our primary elements of the experience of God
in the perception of values, intellectual and aesthetic, in the social
sense, in the sense of the unity of life, are postulates and axioms of
all serious human thought. We cannot prove values nor the laws of
mind nor the laws of sanity, but we see them; and what we see, we
see, even if we do not know why nor how.

Beauty, truth, and love need no argument; they are God, and their
unity or integration is even more God than is their differentiation
as being more organic. We thrill and admire, aspire and achieve
in relation to the universe about us, and that in more and more
conceptual or theological forms, and these things are utterly valid,
more valid indeed than all else for us, for they are the materials of
human consciousness out of which all our mental and moral conflicts
- which are so real for us - arise; they are not merely the uncertain
results or interpretation of such conflicts. We see, we feel, we act, and
we interpret things as best we can; and, till we can improve on our
interpretations of these more immediate experiences, they remain
relatively true for us and necessary for life, and therefore with some
kind of objective or real validity, because they are held amid life, and
so criticised and tasted and purified continually by the experience
of life and social relations. But, once we pass from the *perceptions*
of moral and social values to more *conceptual* experience, we enter,
as in religious forms and definitions, upon more debatable ground.
In relation to these more complex conceptions our aim should be,

not to prove them absolutely true - a thing impossible in the case of developing human forms of thought about life - but to prove them truer than any other views proposed i.e. truer than they are false, which is all that can fairly be asked in a study which is concrete not abstract, as, for example, in the study of education as compared with the study of mathematics - in the latter greater precision and certainty can be found, but its symbols do not exist as anything except symbols. (vide Illingworth, Reason and Revelation).

The question of this chapter is really this - Is religion only a subjective fantasy? It is well to remember that objectivity in relation to any experience, for which it is claimed, is a faith, perhaps a reasonable faith, as I think in this case, but still a faith. The *experience* of a rose in colour and form and perfume is all that one can actually claim – i.e., that there is an experience of such colour and form and smell. "One cannot even say "I see a rose° without a faith in an ego which can be controverted or criticised. If subjectivity can be asserted as characteristic of religion it can be asserted as characteristic of every experience; and once you move from a position of pure subjectivity at all, definition is all a matter of the degree of objectivity (or independence of the personal experience) which you allow. But objectivity is always an inference, a faith. All that we know is experience, and all experience is for us primarily subjective. The blind man does not see the rose, not because it is not there, but because he has no experience of its colour and form from which he might deduce or visualize it. Thus, if we use the word "objective" of experience, we mean that our experience corresponds to some outward and relatively independent fact, which is at least a partial cause of our experience; and this inference can be as readily reached in religion as anywhere else, though precise definition and agreement regarding results are not easy to reach, as, the less abstract a thing is, the less easily is it defined or proved. But in the seeing of a rose, the main questions are again: (1) Is the experience shared? (2) Does it work? i.e., does the universe react to our belief in the rose in a way which supports the belief? The drunkard might see pink rats yet find his experience unshared; but normally our seeing of a rose is and can be shared. And, if we can touch the rose, and so add the evidence of contact and the universe reactions through contact to our seeing, we strengthen the faith that there is a rose there.

These proofs of objectivity in the seeing of a rose are precisely the proofs of objectivity I have been stressing in the matter of the religious experience. If our fundamental religious convictions and experiences are shared, and if they work in putting us into right relations with our environment, then they too are objective, in quality as surely as the seeing of a rose. And there have been men and women who have been quite as sure of God as of roses and in much the same kind of way, though the two facts are quite obviously very different in their whole content and setting and in the types of proof to be required. But this whole question of subjectivity and objectivity in religious experience has little *practical* meaning, because life is not greatly affected by the issue of mere theorizing for, if religion *were* but man casting his own shadow, his moral conflict, which is the prime fact of concern, would be little changed by the discovery. For, as I have said, if we are our own God, we are also our own Devil, and the real facts of the inner warfare remain, the strife between two or more selves, between self and not-self - these things remain as facts of experience with pressure on our spirits and need of solution. Psychology may redefine, but it cannot destroy the elements of human experience of values, of the conscious relations of parts with the, whole, nor the emotional and mental states which are associated with them of love and awe and satisfaction and the like, and of the pains and pleasures of the spirit which are as far apart as the traditional heaven and hell. We need salvation, atonement, integration; and to win our battle we must understand and define it in some such words as religion uses. When psychology has done its utmost regarding religion, the religious man will still possess certain tests of at least a relative objectivity the object of his worship, that show that it is not an individual fantasy nor corporate delusion, viz. in the tests of corroboration by practical results and in the Butlerian test of the analogy of nature by which it can be shown that the arguments against, religion are arguments against all vital human experience.

Allowing for great differences of types and experiences, yet fundamentally and generally religious experience is shared, does work, and is no less real than the rest of life - and for some, the saints of the world, it has been more real than all else in life. The arguments against the validity of religious experience turn out to be arguments against the validity of all knowledge and of all systems of belief and behaviour. After being exhaustively analysed, modified, restated and enriched by the investigations of psychology, it is my belief that religion will not be the loser but the gainer by the testing, because it can answer to its questioners that, in spite of many minor differences, which do not for the most part injure, but enhance it, it is a universal experience with substantial unity of content and meaning; that it does work or effect what it proposes in one's actual environment, not perfectly indeed, as it is human, but really; and that, like all the other valuable inner experiences of life, it is in tune with life and nature as a whole. In concrete things demonstration cannot be perfect and is by a cumulative argument rather than a syllogism, but these concrete tests give us what is needed.

Religion then, to sum up, is not an. individual fantasy of the imagination only, though the creative imagination has its true part to play; it is not an isolated dream out of touch with the realities of actual life. It is in large measure a shared experience, and a universal one at that. If the experience be a delusion, it is a corporate, a racial, delusion; yet, by the general admission, even of its critics, it has been useful and even necessary in the past and possessed of real value; and it is improbable that that value should suddenly cease in our day. It has some kind of objectivity, for it is corroborated, by others outside the subject of it; and not only is it not essentially individual nor local in time and place, but it has had to stand the tests of life in the past and it is based on the instinctive and emotional realities of life, i.e., on the creative, elements of personality. Even if it is a dream, it is a dream coming true. If we have built our religious castles in the air, they have been growing their own foundations; i.e., religious experience is not a baseless mirage but a prophecy or vision of unseen things based on natural law and corresponding to reality. In the test of practice life reacts to it and it works. It has its failures, as all life has, for so much in all our forms is tentative and but partially true; but the story of religion is marked by organic growth, by success and advance; it has not only furthered itself, as the soul of society, but it has furthered the rest of life, and served the best interests of the race, as behind the intellectual activity of the age of the schoolmen or the social activity of our own time there has lain the challenge and impulse of religious life and its hungers. Its forms may pass and die, but the meaning and the life abide.

The real question involved is one of definition and we must not claim for religion what does not belong to it. Religion is wisdom not knowledge; it is faith, not sight. Christ's miracles of faith-healing were done, no doubt, many of them, by powers which we more or less understand to-day and can use consciously now as scientific facts; but He did them before they were so understood. Religion in many spheres has anticipated our knowledge of to-day by a power of intuition that springs out of the right religious attitude to the universe and its parts; and today we recognise that the demand for faith and optimism in disease, which Christ used, is true to psychical laws. But religion has often perceived what has not yet been investigated or systematised; it has apprehended where it could not comprehend because, by its spirit of a true universe relationship, it has been *en rapport* with the heart of things. What has been investigated and has so become known and systematised, becomes thereby scientific knowledge; but, while religion welcomes all knowledge, it has to work in much of life, which is still obscure, as best it can on general principles of mental and physical health. The historical proof is, however, very clear that religion in the past has often been along the lines of reality and nature; and the same is obvious today in the quickened social conscience, in the new scientific spirit, and in other ways. It has worked and reacted healthily to life; it has commended itself to most men in most ages as true, and where it has not, a spurious substitute has had to be invented by an undue straining of other terms or activities; and it has as much objectivity as anything else which has the same kind of material and vital meaning for life. No doubt the question may be with us in various shapes: for a long time to come - Is religion a subjective fantasy, or does it correspond to and find contact with objective reality? If it is not such a fantasy, it must pass the same tests as anything claims some objective validity, the tests of universal meaning and practical value, the test of the response of other minds and of the universe in which we live and its laws, the social test of the experience of others and the practical test of actual results. And, speaking broadly of religion at its best, it has done so and can still do so; and therefore, has all the validity along this line that we can fairly demand.

CHAPTER V

The charges of morbidity, regression and the argument from origins

One of the bitterest attacks made upon religion and its associated experiences is that which claims that the whole phenomenon is morbid mentality, the product of a diseased mind. Parallels for example are adduced of mystical states preceding epileptic seizures or accompanying alcoholic intoxication. But this is certainly a false line of argument. The fact that strychnine or cocaine can produce or rather release energy doses not prove energy to be an unnatural drug-product of itself. If epileptics have sometimes had a strange compensation for their ills in a great religious experience of joy - and many great religious and practical leaders of mankind have been epileptics (cf. Shakespeare's, Julius Caesar "He hath the falling sickness.") it is certainly more probable that the epilepsy is a by-product of, or the price paid by, the nervous sensibility which also makes them great, than that the religious experience is the creation of the epilepsy. And if alcohol makes a man happy, genial and truthful, is that any reason for regarding happiness and geniality and veracity as morbid products of alcohol? The facts stand independently and as regards the alcoholic's consciousness of a larger fuller and freer life, there is no necessary reason why a drug should not stimulate the same nerve centres as do religious exaltation and intensity, and this is probably what takes place. The pink rats and blue devils of delirium tremens are really morbid effects because they are not corroborated elsewhere and have no practical usefulness; but religious experience is not so; it is coherent, it has corroboration, and it has practical meaning and value through its essentially ethical, social and aesthetic content.

But in various forms the charge is made that religion is pathological, a morbid condition of mind and even of body. And one must in fairness recognise the elements of truth in such an accusation. There is a religious pathology of abnormality and disease in certain historical aspects or connections of the religious experience, especially to be noted in dervishism and revivalism. The neurological excesses and weakness of the superficially ecstatic dervish type of worship, from the cases of Saul and the prophets, or the priests of Baal, to the modern "tongues" and "holy rollers" are only too evident as a blot on the religious story – a blot at least to-day, when such things are neither normal nor necessary. The story of revivalism with its hysteria and laughter, its jerks and kicks and other automatisms, its trances and even mental breakdown, makes at times painful reading, especially when one realises in what good faith these weaknesses of the nervous system have been and are exploited by earnest men and women for the supposed glory of God. Even in the early church these excesses and pathological phenomena, while they have value for us in that they stand there for the incoming of a new and vital but unaccustomed impulse, yet represent the human weakness which could not yet absorb and control that impulse; and it took some time for the new ecstatic states of the first Christians to become co-ordinated and directed and estimated aright by the sober judgment of men according to a true scale of values. But pathological as such experiences may seem, they are not peculiar to religion but can be found, especially in primitive peoples, associated with such activities as war and sex especially in the dances which are characteristic of preparations for war or of nature festivals, and are often heightened by intoxicants or other drugs.

Of course, it may be answered that in primitive peoples these phenomena may be classed as religion, but so may everything else for all their life appears as bound up with religion in some measure. By specialisation however we today speak of war and sex and the like as secular, but that is purely a question of definition; at any rate from the standpoint of this book religion means primarily a felt universe relation, which these things are not primarily. However, one recognises that in religion, as in other spheres of life, and perhaps .in greater degree than in other spheres, there has been genuine morbidity apparent in many characteristic phenomena which have been valued and worked for; but in sober fact all our life has its morbidities, and the more vital the sphere of life, the most obvious they will be. It is hardly too much to say that modern students of religion and modern religious leaders agree in deploring these pathological elements of past religious experience, and perhaps especially in the subhuman experiences of the crowd, and do not care to discuss them as true parts of genuine religion. It is not for such experiences that 1 am claiming the word "religion" as representing today a healthy and necessary element of life - they represent rather failures in adjustment. A true mysticism at its most remarkable can remain quiet and controlled and both socially and individually healthy and useful; and if some souls are "carried away" by religion, so are others by music or by nature or by nature or by sex. But it is not morbid to feel keenly or to be supremely happy, and true religion has on it the marks of superlative health rather than of disease.

But the claim is being made by many opponents of the churches today that both personal religion and corporate religion represent a morbid state, of the human mind. If so, its most morbid souls, like Christ or Jeremiah, have had an extraordinary power for practical usefulness and an extraordinary influence for all that we recognise as good and healthy, and for making others sane and socially progressive! Here we have the tests of power and fruit, and I think most of us recognise the essential truth of Christ's dictum, "By their fruits ye shall know them" If ever there was a religious experience it was that of Jesus, full of a felt communion with God, of mystical raptures and visions, but also of ethical content and social influence in goodness, health and power. The reproach of morbidity is hurled constantly at forward movements in the spheres of human belief, ethics, and conduct; but the sequel in actual life has usually shown that the unfriendly judgment is much the more morbid of the two.

Another semi-psychological attack, that is allied with that which I have just discussed, charges against religion that it is a regressive and reactionary activity of the human mind. Most morbidity like most sin is regression, the return of the mind to lower levels of life in the past, to the animal or to the savage, to the world of fear and suspicion and superstition out of which humanity and civilisation have lifted us. But it is claimed by some that the religious type is an atavism, a return to the superstitious and childish mind; in other words that religion is "infantile regression." This accusation has really two forms or lines of attack, the first (which I now propose to consider) being the psychological, which claims that man, having reached his adult stage in the modern world, yet tends, with fear and the remnants of superstition in lower deeps of his mind, to go backwards and find comfort in becoming a child once more, and in the long- wonted activities and thoughts of the child stage, seeking protection like a baby instead of standing on his own feet, and pretending that he is in his father's or mother's arms when he is really a full-grown man, facing a world of problems and dangers; in other words that man in religion represents the ostrich burying its head in the sand, because of some old habits of running away from facts and dreaming dreams. This view seems to allow some justification to the savage for being a savage and a child - on what principles it is not clear, except that he cannot be anything else - but one would imagine that, if a grown man sought to be a child that he might have protection, it is because as a child he *did* have protection, i.e., that behind the infantile regression there lies some experience of parents or of a father. There is little evidence in history to suggest that going back would in fact make life easier or happier, yet one does recognise, for example in the religions of authority, a real tendency to simplify life by accepting the views of others, as a child, not having the power to face life independently, receives instruction, direction and protection from parents who tell it what to think and do.

Such infantile regression does seem today to exist, if one compares the more individualised and free with the more collectivist and dogmatic forms of the church - the bulk of the membership is back in the nursery. Thus, there is probably some truth in the charge as against certain types of religion which have rigid systems of authority; but the charge is usually preferred against religious experience rather than doctrine; and there it seems much less definite and pointed; for it is not always easy to see where the regression is, nor what a man gains from it; and it is just as certain that there are childish elements in every normal experience of life. For, as I have said earlier, there is between man and the universe of necessity the relation of creaturehood or dependence. In some sense the universe is a parent even for the most sceptical mind; from it men have come and to it they owe all they have and are. Thus, to stigmatise religion as infantile in part, is but to state the sober fact of man's derivation. It would be serious if it could be shown that it was nothing but childish, but every venture of thought and action by the adult religious man - and history is full of such ventures - disproves the assertion and shows that religion is adult as well as childlike in its meanings, i.e., that it covers all life. The child element in religion, the implicit relation of sonship, is merely a proof that religion is dealing with all life, with the roots of life which lie in our past, as well as with the surface of life in our more adult present.

Thus, some regression to primitive elements could be no real objection to religion, for primitive elements are in all human experiences; it would be serious if it could be shown to be *only* a regression to primitive forms, but that charge seems more or less obviously absurd on the face of it. Our present religion is not the religion of primitive man nor like it, nor is our religious experience very like his in those respects which we regard as primitive and out of date in other spheres as well as in that of religion. Nor is the charge of regression in itself always a serious one. In the first place, though regression is usually wrong and often synonymous with either sin or insanity, it can be healthy as life can become so artificial, so sophisticated, that a regression to a more natural stage may be advisable, even if only for a temporary re-energising of life. Thus the post-war dancing craze in 1919, with its jazz and abandon, was probably in part just a regression to a more savage state with more primitive sex arrangements and a more primitive music of little tune and such deliberate monotony of rhythm, or with complicated syncopated rhythms - for rhythm was highly developed before the coming of melody and thereafter became less complex – so representing savagery; but in part it was the attempt of a world to re-energise itself in natural and less sophisticated style after the weary war years, and so may have even yet a relative justification.

In the second place, granting that regression is usually evil and morbid in life, let us see what the argument actually amounts to as against religion, as we look back at its beginnings - the argument from origins. Here the historian takes up the running from the psychologist with a second line of attack, and the charge becomes chiefly one against the origins or original forms of religion as being in themselves evil and unworthy and so incapable of producing in later religion a true or valuable adjunct of life. In other words, it is claimed that the roots of religion are bad, and that religion is among us always the regression of the human mind to those roots and so to the undeveloped and relatively evil period of the past to which they belong. Here the claim is that religion is morbid from its foundation in history as well as in experience. In itself this view is not very clear, for the historian can hardly proceed to condemn religion in itself as it first appeared - it was a necessary or inevitable development, whatever its defects, and the beginning of most of the modern professions and studies - nor can religion *at its beginning* have been a regression, for it had no religious past to regress to; and one must recognise in fact that religion advanced with man's advance and so is, at least a progressive, as well as a regressive activity, in some degree. Let us then at this point turn to the historical question of religious origins in the distant past and see where it leads us. We come here to the second line of attack on religion as retrogression; the attack of some historians of comparative religion, seeking to damn religion by its origins and to make validity depend on pedigree.

Like all human experience religion contains its primitive elements of undeveloped and instinctual gropings and forms, of savage and pre-savage material; but in the long process of human development these primal elements have been co-ordinated, sublimated and developed into complex and civilized forms as religion has grown and progressed. But some scholars tell us that the whole process is rotten and condemned at its root because its root consists of superstition, of discredited activities and sentiments of uneducated groups dominated by uneducated but cunning charlatans in shamans and medicine men. The actual history of religion in historical times is a history of ethical and social development in more and more reasonable and useful forms; it appears almost as the heart or soul of the forward movement of mankind. But some would today sweep aside all in this movement that is specifically religious on the ground of questionable or unworthy origins. From the beginnings of organised society all important activities of life have found their sanctions and direction in the life of religion and under the control of the representative of religion, the priest whose early office laid the foundation of so many distinct human activities and professions in politics and law, in medicine and art; but it is proposed now to sweep aside, as condemned by origins, all that is specifically religious or non-scientific in this process of man's upward climb.

Now if the validity of a present activity is to be decided by its historical origins, where will the activities of science and philosophy themselves be? For all human origins are lowly and today can be described as unscientific and superstitious. If the roots of religion historically are in magic and superstition, in fetishism and totemism, shamanism and animism, and phallicism and polytheism, in the obsessions and fears and primitive mentality of early man, so too are the roots of all the important intellectual and cultural activities of our time. No question of validity can be settled by origins. It is by making mistakes that man learns; the quest of truth finds at first very little, but it is the quest which matters, and which sooner or later leads to real truth and power. And, again, it is obviously impossible for reasonable men to explain present life or any developed life adequately in terms of past life with its simple and undeveloped and so often scientifically erroneous forms; the higher is not adequately explicable in terms of the lower. In other words, life may be derived genetically from the past, as the peacock from the amoeba, or man from the fish, but this derivation of the material of life does not fully nor normally account for the present forms and complexities of life; there is a present as well as a past cause of life, an involution of the supernormal as well as an evolution of the subnormal. Not only our historical past but the present active and purposive life of the universe are needed to explain the present condition of life; the past provides the material, the present formative influences the emerging forms and complexities of life. And to this vital and purposive and progressive life principle one can give no better name than that already used so often by me, "God". Hence religion, like all else in life, can only be truly explained or its validity discussed in terms, not of a lower past, but of God and the life of all that lives. Religion has both derivations, like all human experience, the lower and the higher parent, or nature and God. Water cannot rise above its own level; and the religion of the past can give no true or adequate account of the religion of the present, for life by general consent is creative and emergent.

Yet one must recognise, of course that present religion does spring out of primitive religion, and that the human instincts involved in the making of the latter are to be found in some measure in the former. But the continuity of human experience amid all its changes and advances is no argument against its own validity, even if its early forms seem to us now futile and absurd. Our forms, which we value so highly, will probably seem futile and absurd to our more informed successors, and they may despise us; but they will have climbed to their better views on our shoulders, and therefore we have a relative justification; and in the same way primitive religion with its errors and superstitions has its relative justification as perhaps the best possible at that period and as a necessary stage.in the upward march of man. All things are relative, even truth; and it is intellectual blindness which leads men to undervalue and despise the ladders by which they have mounted. Judgments of truth and value are relative to circumstances, very largely; and if we are today able to hold to present religion - as I think we are - as being truer than it is false for our day, it matters little or nothing that its origins may be found, not in a Garden of Eden or journeys of angels, but in totemism and the various magics of the witch doctor.

I remember a philosophical friend of mine, now dead, who was strongly imbued with the modern creed of specialised and

departmental science, telling me that the day of religion, as an attempt
to provide short cuts to the understanding and unification of life, was
gone, and that the modern clergyman was but the medicine man of
primitive history in a more civilised dress. Knowing something, as
I did, of the work and practical value of the official representatives
of religion and of the past and present necessity, for the mind, in the
search for individual sanity and social health, of the attempt to unify
experience in the way religion does, his friendly jibe did not in the
least lower my opinion of the minister of religion, but it enhanced
enormously my appreciation of the work and meaning of the witch
doctor or shaman of the days of old. To us today he may seem a
monstrosity, but in his own day he was often the ablest man of his
community, a great figure, the embryo or forerunner of minister,
doctor, lawyer, scientist, and philosopher all in one. He formulated
the earliest philosophy of the universe, a practical philosophy of life
and its relations so far as he could, not a mere theoretical attempt to
understand his environment but an attempt to harness it and use it
for man's ends. That is, his work was religion; he attempted to make
man at home in the universe, to make use of it for human purposes
i.e., to find peace and power; and religion has with growing success
done the same ever since. Nothing has so killed fear as religion,
and fear is the chief enemy of primitive man; nor is it dead yet
though its power is enormously reduced. As Mr Shaw has written
in all seriousness, "All courage is religious; without religion we are
cowards." And the history of religion is a history of the conquest of
fear and of the finding of peace and power in the larger issues of
life. The primitive priest succeeded in some measure, or he would
have disappeared as a useless figure; and the whole story of religion
witnesses to the remarkable achievements of man's search in religion
even more than to its errors and failures.

It is by religion that crises are passed; and the past history of man
must have been full of crises that called for the utmost of faith and

courage to surmount them. There must be in man, and especially in his religious activities of mind, some kind of intuition or instinctive knowledge, because religion has anticipated so much of value in personal and social life, in matters for example of individual health or social relations. Christ's miracles of healing, as I have already said, were performed about two milleniums before scientists professed to explain how they - or some of them - may have been done and could now be done. Christian doctrine, with its roots in the Old Testament, anticipated by nearly two thousand years the modern democratic view of the citizen and the state. And, whether by intuition or repeated experiment, religion has again and again succeeded in anticipating the later findings of scientific investigation. The medieval church had a working and elaborate system of psychotherapy in confession, penance, and the Mass before the word was coined; and in every age religion has done things of enormous importance for the life of mankind, above all in relating man consciously, and in large measure reasonably, to the world without him, and in promulgating and practising with considerable success the laws of mental and spiritual health. Even on the admission of the later investigating scientists, man has always *in practice* been ahead of our human systematisation of thought, and nowhere is this more obvious than in the domain of religion, where we are concerned with the deepest social values of our humanity and the conditions of our sanity and mental health. The early "charlatans" of religion, so called, were not infrequently like some of the so called "charlatans" of medicine in recent years, pioneers, at least in part, of advance. No man could today overthrow the study of chemistry because of its undoubted descent from supposedly superstitious alchemists, nor the science of astronomy because of its early and now despised astrological associations. So religious genetic associations with magic and the like cannot affect our opinion of its present value.

The ladders by which as a race we have climbed up we may find to be very far from perfect - our forms always are so - but the reality,

which has created and used these ladders or forms is a serious part
of life, must still find expression, and must ever continue to advance
and to put the past and its ways out of date. The present, of which
we are so proud, is continually being transformed into a past which
we despise; but the contempt at least is historically ridiculous, and
only manifests our failure to judge things aright in their context and
relations as parts of an unfolding universe life. The validity of an
experience cannot be disproved by an examination of its primitive
ways and forms, though a presumption of proof in its favour may
sometimes be gathered from these very ways and forms. If we are
to find in life any knowledge of truth at all we must admit that
human progress is by partial truth, the progress being measured
by the proportion of truth found at different stages, as judged
from the standpoint of a later time. Our present-day knowledge,
we know, is itself but partial truth and will be modified and even
largely condemned by our own successors, who will nevertheless owe
much to our partial truths. Einstein displacing Newton, and Freud,
Aristotle are but cases of a continual movement of thought upwards
with a steady discarding of past views and achievements, regarded as
wonderful in their own day but transient nevertheless.

The function of a present is to create a future. No doubt the
wisdom of the past in religion as in other matters was often a rule-
of-thumb wisdom, but nevertheless it worked in some real measure,
it stood for real discovery and value. The laws of mental and spiritual
health were seen long before they were understood or systematized;
apprehension precedes comprehension, and truth as wisdom comes
before truth as knowledge in the scientific sense. At any point
the quest of religion was truer than it was false because it was a
necessary quest. Thus, chemistry is the real child of alchemy, and
astronomy of astrology, and religion in part of magic, for speculation
and experiment preceded knowledge and system; but these early
forms were justified in their own day as true expressions of the same

instincts or urges as have to-day created modern science-and social Christianity. For speculation and experiment are but faith in action, and faith is one of the fundamental human activities of religion, especially of personal religion - venture upon vision. Contempt of our own racial past is puerile, not intelligent; but life being kinetic, progress involves the continual restatement of truth and the going out of date of earlier forms.

We must then distinguish carefully between origins and values, between the validity of the partial truths - to us relatively false - by which as a race we have reached our present standing, and that of those which we today ourselves hold - still partial truths, no doubt, but to us relatively true. All our so-called truth is compounded of partial truth and partial error, and God's method of educating man is by such half-truths, i.e., by illusion. It is very important in this connection to differentiate clearly between illusion and delusion, for the historical growth of truth is largely by illusion, while true delusion is never a help but a hindrance. If we have put a walking stick in water, we have all seen it bent. It is not really bent, yet if a primitive man, ignorant of the refraction of light, spoke of seeing the stick bent he would be giving a true witness so far as he could, and yet he would be the victim of an illusion. His view would be false in fact, yet it would represent truth, as being a genuine and normal experience of men of his type or development. The walking stick bent in the water is an illusion; the rats and snakes of delirium tremens are a delusion. Illusion is partial truth; it is a mental misinterpretation, in part at least, of actual facts; delusion is an experience which has no factual counterpart, though of course it must have an adequate cause like every experience; but, the content of the experience itself is a deception, not a half-truth. The progress of our race has been and still is by illusion - by alchemy, astrology, and magic for example - and this is as true of religion as of any other aspect of life. Any other view of the progress of knowledge gives us a static rather than a dynamic view of life, and life today must be interpreted in terms of a philosophy of motion, not of rest - probably not rest but motion is eternal. It is this fact which has given pragmatism its great grip on the mind to-day, and no one is immune from its fundamental conceptions of organic growth and relative justification. If nature habitually responds to a certain theory of life, while we cannot affirm that its form is actually true, yet relatively the theory must be true, i.e., contain truth; and all our knowledge of truth like all the growth of life, is gradual and progressive, and therefore relatively true for the past and relatively false for the future.

Growth like all movement is more or less irrational from the standpoint of the old static philosophy of rest, but it is an obvious fact of experience. Definition is the attempt, to catch and describe phenomena at rest, and is therefore static and inadequate in all the phenomena of human experiencing; therefore, as soon as a definition has been made, it is at once partially untrue, for it stands still while life moves on. The views of practical life which work, in that nature responds to them as expected, are true for us at least as practical truth, and so often as religious truth, where scientific fact is not known or available. Hence, the impossibility of adequately defining man or sin or salvation or goodness, except perhaps as ratios or relationships or abstract ideas corresponding to reality, but not as themselves concrete reality, Thus, we see that theology can never be really fair to or fully adequate to the expression of religious experience. It is not, then, to be wondered at that theology has always a host of critics among such living thinkers as have failed to develop the historical sense of perspective and relativity. All human theology has had its measure of truth, if it has lived at all; but no human theology of the past has been sufficient as an expression of the experimental facts which it professed or professes to embody. Often, too, our theology must appear at points illogical or inconsistent, for not all the values and experiences of life are yet commensurable in our pedestrian thinking; and the urge of common sense or reason towards unity and coherence is rather an aesthetic rather than a logical imperative of our nature. Definition we must have for the purposes of record and effective progress, but it is well to remember that experience is larger than definition, religion than theology, and life than thought.

CHAPTER VI

The charge of delusion

So far, I have spoken in a general way regarding the accusations against religion of subjectivity, morbidity, regression, and low origins and in a brief way, too, have dealt with the question of illusion and delusion. I wish now to turn to a more particular and widespread form of the modern psychological attack upon religion as delusory and examine its foundations and implications; I refer to the common charge against religion that it is merely the product of human wishes and fears, and so a subjective delusion or a kind of dream, thrown up by dominant cravings of our imperfect human nature and having no basis in objective fact. Is religion a subjective delusion due to human desires? I have already dealt with the question of the subjectivist charge and to some extent with that of delusion, but I wish at this point further to consider the premise on which this particular argument that I have just quoted is based, viz., that what is based upon wishes is suspect and unsound. The first point which falls to be noticed is the obvious fact that, if religion be attacked as a product of human wishes, the same attack can be levelled against most of our human behaviour and activities of mind and body. Action and thought, not only in religion, but in all life, are the outcome of wishes and fears, and without them we should do and think little or nothing, for we should be without the emotional forces or motions which initiate activity, whether intellectual or physical. That a phenomenon should spring out of our wishes cannot condemn it, for practically everything in life would fall under the same condemnation. If religion merely dreamed and never tested its dreams, i.e. never sought for the objective reactions of environment to its wishes, we might perhaps condemn it, not indeed as delusion, but as unverified thinking; or, if it failed to verify its dream when tested, we might then condemn it as delusion; but: in actual fact men have always been testing their religious faith - all life does that for them even apart from any deliberate trial - and have been proving it to be substantially, or at least partially, true by the touchstone of results. Most of the critics of religion will and must admit this partial success, but some will simply put it down as coincidence, while others will ascribe it to supposedly non-religious or scientific elements which have been mingled with the specifically "religious", and which have therefore helped to foist upon the world a specious fallacy by their unholy alliance with the religious factor. Not a few of the critics will say that religion has done its work and had its day, but that, now that we are able to remove from it actual scientific elements of value which have been embedded in it and are not truly of its nature, its day is gone.

This divorce between religion and scientific truth seems to me quite unjustifiable; every age recognises some of the elements of truth in the religion and even the superstition of the ages that are gone; but religion is always giving shocks to science by the continually new tracts of it in which scientific truth is being discovered, as today, for example, the practices of suggestion and psychoanalysis have been recognised as belonging to religion long before they belonged to science. Religion his often shown itself to harbour error and falsehood (as have other branches of human thought), but it has also given clear proofs of its possession of effective truth long before that truth was consciously realised and systematised. The modern attack, then, does not claim that all that belongs to religion is false, but that the specifically religious part of it - whatever that be - is false, a dream thrown up by uncontrolled and rebellious and unjustified human longings, and aspirations. Without seeking to define what in religion is specifically religious, let us accept for the sake of argument the assumption that there is a "religious" element in religion as distinct from a scientific, and then let us ask whether the charge that this is created by human wishes would be a condemnation, if true. Of course, one might begin one's apology at a different point, viz., by seeking to show that religion, properly so-called, is not a mere product of human hopes and fears but in part at least the product of experience, of the action and reaction between subject and environment; or one might seek to prove that the hopes and fears in question had some objective meaning and corresponded to objective facts and results, i.e., that religion has a scientific validity, as I believe it has. But let us go more deeply into the question and ask at once whether it is a condemnation of a system of life or thought that it should arise out of human hopes, fears, and wishes.

Here modern psychology has itself largely won the case for us already, for the study of psychology in recent years has made clear the enormous importance of the wish - and fear is only the negative or inverted form of the wish – as creative of life, i.e., wishes create, and fears conserve. And if there is one truth more than another which modern psychology is teaching us today it is this - that, while wishes may be found in morbid forms and associations, yet eventually they are in their own degree good, all of them – "libido is God" - and that through them we have an immediate contact with reality. Morbidity of wishes is due to misunderstanding and misdirection; and discrimination of them is necessary for a right adaptation of life and for advance; but the wishes or desires *per se* proceed from nature as the architects of a growing life and therefore have some intrinsic validity. They do not come ultimately - any of them - from arbitrary and diseased elements in life, though the mentality as a whole, which directs them to specific ends and through which they filter into action, may be or become morbid in part or even predominantly; but they come from the purposive bedrock of life and put us into immediate touch with real factors. We do not make our wishes, not even for example the wish for immortality or survival, so often discussed in this connection; they belong to nature, and so to God, and are normal means of creation and progress. They are means to life coming from life to make and enhance life, and they have a real relation to facts. No one knows these truths better than the psychoanalyst, who does not attempt today to destroy wishes but to get them sincerely faced and recognised, and to educate the discriminating mind, and so to redirect or, if necessary, sublimate desire. But our wishes are not to be despised or condemned in themselves; and, if anything can be shown to proceed from them, it is antecedently worthy of respect, and probably has a real relation to and meaning for actual life.

This system of wishes, if religion be such, is at any rate subjected to considerable and continual strain from the facts of life and the reactions of our surroundings, and, if it is to continue to hold an honoured place in our judgments, as more or less educated men and women, and to be a source of strength and comfort to our race, as it has been in the past, it cannot afford to be completely at variance with the facts of ordinary experience nor insusceptible of modification by them – and this has always been true; it is not merely our new, scientific age which has tested and restated religion. In actual fact our theology has been and is being continually modified and restated in relation to all our knowledge, i.e., it has the tokens of life and of concrete significance for life. The truly objective test, of course, always remains; "Try it and see"; and as religion is being continually tried, and as it is indeed of the essence of a living faith that it should be venturing and proving itself, the friends of religion have no great cause for fear. Their religion is at least as fully proven in life as the non-religious philosophies which are opposed to it or offered as substitutes, philosophies often negative rather than constructive, critical rather than an activity of life grappling with life. Our wishes precede judgment; and, if we cannot trust our wishes as guides to something of value, we have no sure footing in life at all; for from its lowest conscious forms upwards, life and growth are based upon instinctive tendencies, impulses and emotions, which form themselves into wishes of a more or less conceptual kind. For the self-conscious mind of man discrimination is of course essential, but to insist upon the need of discrimination does not deny the inherent and fundamental validity of the wishes concerned, nor can it condemn as fantastic and delusive a system which springs out of them. Disproof must be sought elsewhere, if it is to be found at all.

If our religion did not spring out of our wishes, we might well suspect it, for then, it would not be on a par with the rest of life, which certainly does so. It is the modern psychology of desire or libido which has routed the false ascetic and moralistic caricatures of religion that have valued the unpleasant and the conventional as against the spontaneous, personal, and real. Modern psychology has not destroyed religion, it has destroyed Pharisaism and Puritanism and all systems that have valued conscious repression and self-mutilation as, good in themselves and pleasing to God; and it has rehabilitated the religion of grace and feeling and taught us to value self-realisation and unselfish service far above self-mortification, and spontaneity above imitation. It is our wishes which are creative of better life and thought rather than our reasons. It is because we wish for a better world that we become reformers to seek it; it is because we wish God to be at least as good as ourselves that we find it hard to believe in an eternal, divinely imposed hell or in an arbitrary reprobation of souls. Reason helps our wishes to fulfilment, but it is our wishes which lead us upward and onward in aspiration, thought and action; coming from God, fundamentally, at least, good, they produce in us that divine discontent which makes us seek the things that are permanent and satisfying, seek in fact to –

"grasp this sorry scheme of things entire
and shatter it to bits - and then
remould it nearer to the heart's desire."

Our wishes are really on the side of God, though our fears – those negative and inverted and cramping forms which wishes have assumed in particular stages of development as sentinels of life - and which are so often the Devil for future stages of life - often range us against Him in our weak egoism and timidity. Fears are got unjustified by circumstances, and they are related to desire; but they are not desire in its positive and creative form but paralysing, negative and conservative in meaning and activity. In life generally negatives destroy and positives build up, and, if we can but trust our wishes more, rather than less, we shall not only cease to tremble for our religion when we find its close, relation to our wishes, but we shall have a religion worthier of our hearts and minds at their noblest and best. That which is not yet can be made to be, if we do but desire it enough; for through our wishes, our passions, our enthusiasms, our loves, God (or Life) is making here and now a better world. Some things in our religion, no doubt are better than the actuality around us and so do not yet correspond to human facts, but the presence of the wish in our hearts is the first step to its realisation in actual life. Thus, not even our unfulfilled wishes, nor those apparently unrelated to present conditions can be condemned, for they may be the architects of a better order of things which is not yet in being, but which through our wishes may become real for us or for our children. So, I would, plead for a revaluation of our desires, even those seemingly most suspect or dangerous, for a larger faith in the scheme of life and its progressive meaning, and for a curt rejection of all criticisms of our best and highest thinking which would condemn it as unreal because it is the offspring of our wishes, a beautiful dream. There is a great deal of truth in the philosophy of the "As if" (als ob), or in what Cabell calls "dynamic illusions".

Dreams are the stuff that man's life is made of; the creative imagination is one of our best gifts. Is our wish a dream? Well perhaps it may yet come true if we will continue to dream it; perhaps it requires to be pruned and remoulded in its conceptual form by a more perfect discrimination of it, or reinterpreted by a more complete surrender to it; but condemnation out of hand is both ignorant and futile. If we wish a thing it is at least likelier to be true in some sense than if we do not wish it, or all our present-day psychology is misleading and false. Above all, a system of religion, which is founded on human desires and emotions - the highest form of desires and emotions come within our experience - which is found to have some sort of universality of content and meaning, which is amenable to reasonable thought and experiment, and which has produced good results in character and society, is not likely to be a purely subjective fantasy or delusion; it is probably as objective as most other things in our higher ranges of experience. The marks of a subjective delusion are its impotence and its lack of corroboration in others; the marks of the best religion are power and a modified universality of acceptance and even of form. In Jesus Christ and in His truest disciples the fruits of the faith have been venture and freedom, love, optimism, and the like - all healthy, sane, and social things; and even our Christendom's failure is not the failure of our Christianity but rather one of its proofs; for men to-day have realised clearly that it was because we were not Christian enough that we failed, and that our remedy is not to throw Christ over but to accept Him more fully. And even professedly non-Christians, like Mr Shaw or Mr Wells or Lord Russell, have seen and proclaimed in measure the same truth.

The true fruits of religion pure and undefiled, as known in history, have been and are individual usefulness and social well-being; and these are not the natural outcomes of delusion. And religion which has not conformed to this higher type does not win the serious or lasting approval of those who are acclaimed as religions leaders even by uneducated or morally undeveloped men.

Those who know religion both as an immediate reality or awareness in life, and as a practical power to do, to endure and to love, will have no fear of the future of our religion at the hands of psychologists. It can only come forth purer and stronger and richer from this, as from every test of every school of thought; and what does not ultimately and actually stand the testing is no loss. The same stars can still guide us as guided our Viking forefathers, though to us the stars may theoretically be very different things, to them lamps hung by the gods in the sky, to us other worlds or flaming suns. Our experience of the stars is substantially the same as theirs, and their value to us is certainly not less than it was to them, but greater, in as much as we can use them more for the practical purposes of life. That is, while our experience is substantially the same, our theories or interpretations have been greatly readjusted.

Interpretation may change but facts abide, theories may go but realities stay; what does not in the long run abide testing is not real, and we are better without it. But science will never genuinely hinder us in our religious life and quest by any of its searches; it can only help us in the end, because truth is truth and power is power, no matter where truth and power be found, and no matter what changes our definitions may suffer in the process of sifting. And religious experience will abide because it is truth and power, amenable to thought and answering to the tests of corroboration, of coherence, of circumstances and of practical results. If it be found true in fact it cannot become false in theory; in other words, that part of our religious life and experience and thought which is true will remain true, and our human theories must fit it, not it fit our theories.

The charge then, that religion is the creation of desire running riot, a dream thrown up by dominant cravings, is a very partial and prejudiced one, unless it can first be shown that these particular cravings find their satisfaction in other better ways or that the dream in question is useless and degrading; but in fact, these cravings have no other adequate outlet nor is the "dream" in question useless and degrading but creative and elevating. Indeed, if the wishes involved could find another adequate outlet, it would be a religion of a not very different kind, for there is a kind of inevitability about the functioning and satisfaction of desire in any given set of circumstances or in any continuous process of development. That which we call, religion called by some other name, but achieving the same ends of individual and social integration, of peace and power and personality, would be much the same. Wishes are driving forces which cannot be ignored, and in some form the wishes concerned in religious experience must express themselves concretely; and the wishes being given, and the environment given, the form cannot well vary much from that which we know (varied as it actually is at present) though terms and definitions might vary, if invented by enthusiasts who claimed to be anti-religious. Human wishes are the initiating and driving force of all human thought and behaviour, and the wishes for peace and unity and power and for the discovery of meaning and worthwhileness and kinship in the life about us all recognised and approved in measure by "non-religious" thinkers as well as "religious" - cannot be denied or evaded. They must have their way in so far as they can fashion a world view which is both satisfactory and reasonable; and in religion at its best such a view is to be found, though future generations will no doubt find one more satisfactory and reasonable still by more accurate definition and more sensitive and more comprehensive appreciation of life.

But in religion past or present, for all its mistakes and defects, effective truth for life has been found and used. We do not make our wishes, though we have some control over their more conceptual forms which are not simple but complex; our wishes fundamentally make us and, incidentally, our religion; our business is to understand and direct them in the forms of their activity, but they belong to nature and to God as means to life and as kin to the deepest facts of our constitutions. The psychoanalyst knows this to-day better than most; he can do nothing to still desire nor can he thwart it forever; his business is to help us to see and feel clearly, with all the facts of the situation before us, and so to make the soundest and best available adjustments of life to life. Thus, the most that a fair critic of religious experience and forms can really succeed in doing is to make religion as true and reasonable and effective as possible. Bertrand Russell's freeman's worship is as truly a religion as that of Archbishop Temple and only God knows which is the more really suitable for the individuals concerned, though it would not be hard, in the given circumstances of our day, to determine which is the more useful and effective for the great mass of our people.

What springs from desire is antecedently worthy of respect and probably has meaning and reality. Scientific truth as discovered up to date does not yet carry us far into the inner life and leaves the greatest things of experience still undefined and uncoordinated for life. And the noblest and most effective element in religion is a divine discontent with things as they are, compared with what we see, or think we see, that they might be; for the heart's desires are fundamentally on the side of the angels, on the side of God and man and the future. Fear and impotence often deter or thwart us, but our religion is usually better than we are; it is a means by which men raise themselves above their normal selves, and, limited and unsatisfactory in many ways though it may be, it has more in it of love and trust and faith than has normal secular life, i.e., it has more social meaning and helpfulness. Desire and passion are power, and religion exists to awaken and feed and direct them. Thus, in place of rejecting our wishes and their works, we must revalue them, make the most of them, and cherish tenaciously our best dreams. The actual is often the enemy of the truly real, and religion is an energy of man seeking to fuse the actual and the ideal in life, into a better reality than we have. Religion is not, as we know it, for the most part a regressive but a progressive or futuristic activity of the soul or higher life; and it has upon it, not the marks of a morbid delusion, but the marks of truth and of creative power.

CHAPTER VII

The charge of self-projection

I turn now to another important question raised by the psychologist critic, which has filtered down into the thought currents of the ordinary educated and thinking man or woman, and which now constitutes perhaps one of the strongest of his doubts regarding the validity of religious experience. Is not this religious experience of God so-called, or this communion with Him, merely a kind of spurious or imagined contact with oneself hypostasised into a separate entity? Is it not merely a projection of one's own mind, passionately and imaginatively objectified, with which we have a seeming contact and carry on conversations as men are often conscious of talking with themselves?

Thus, a man is quoted as having been overheard to say, "Did you fall?" "No, I did," as though he were two men. We must today recognise that much of our ordinary thinking is conversational, that we talk and reason things out with ourselves, as though we were two persons, and even with the full use of the physical adjuncts of speech, gesture and facial expression, though we may be quite alone. Is not religious experience so-called a talking with oneself; an emotionally realised contact of part of ourselves with other parts, conscious or subconscious, imagined or real? Is our experience of communion

with God a real thing or illusory? One might of course apply here
the practical tests of objectivity spoken of earlier; but some of us
no doubt wish to feel a certain *reasonableness* about the ordinary
Christian view of this experience before we proceed to test it by
venturing upon it and so finding out practically whether it responds
in a way that demonstrates an objective content in it and a meaning
in the experience which is independent of ourselves as ordinarily
conceived and known i.e. independent of our normal selves. And we
have a right to ask for such a discussion and for such a measure of
reasonableness in the faith on which we propose to venture; for God
never asks us to venture except upon that which we believe probable
- not certain, indeed, for certainty we can seldom if ever gain in
concrete life, but probable. Let us then consider the matter from the
standpoint, not of action, but of thought. Is communion with God
a real valid experience? Is it communion with God or with our own
selves, for example with our own best self? Is religious experience
merely self-projection, "a chasing of our own tails," as it were?

Here, as usual, the difficulties are, I think, largely difficulties of
definition, and unfortunately in this section of our thinking clear
definition is almost impossible, for the whole question is bound up
with the mystery of personality. If we could define "personality"
I think we might be able to give a much clearer answer to the
questions posed; but we cannot – it is too big for us as yet, but it is a
growing, not a fixed, condition; and therefore I must be content with
the statement of two main points as indicating the lines along which
I should personally meet such a criticism. In the first place the reality
of this religious experience has been tested by thousands and found
to be verified in its results. The hypothesis of, or faith in a personal
life or being, a personal spirit or consciousness, intelligent, loving and
powerful, much greater and better than ourselves has been tested and
proved over and over again in comparatively recent history; but the
proving has been so intimately personal, of necessity, that conviction

here is never transferable in a degree which dissolves doubt in others; the proof must be experienced to become convincing. For one reason or another you may not yet wish to venture your all upon such a hypothesis as this personal objective God of Christian faith; but at least in fairness you must recognise that in Christ's life and in Christian biography the hypothesis has responded in a real sense and in crucial ways to the tests of objective reality. So, William James and others regard contact with "a more" as proved i.e., something greater than our ordinary self-conscious life, yet akin to it.

And the second point which I would make in this connection is that the antithesis between communion with God and communion with one's own best self is largely unreal and very misleading. The whole conception of immanence destroys or resolves the antithesis. God and man are not opposed but akin, not apart but vitally related - of the same stuff, as it were, and the same life; consubstantial, not identically exclusive spheres, but interpenetrating. The divinity of man and the humanity of God which constitute our ultimate Christian faith stand for an essential contact between the two. The contacts of spirit even in human relationships are not physical and external but inward; they may be conditioned and enhanced by physical factors, but the experience of communion of spirit with spirit is an inward one. But our relation to God is much more immediate than our relation to our fellow men; they are in a real sense largely outside us, where God is not, for God is very definitely within us, immanent in our values, our judgment, our conscience, our aspirations and enthusiasms, our shame and self-reproach. Man is made, we are assured by theologians, in the image of God; his relation to the central life of the universe is at least as intimate as, for example, that of the inhabitants of London, possessed of wireless receiving sets, to the London broadcasting station, and is at least as inexplicable without a very exact knowledge of the ultimate structure of life. Personality and spirit we cannot define, but it seems clear to-day that they are not limited by physical forms and distances but can be in some immediate way in contact, receptive and susceptible of continual action and reaction.

There is a sense in which we must be closer to the central life of the universe than we are to the life of our neighbours. Thus, even if God be conceived of as objective or external to us, He is obviously less so than is anything else in our experience, if we are His offspring and akin and if "in Him we live and move and have our being," But it is important that we should not commit the error of defining God as another man, another individual than ourselves, only greater, wiser, stronger and better. God is not a person in just the same way as we are, though He is personal i.e., He is not an individual. Rather He is (among other things) Personality, of which we are but partial expressions. Men have often claimed communion with other persons who have passed out of our human sight, saints and friends; but such communion is not the same thing as communion with God; it is external to our personalities in a very real sense, while communion with God is within, an inward thing. Our kinship with God and our sense of communion with Him is not the contact of two mutually exclusive things; it is rather the drop's sense of the ocean of which it is part. Our lives are in some sense functions of God, not mere creations of His will and technique, but parts of His very life; for our God is an indwelling spirit who is one with us even while He is distinct from us, as the ocean from the drop.

If our communion in religious experience is with our own best self - let us grant it, for the sake of argument, in this crude form - who after all is this best self? Is it not God? Some men have told us that this communion of ours is *only* with this best self, just as superficially as men have talked about man as a *mere* animal - though what a mere animal is no man can tell us - or as others have talked about Christ as a mere man - though they do not know what a mere man is. "Merely with our best self" will not condemn the religious experience of communion, especially if we can show that our best self is in a very definite sense God, is in fact more truly God than it is as yet ourselves. And such I believe to be the case. Let us look briefly into this question.

In all human experience we have a consciousness of the macrocosm and the microcosm within the one mind. On the one side is the macrocosm, the universe, the ALL, which for us includes all of which we have had experience, and besides what is reached by analogy and inference; on the other aide is the microcosm, the mind or soul of man, in which the macrocosm is mirrored, and through which alone it can become real for us as individuals. For us the universe means our experience of the universe, however gained and however extended beyond our physical contacts; and our mind is the same thing, viz., our experience of the universe, however gained and however organically systematised, and, related and reduced. So, in the experiences of religion, i.e., of ultimate social or universe relations and principles, we have these two elements, the larger and the smaller, the macrocosm and the microcosm, which can only together become real for us through the smaller, and through the capacity of the smaller to receive, appreciate and rationalise the larger, i.e., through the kinship of the two - our soul and our total environment. These two elements in our thinking, macrocosm and microcosm, or universe and soul, are two forms, however different, of the same reality, the one life of the universe; and so, the God who is the ALL, is also in the truest sense our own self at its best and fullest. The reasonableness of the universe is a fundamental assumption of thought, and it rests upon the belief that we are akin to it, consubstantial and one with all that exists, even the highest; we belong here; the universe is ours and we are its. In ourselves we find the theological doctrine of the two natures of the true or ideal man, to be more than a Christological formula, to be in fact an expression of essential human experience. All day long we are at war with ourselves, the lower with the higher,

the animal or brute with the divine. At bottom man is of God; His
foe is his lower self, at heart where it seeks to dominate; His spirit is
his higher self, a spark of the divine essence. With the body of God
his whole life is one, with the soul of God his best self is one.

It is this higher self of man which recognises all divine revelation
because it is itself divine. It urges us upward and rebukes our failures
and our sin. We cannot escape from it; it is our Judge. Here we touch
the mystery of Personality and of Immanence - God in man. As
Blaise Pascal wrote in his Pensées:

*"The true and only virtue is to hate self and to seek a truly
lovable being to love. But we cannot love that which is outside
ourselves; we must love a being who is in us and is not ourselves;
and this is true of each and all men. Now only the Universal
Being is such. The Kingdom of God is within us, the universal
God is within us; is ourselves and not ourselves."*

Here we have the doctrine of love as extended self-regard and
of two selves, one loved and the other felt as "hated". And they
are basically true. Love, sympathy and understanding proceed
from within out. We first love ourselves or pity ourselves, because
in ourselves we have the one reality of which we are perfectly and
immediately sure; and by the extension or projection of our own
feelings and consciousness to others we come to love and feel for
them. But our God cannot be wholly outside ourselves or call forth
our reverence and love as transcendent and external; He must be and
is immanent in us all. We cannot love that which is not ourselves
in some sense, and yet we dare not love ourselves on our ordinary
level. Our love and reverence must be given to our higher selves our
more or less as yet undeveloped spirits which are craving for better
things. God alone it is who is both ourselves, and yet not ourselves,
i.e., our best self and the foe of our worst. This mystery of the two

natures is a universal human truth, and one might adduce further confirmatory quotations from such psychological students as James and Pratt, Holmes and Waterhouse.

Why is it that suffering teaches us sympathy? Because we are able to project ourselves into the circumstances of others and so imaginatively to carry their pain into our own experiences, and, feeling it there, to pity them, for it is ourselves that we are pitying in an extended form. Again, it is not so hard to take the forgiveness of others, it is not so hard to accept the forgiveness of a transcendent God - an external Judge; but it is very hard to forgive ourselves - though quite as necessary. And why is it hard? Because our best self is God, and to win the forgiveness of the immanent God calls for a real change of heart, purpose and action - we cannot easily humbug ourselves, certainly not for long; we must be convinced of our own sincerity of purpose and that is not so easy for us, having once doubted it. Why is self-respect so important that to lose it may mean suicide? Because our best self is God. Why is self-confidence of such obvious value and self-depreciation so paralysing? Because at its best, self-confidence is faith in God, and even at its worst it has in it some elements with this same value. Why does the mental suggestion of some good in our health, or of courage or humility or calmness, work as it does? Because it is in a sense true already, potential but real in us through our best self which is divine. Why do we thrill with a sense of blessing and satisfaction when, at a cost, we have done our best and kept the flag of our worthiest faith flying? Because our best self is God, and He is blessing us within. I can still remember the thrill which I once felt as a little boy - so do seemingly trivial things impress themselves on our memories - when, after a struggle, I gave the minute gift of a sweet to a still younger child who was crying, no doubt at some cost in self-sacrifice. That strange sense of pleasure or joy, of harmony with a greater, nobler, and more beautiful life, was even then the approval of God within; such experiences can be very vivid and humbling and are not easily to be explained on the normal level of human experience.

This whole question is one of the most troubling for men and women of honest and sensitive moral natures, impressed by the current scientific but probably false, and certainly un-psychological way of treating reality as external and objective, and so suspecting what is inward and subjective as deceptive and misleading, though it is actually more primary in all our experience or knowledge. Men are deeply worried about such questions:

1. *Is God but a shadow of ourselves?*
2. *Do we ever create God, or did He create us and through us these thoughts of Himself?*
3. *Is He a projection of our minds as on a cinema screen, or is it God, shining through us as the lens, who casts the picture Himself?*

This latter I think is the truth, that through us as a lens. God is projecting Himself; and the question whether in fact we are projecting God, or He is projecting Himself *in* us is a matter which can only be settled by living and finding which is the more probable. But men are troubled by these questions because they feel that they are in danger of losing something of great value, viz. their faith in God; and their very worry testifies to the felt importance of religion and its professed truths. There is no doubt that in religious experience power has been found, but many writers feel they have adequately explained the matter by calling it a case of suggestion. By suggestion power *is* obtainable, as much modern investigation, especially in psychological medicine, has shown, and religion is undoubtedly, among other things, a system of suggestion with its inherent powers - perhaps the supreme form of suggestion. But whence does the power associated with suggestion come? It is rather absurd to claim that we grow by suggestion and yet that this suggestion has no objective meaning or value; for whatever changes us as we are, must from somewhere other than ourselves as we are, i.e., in some sense from without our normal selves. It is surely most natural to assume that the faith-state puts us in touch with power which does not belong to our ordinary or past selves, though it may come from a future or ideal or better self, at present unconscious, or subconscious, or from God in some still more objective form. But religion with its obvious power of growth for character can hardly imply that man is climbing up a rope hung on nothing. If the power of suggestion is true, there is some real and objective object allied to the subjective activity which produces that power; if there be a real climbing up a rope, the rope is somewhere attached and firm, even if that somewhere be beyond the clouds, i.e., beyond our present definitions and power of comprehension.

Religious experience has given men passion and aspiration and guidance, it has made for progress in personality and society, probably by the inletting of God, who is social personality. Our relation to God is probably, as William James thought of the brain's relation to mind, transmissive; and He has only been believed in without because he has been found within. These views are of course not analysis but synthesis, not logical argument so much as the statement of a position which may seem reasonable or not at first sight, yet which as a hypothesis, fairly tested, seems to be justified and to work. In religion as in science the method of induction and hypothesis is probably satisfactory here; and the faith of religion is that man is in the image of God and of His Kin. All scientific advance is by hypothesis to which nature reacts favourably, and this is such a case. Even the materialist would admit that there is a vital sense in which one must be closer to the central life of the universe than to one's best friends. Our relation to God is a relation with the centre of life; our relations with men are on the circumference of life; that is, our contact with an other man has as its symbol an arc, but with God the symbol is a radius.

All our growth in knowledge proves our ordinary assumption of the rationality or commensurability or kinship of the universe with us, i.e., the laws of thought are not human inventions but human discoveries of ultimate facts. All our advances in power, in the perception of beauty and in applied knowledge show that we are akin to the life, physical and psychical and spiritual about us, one with it. And by the incoming of the higher life of God, as we grow fit to receive it, we are developing upwards into personality and into a more divine nature, into a truer likeness to Him in whom we have our being. From our neighbours we are shut off by higher walls than from God, and growth in personality and in goodness is by the lowering of the walls between ourselves and our true life, as also in the case of our neighbours.

This whole outlook is one of the main thought currents of our time, not new in fact but new in emphasis. Faith, suggestion, religion work for us through this higher self, the part that is yet outside the door of our normal life, potential but real, waiting for our receptivity and venture. In the deepest sense it is the ideal, not the actual, which is real and the master of life, the God in us; and the transmission of God from potential and ideal to the actual and normal in our life is by that faith-state of receptivity towards the highest which gives religion its power.

But this God within us is not only within, He is without too; not only immanent, but in some sense transcendent; He is indeed our link with the whole universe, our means of contact with all personality, with all life indeed; for all life, like matter, is continuous and one. For if God be the spirit that is in man, He is also the inclusive ALL The God we find immanent within, is transcendent without; He is not only Personality, He is Society. The microcosm of the human spirit is of the same stuff as the universe of spirit, not merely of like stuff but identical, consubstantial. We are parts or members of a divine body - as the apostle Paul pictures the relation of the Christian believers to their divine Lord. Sometimes men profess to find great difficulty in conceiving of God as both immanent and transcendent; but surely, we may picture to ourselves the relation of God and man in the same way as St. Paul does that of human and divine in the figure quoted above; we may conceive of a body composed of living cells, each with its own life, limitations, boundaries, functions and relations, yet each a part, however minute, of the larger whole. Each such cell might have its own consciousness - in the world of spirit it is so; yet the whole has also its own overriding consciousness. Such cells will have their nuclei, their walls of division (or their egos and individualities), yet all will be co-operant and one, in the body they serve. We do not even know, if the separate cells of our physical body have a separate psychic life, as is not impossible; but we ourselves have - or are - the consciousness which pertains to the whole body. In the world of spirit, then, ours is the cell consciousness, God's is the body consciousness. Walls divide us from one another, each has his own nucleus of life; yet in God we are one, and especially if we are in health and co-operating, though, like cancerous cells, we might be malignant and injurious.

Thus, it seems reasonable to regard human lives as cells in the body of God, healthy or malignant members of a universe life. In this way we can get a meaning for transcendence which is congruous with our meaning for God's immanence, a meaning which makes of transcendence a real and a reasonable thing, without requiring us to postulate a distinct portion of the physical universe as alone truly transcendent or ultimate; for this figure of the body makes of transcendence a psychical fact which can coexist with immanence without having a separate body, as our soul coexists with our body. And important as immanence is, transcendence for religious experience is at least as important. That which marks off religion from ethics, the practice of the good life from the scientific classification of moral values and states, is the dynamic or practical element which we call power. Living religion has consisted in man's discovery and use of a power not (as yet) his own, though coming from within, and in all such vital religion some idea of transcendence has been found necessary to convey man's sense of contact with something greater and better than himself, as he knows himself and he is at the moment; a sense of contact with goodness and with power as yet ahead both of his definition and his grasp, i.e., with God, to use the ordinary word; a contact too which is beyond his ability fully to comprehend but by means of which he can grow in power and apprehend new truth. Whether the word "transcendence" be satisfactory or not, the experience involved is a real one, perhaps the most real of the experiences of moral growth - the experience of a moral power, seemingly objective or external to ourselves, and only vaguely seen or grasped yet sufficiently so for a measure of victory and progress, but which, as we grow, we see and grasp more firmly, though the vision and the power alike, both continue to pass beyond both our understanding and our reach. However, the experience is best explained, it is just such an experience that is involved in our moral struggle upward - the sense that *we can*, because in our universe, (i.e., in God), it is inherently possible - and that has been perhaps the chief mark of religion on its ethical plane. Such too, has been the chief reason for the practice and continuance of prayer.

Both immanence and transcendence are poor words, but we can as yet do no better, and therefore we must use them and so affirm the experiences on which they rest. If then the transcendent God functions as immanent in man, the experience of communion with one's own best self is obviously communion with God, not a mental fantasy but the deepest reality of moral and religious life. And if the reality or validity of the experience in question still be challenged, the answer for a reasonable mind can be given in practical ways, through community of experience with other men (which removes the experience from the individual plane to the collective, from the

subjective to the relatively objective), and through its outworking
in practical results, when tested as a hypothesis of life. We know
today that ideas and our faith in them are not abstract things but
are a power; and that their truth as real (even if not in the past
actual) can be shown by their effects. And in these methods of proof
religion is at least on safe ground, for we knew that others share our
faith and that it works. Many of us, further, have been conscious of
definite communion with God especially at certain moments when
the unseen world seemed to open its secrets to us and we knew God
- not merely knew *about* Him - moments of certainty, of conviction
and of great moral consequence for future living. Such moments,
when God has passed from being a mediated inference to being an
immediate object of conscious knowledge, are very precious to us,
not only for the clarity and certitude which they have possessed, but
for the ethical quality of the experience and for its power to release
our highest desires and to accomplish our truest achievements in
practical goodness; and upon such memories many of us still live
and conquer.

Thus, if we conceive of the totality of the universe as the body
of God, and its integrated life or unity as the soul of God, bearing
the same relation to the body, of co-ordination and direction, as
our minds to our bodies, we can reasonably conceive of our lives
as cells in that life of God, as parts of His body in immediate
relations with His mind or will; and in this way it is possible to
reach a joint conception of immanence and transcendence without
raising conceptual difficulties which may make the whole idea seem
irrational. Of course, the transcendence, like our own personality,
passes far beyond our definitions and understanding, and of it we
can only give a meagre account based on our own experience. What
is more the life of God as immanent in other human souls is objective
for us just as truly as the integrated unity of God's own mind; that
is, we can claim objectivity, not only for the transcendence of God

proper, but also for such spheres of His immanence as are outside our own experience - and the experience of other souls is that in a very large degree. Here is a treasury of life and power which is not ourselves - so far as we can define ourselves in terms of past or known experience - and the vital meaning of religion has to do with this fact of a God lying outside the circles of our actual lives as individual souls. But, through the immanence of God, it is within us that this life and these powers are found and used. The current of life is against us - the doctrines of original sin and racial heredity stand at least for that experience - but nevertheless we can make our way upstream. There is power to move upwards. In dealing with prayer as the laying hold of such a power, Pratt has somewhat sarcastically dealt with the argument advanced against prayer that it is hocus-pocus and bluff, such as is the faith which enables bread pills to cure, a morbid body because they are *believed* to be other than bread pills. Prayer has in fact given men, power because they have believed in its *objective* significance. Take away from the invalid the belief that the pills have in them some potent drug, and they fail, to affect him, being but bread. Deny objectivity to prayer and you kill the goose that lays the golden eggs. In other words, you cannot at the same time admit prayer to be a source of power through suggestion and yet remove the validity of the suggestion; you cannot accept it as a means of power independent of the belief that it is; you must choose between objective validity and impotence. To kill the goose that lays the golden eggs seemed a fine thing to do in the infant story, but it was a mistake; and in religion the killing of the belief in a valid *object* of worship and prayer will do precisely the same thing - it will impoverish life, not assist it. The practical or pragmatic test of truth can only be satisfied by the religion or belief which does work and change life.

Thus, our business is the transmission of God, the opening the door to Him who stands and knocks, that He may more and more come in and lift and empower and enrich life by a process which is both a personal growth and a divine incoming. Words are but poor counters of the experience, but it is as real as any experience can be. Definition is never easy in the important things of life; all great ideas or experiences like life and freedom, beauty, and love, defy us in large part; but the experience of God is the truest and most vital of all life's experiences. If then the transcendent God functions as immanent in man, the experience of communion with one's best and truest self is communion with God, as He passes, continually from transcendent to immanent, or objective to subjective, in our experiences. Even if God be regarded, as by some, as only an idea, what after all are ideas? Dreams and ideas of moral worth have power, that is they are real in some vivid and vital sense. Readers of the famous story, 'Loutre', have seen the strange outworking in fiction of the extraordinary power of an idea. But, if for some persons God is still largely an inference or a mere idea, drawn from experiences or from moral values, others have had a consciousness of felt communion with God and of the sudden unity and meaning of all life, a certainty of conviction with great ethical and practical consequences. Such experiences are very precious, not only for those who have had them, but for others who have not, if they on their part are convinced of the honesty and ability of those who claim them; and upon them, these moments of the mountain top, the race has lived; for they have given life its peculiar value and meaning and glory. But the final proof and test of religion, as of all life, and not least of the Christian's faith in God, is "Taste and see." and the religious man or woman who has tasted and seen has little fear for the ark of God, or the future of religious truth, or of the religious experience however *it* may be stated and defined in days to come.

CHAPTER VIII

The fact and experience of God

In this chapter I wish to sum up and enlarge upon my earlier references to the conceptions of God and then, in the following chapter, take up the question of the experience of communion with God which is claimed as the completest and profoundest and most effective form of this religious experience, and which is certainly the most characteristically religious of all the experiences which are claimed as belonging to the domain of religion. The first question then is "Who or what is God?" One might approach the whole question from some popular standpoint along such lines as that of Bernard Shaw's dictum, quoted earlier, that religion is that which gives us courage. Indeed, if one might add to the quality of courage such qualities as that of tenacity or patience, or, again that of purpose, one would reach a very sound practical description of personal religion as that from which individually we draw courage and patience and the like, and a life purpose; in other words that which gives life meaning and value, or worthwhileness, peace, and power. This may be found in measure by one in stoicism, by another in patriotism, by another in family love or service by another in self-development, by another in herd-regard or the esteem of his fellows, by another in self-respect and a lofty ethical code or ideal; but most of these reduce themselves to some form of self-regard, less ideal or more ideal, in self-protection, self-interest, or self-respect; and at its best this self-regard is a worthy self-respect which makes the judge of one's life one's ideal self, so that one's highest ideals, conceived as personal and identified with one's whole life, become one's judge, and so one's best self, or what we call conscience, is the spectator and adjudicator upon all one's thought and conduct. But this best self, as I have said, is one of the most obvious meanings of the word "God," so that, if religion be that which gives us courage and tenacity and a life purpose, it is from God or the ideal self that the power comes. God can thus be conceived as the true Self; in like ways God can be conceived as the All or totality of life, multifarious as it is, with which we are kin; or, again, as the true One in whom life finds its integration, its centre, its meaning and its purpose. Theology is not in itself unnatural dogma but reasonable interpretation of life, and especially of its universal experience and meaning; and, along the three lines briefly suggested above, God can be used as the effective symbol of life on its physical, psychical, personal or ethical sides, as the beginning and meaning and end of nature, of mind, and of personal or social relations, or one may say, of body, mind and spirit.

I have attempted throughout this study of religious life to deal with my subject from the standpoint of universal human experience rather than from any ecclesiastical, theological, or specifically "religious" or pious point of view, and I propose to continue to do so in what follows, viz. in my attempt to define the term "God" more systematically and precisely than I have yet done, as a basis for an adequate discussion of the experience of communion with God.

In seeking to give the word a true definition with universal meaning and content one may begin by pointing out that the word stands in religion, in the first place, for the sense and evaluation of life as a single thing or entity, rationable, coherent and akin to ourselves at every point - the fundamental assumption of our increasingly successful attempt to understand life, i.e., to reduce it to our own terms; and in theology or philosophy it stands for the corresponding interpretation of the universe, or man's completest experience, as a single coherent system.

Life is urged on by many values, but the vast majority of men believe in the fundamental unity of these values as parts of a coherent system, whether at present we can truly relate and evaluate them to our satisfaction or not; that is, the vast majority believe in some sort of theism or worship of one God, one focus of life, feeling, knowledge and power, whether they call themselves theists or naturalists or atheists or agnostics, or what not. As nothing can be actually denied till it has been defined, the common denial of God means no more than the denial of a certain conception of God, not a denial of the real fact which, in one form or another, all sane men affirm. The unity of the system of life is accepted by most scientists and philosophers, quite apart from religion, and this is the fundamental element in theism, or the belief in a theos or God. And even pluralists or our modern polytheists usually hold to some kind of unity, kinship or system of actual life. Thus religion, unlike the deliberately specialised work of particular sciences, is the seeing of life as a whole and as a unity. Real pluralists or polytheists must be very few, for to deny to the universe what you must insist upon for your own life is absurd, in view of the fact that only through your own experience do you know the universe. In our own thinking we must find unity; the rational impulse is the impulse to unity in our thought life; and, if we cannot find this unity in some real measure, our minds become seriously dissociated and we lose our sanity. Complete unity is not yet possible to us, but a preponderating measure of it must be achieved if we are to survive the struggle, and to this end we must believe in this unity of life. Moreover, all the growth of our knowledge has been in the direction of such unity or coherence in nature and in all our experiences, and the hypothesis of that unity has been progressively justified by its fruits. The onus of proof is upon those who deny the kinship and coherence and unity of life, which is a postulate of our consciousness, not upon those who affirm it.

Starting, then, with this idea of God as a symbol for the unity, coherence, and kinship of all life i.e., for an integration of the totality of the universe, we find on investigation very different levels of belief in God as this fundamental idea has been developed and interpreted. Even in its lowest terms it must for us include the moral and mental as well as the physical universe, i.e., all the materials of our consciousness. But, as the word has unfortunately become at times a kind of party flag of church or sect, we must not be unprepared for the denial of the word even by those who admit the content of it. Many an atheist may really be a better theist than the orthodox believer of the churches. Many who refuse the word "God" will even admit, in addition to the idea of unity, the idea of goodness or of power or the like, as part of their universe sense. I know one professed atheist who claims a sense of nature which is not very removed from the ordinary worship of God. I think this is quite a common type of experience among, Hellenists, nature mystics, specialised scientists, artists and others. And the instance I gave earlier from the German book "Die Arbeiterfrage" is very illuminating as representing a similar attitude among very ordinary people, where the majority of those who found no meaning in the church's doctrine of God found the same moral idealism and sense of power for goodness in their sense of nature i.e. in a beauty mysticism. Here again it was not the reality which was denied, but only the term which was unpopular. One might here quote George Macdonald's verse

> *"I see Thy light, I feel Thy wind;*
> *The world, it is Thy word;*
> *Whatever wakes my heart and mind*
> *Thy presence is, my Lord."*

as a Christian statement of the same ultimate religious reality, by whatever name it be called.

In the above cases both theists and atheist had an ethical experience of values, revelation, desire, and power in their conscious relation to the universe about them, in which we may find the elements of a common worship and service of God or life; and it cannot be too strongly reiterated that religion is not an attitude towards a concept, "God" but towards life, and that the concept is only valuable if it be useful to any as a means to life. At our present stage of thinking it is probably the best means we have of visualising that fundamental rational, ethical, emotional, and purposive unity of our life, of our values and our personal relationships, in which religion consists. But the emphasis here cannot be put on any one aspect of life, neither on feeling, with some mystics, nor on sex, with some psychologists, nor on thought with some metaphysicians, nor on behaviour, with some modern philosophers. Life is one, in its variety we yet find unity through relationship and proportion; and religion too must be one, and fair to all elements in their due proportions and relations. The modern study of religious experience has made it clear that there are varieties in the avenues of approach to religious truth and experience, and a variety of types of temperament; and it is no longer reasonable nor possible for any man to try to fit his experience, into the grooves of another's experience, nor to demand it of others. And along with the intellectual comprehension of the variety of life in every aspect there has come a fuller emotional realisation of the solidarity of the race and of the substantial unity of human experience in all its essential elements. Therefore, our terms must, to be valuable, have no partisan, but a universal, meaning. And such a universal meaning the word "God" undoubtedly has, if we have the patience to trace it out. And how well worthwhile is the search! In one of his commentaries, Dr Alexander Maclaren says of this unity of God in human experience, "Blessed are they who are delivered from the misery of multiplied and transient aims which break life into fragments, by steadfastly and continually following one great desire which binds all the days each to each, and in its single simplicity encloses and hallows and unifies the else distracting manifoldness."

I have spoken of the idea of "God" as implying the unity, coherence and kinship of the universe, or total experience of man, both in the sense and domain of values and in all the relationships of life. But like most of our great terms, the word has a long and complicated history and represents not a simple, but a composite idea, behind which lies along development of experience and of its philosophical, theological, and scientific formulation. Yet these above are the two main divisions of the content of the idea of God, what we may call principles, and what we may call social values and relations; for as individuals we have two kinds of relationships, relationships towards the universe as a whole, which we may call the sense of principles or values (i.e., a relationship toward the unseen which we may call central) and relationships towards our concrete environment, in particular our fellowmen, (i.e., a relationship towards the seen which we may call peripheral). The two are, of course, ultimately related and interdependent; but such a division is I think a fair one, and it corresponds to Christ's great summary of true religion or true human behaviour as "to love God and to love one's neighbour." Thus, our idea of God includes obligations or relationships towards things seen and unseen; towards the unseen the chief virtue of man is what we call worship which includes homage and service; towards the seen the chief virtue of man is what we call love or social and self-forgetful benevolence. But the word of 'love' in the sense of positive passion may be used of both, for worship too is love. The word "God", then, stands in an ultimate sense for our Universe and also in an ultimate sense for society; a true relation to Him as the focus of all life, personal or impersonal, involves a true relation both to principles and to our fellows, for God is the exclusive One and the Inclusive All. Here then we have a word which simplifies the question of moral obligation; if we can think feel and act in terms of, and for, the whole - for God - we shall do our best for every particular part, for the world, for humanity, and for self.

Hence religion is the art of life and theology its science - the service and the doctrine of God. Further, this inclusive and unified, yet social, idea of God must include the note of personality, which is perhaps our chief modern value. Personal and moral values depend largely on relationships. Goodness is a personal relation to God or to one's neighbour. It is in personal relationships that our highest values find their best or only expression; it is in personality that most of the real worth of life consists. Perhaps the chief argument for immortality is that the main worth of life and its ethical values have no permanence, except through the permanence of personal relationships with God and with other lives. All the highest things we know and value revolve round personal beings and their relations, and in God we must find not only a source and explanation of these social and personal values and relationships, in particular the worth of love; but we must find the pattern and inspiration of them and the power to achieve them, for the purposive process of life is the growing expression of what is already potential in our lives and their environment, i.e., it is the realisation of God. We cannot possibly as rational beings believe that God is unlike us; as rational beings we believe in the ultimate commensurability and consubstantiality of the universe, and therefore in God's kinship to us, however short of Him our growth may be at any point. Therefore, by a necessity of our own nature (which is the handiwork of God) we must conceive of God as in our image if we believe we are in His; and consequently we must find in His those elements which belong to the highest development of our own natures and which we specially value such as emotion, intelligence, power, purpose and freedom. All these help to make up our composite idea of personality; and it is impossible for us to believe that God can be less personal than we, in so far as we use the word "personality" in a positive and uniting, not in a negative and divisive sense. It is perfectly true that the personality of God may be something infinitely beyond ours, as the consciousness of man is at an enormous remove from that of a garden slug; but, as the consciousness of the slug is a step on the same ladder as man has climbed, and the human consciousness, though higher, is yet along the same line development, so we, believing in the organic unity of spirit or consciousness throughout the universe, must believe that the consciousness of ultimate and universal being is along the same lines as our own being, and , while it will transcend it, it must contain the same elements of value, in higher forms, probably, than ours, not in lower. What is of real value in man must be in God, and the personal mystics at least *have* found in God the satisfaction and completion of their personal values and hungers; and if there be in God a super-personality, as is often claimed, it must at least contain the positive values of personality.

The development of personality cannot land us ever in impersonality, which is subhuman; therefore, we must, to think at all reasonably of God, our ultimate symbol of life and experience, credit God with personality, including at least all our attributes of emotion or affection, intelligence or thought, power or activity, will or purpose, and freedom, or some kind, of sovereignty over all the lower reaches of life. That is, God is not merely a unity of values and relations, but a personal unity of these things, a personal (though not an individual) life in whom they cohere and function. This leads us to the personal idea of God which, in the records of the Christian revelation, crystallised first into the Old Testament doctrine of a divine King and later into the Christian doctrine of God the Father, to be enriched later by a still more human evaluation of divinity as found in an ideal manhood, set out in the doctrine of the Son and enshrining the Christian conception of man's goal and his fundamental kinship with ultimate being as revealed in the life and work of Jesus of Nazareth. The development of the doctrine of God has been the correlate and symbol of the development of man's sense of the values and meaning of his own life and experience in its universe relations. Through that doctrine and its practice, he has in fact raised himself and ennobled his life, and so proved the doctrine's essential reasonableness or coherence with the laws and creative powers of nature. The Christian doctrine of God as revealed in human life is becoming truer and more obvious every day by the process of ethical and social development; the doctrine, however imperfectly as yet, is both a means and an end; by venturing upon it men prove it and come, to restate it better. The idea in itself is an inspiration to venture; and, if the subsequent proof be sometimes but partial, it is not God who is thus disproved in part, but the inadequacy of our definition, which benefits thus both from the success and the failure of honest religious experimenters. The final proof of the personality of God lies, of course, in such venture; and in the lives of Christ and the saints, and often in our own, we have tested that faith and found it bear our weight and grow stronger and purer by exercise.

In modern treatments of religious experience much stress has been laid upon awe or reverence as the fundamental religious emotion; and this stress has been for good, even if some of the analysis of the religious consciousness involved have been very unconvincing. Now awe does not mean fear, it does not stand for depression nor even for self-depreciation. In its true Christian form at least it connotes, not human insignificance, but human significance seen against the background of the sublimity of nature or the universe. True humility is neither self-exalting nor self-depreciating, as Hadfield has said; it is self-forgetting. True humility or awe is the feeling most of us would have on a lonely moor beneath the silent stars. The experience might mean discomfort, or it might joy according to our mental attitude or state, but it consists in the getting of a universe perspective in some measure, a sense of ourselves as seen in real proportion against the background of a life bigger than out yet comprehending and oaring for ours. Perhaps with our tendency to megalomania the immediate result might be self-depreciation and even despair; but the truest result is the conscious losing of oneself in the larger unity, the sense of surrender and of homage.

"Now all the heavenly splendour
Breaks forth in starlight tender,
From myriad worlds unknown;
And man the marvel seeing,
Forgets his selfish being,
For joy of beauty not his own!"

Worship is the attitude of mind and behaviour which corresponds to this intellectual and emotional sense of the universe or God; while, on the side of our particular human relationships, the peculiarly religious attitude and behaviour which follows upon such a finding of our true selves in the perspective of all life is the attitude of love or benevolence which is also self-forgetful and full of surrender, i.e., we live henceforth and consciously in and for the whole. Here, then, we have the essential notes of true and practical religion, a surrender of self and a readjustment of perspective, in the conscious experiences of universal and social reality, with the attendant emotions of awe and benevolence, in the activities of worship and love. Society, to deserve the name truly, can only be built on love, the ideal social relationship, first realised in sex and parenthood but later extended to all life; and here God stands for Society on its ideal, as well as its actual side, i.e., for the true integrations and relationships of the Many. And our individual relationship to the universe, to be healthy, real and practical, will be one of awe or reverence, not of fear, but of a true evaluation of oneself with God, against the background of all life; and here God stands for the Universe or the ultimate One. To God as one we give worship; to God as the many we give love. And hence it is that the truest ethical religion of today calls God by the name of Love and bids us worship Him.

Thus, as love, God is the integration of life as one and yet many. In such ways God appears as the completest integration of our experience and of our values; of physical, mental, moral, and social life. Thus, God may be compendiously spoken of as the All in All. As the All, He is the body of life in its powers and parts and differentiation, as time, space and all dimensions, as matter and form, as energy and power, as motion and development - the stuff of life. As *in* all He is the One, the soul, or directing and integrating centre of life, with all the attributes of soul in affection and emotion, intelligence and will, purpose, freedom, personality - the living cause of life. Thus, God is the integration of all that makes up our life on its physical, psychical, ethical and social sides, both in the lower sense of its totality and in the highest sense of its unity and meaning. As our body and soul, however diverse, are integrated into one in a real sense, so in God we have an integration of all the diverse elements of life, with a personal character and unity of control such as marks the highest human life. No doubt there is much in God that human experience cannot touch nor fathom at all; but of our universe sense and activity, which we call religion, God is both its content and its focus. If to this it be objected that we have no real universe sense at all, and that our experience can at its best be but an experience of parts, I should reply that I am using the words, not in a static, but in a dynamic sense, as representing our growing approximation to a universe sense in our every increasing scope of experience; and secondly that our universe sense must normally be taken as meaning our sense of our total environment at its completest and most unified, our sense of the greatest social integration known in our experience.

And in actual fact in the records of religious experience at, its clearest, and especially in mysticism, this sense of God, this universe sense, has been expressed in very simple and convincing ways, and in ways which contain the sense of finality and completeness. Potentially no doubt our experience might cover all things in the universe, and in religious experience there has at times been this comprehensive but growing sense of God, or of a universal object of worship and service; of which I hope to speak later in dealing with communion with God and especially with mysticism. This universe sense may, then, be spoken of more scientifically as a growing approximation, and, in terms of the greater or the lesser mysticism, as a definite experience known in some measure to all men. After all our thinking is such a universe activity; every definition implies such a universal faith or experience. In defining "sincerity" or "man" I pass from the particular experience of individual acts of sincerity or of individual men to a universal conception of each; therefore, it is natural that in religion I should find the same value, the same necessity and the same reality in universalizing my experience to cover both the actual and potential and even the ideal, or the whole of life so far as I know it, or infer or imagine it.

The difficulty with most scientific minds at this point is the personality of God. They assume personality more or less as something dividing individuals and cannot use the word; or they are shy about attributing to God the limitations and the possibly undeveloped, or, to God, unimportant activities and debilities of our minds, such as anger, excitement, wonder, fear, anxiety and the like. But these things just mentioned may be defects of growth, imperfections or by products of our development, though in a sublimated and more developed form they may have more permanent value. We cannot be minute in our description of the content of the personality of God; but at least it seems truer to define personality as positive and integrating, than as negative and divisive, and so to claim with Lotze that we are growing in personality i.e. towards God, who is Personality. And it is on the side of values that we approach the personality of God most satisfactorily; personal qualities at the highest, being for us the supreme category of value, must have meaning for and place in God, who is our ideal and ethical inspiration. In the new realist conception of God (vide Alexander) the divine is that which lies beyond us at our present stage of development or emergence and calls us forward i.e., the potential but unrealised vision of what we may be. And, even if this something be super-personal, it must none the less contain and use all that is of value in personality. For example, the steps of biological development have been briefly, matter, life, consciousness, and self-consciousness; but life uses matter, consciousness is built on life, and self-consciousness, lies beyond but incorporates consciousness. Thus, it is natural that God, who lies beyond us, should possess and use whatever is of value in the higher as well as the lower reaches of our natures.

Unfortunately, so much of our experience of life is circumferential and not centripetal; we are conscious of our relations to the people about us and to the natural objects near us; but the religious experience of God, though it has its relation to all life, is specifically and characteristically centripetal, an immediate experience of our own lives in relation to their proper centre, which is at the same time the centre of all others' experiences. The mystics are those who have had a strong central as opposed to circumferential experience; but in some measure these experiences belong to all human souls if they can but recognise their facts and element; and it is central consciousness which is the chief and most characteristic experience of religion, communion with God.

Let me say in passing that it is not easy, not even reasonable, to seek to account for a complex universe like ours by a simple unity in our doctrine of God. A complex universe in continuous activity seems to imply a complex of ultimate elements that interact. It is here that we come to the Christian conception of God as a Trinity in Unity, elements in God fundamentally one, as our mind and body are, yet incommensurable or ultimate. As in man we perceive a creative activity of hunger or desire, a limiting and discriminating activity of thought, and a practical or integrating activity of action; so in God we recognise the creative element, which we call the Father, the individual or discriminating element which we call Logos, or the incarnate and eternal Son, and the integrating or social element which we all the Holy Ghost. It is not my purpose to enlarge upon this valuable credal pattern of the Threeness of life, but I would simply point out here that it explains and covers many aspects and levels of life, as Body, Mind and Spirit, as Desire, and System and Life, as sub-personal, personal, and super-personal, as father, mother and child, and so forth there is abundant evidence of threefoldness in our lives. But it is at least probable that the ultimate unity and unit of life in such a complex and developing world should be complex rather than simple, and should contain in itself the seeds of movement, development and creative purpose. Thus, in God it is probable that there are elements sub-personal and personal and super-personal, in harmony with our experience, but passing far beyond it; and yet, that the three are one God, one life, as desire and reason and action are one in us. I do not anticipate that all will gladly accept the Trinitarian form of this complexity, as the subject has been so controversial in the historical progress of theology; but at least I think a complexity of life in God can reasonably be postulated, and in some such way as is found in the orthodox doctrine of the Triune God, i.e., of primal elements, incommensurable in thought, but integrable in action or actual life by virtue of life's very constitution. No simple and lonely monad God is sufficient to account for life as we know it; and even if we do not accept the creeds of the church or of any organised religious society, yet they may be found suggestive in such ways as the above.

Again, the doctrine of relativity today, as applied to morals, has shown us that in a developing and kinetic, not static world the absolute stands, not for a point, but for a direction; and that evil has no meaning except as relative to good i.e., that there is no positive principle of evil, but only, for example, the pull and contrast of our lower past against our higher, i.e., of our past against our present and future as that lower is embedded in our heredity and in society – while goodness has a positive value as the activity of the maintenance, development and integration of what is useful and valuable in life. Thus, goodness is the direction in which, by growth in valuation and achievement, we are developing as a race; evil is any point on that line behind the points we have individually or socially reached, and the truly good, or the better, is always ahead of us. So it is easy today to think of God, the source and end and unity of our values, as good and not evil, as free to do good without being free to do evil, as indeed the fount and inspiration and power of goodness - "there is none good but one, that is God", and all our true goodness is the expression of God.

CHAPTER IX

Communion with God

But if God be such - real, good, personal, and one, yet all embracing - can our minds enter into a conscious communion with Him? i.e., into relations of a kind not entirely dissimilar from our fellowship with men. The affirmative answer implies a consciousness of being both one with God and yet different from Him. The believer in mere pantheism, mere immanence, may find some difficulty in an affirmative answer, so far as definition in language is concerned; for all things will seem to him but functions of God, and, apart from the separate phenomena of the flux of experience, there will seem to him no God with whom one can have actual communion, no one personal being in which our personalities can find satisfaction and completion. But Christianity ever stands between pantheism and deism, between immanence and transcendence, finding in experience, and attempting to find in theory, a fusion of the two ideas of God, as one with us and yet as different and so over against us.

I have already discussed the question of this communion with God in some measure as regards both the experience of immanence and that of transcendence, i.e., the consciousness of contact with God as our own best self, and the consciousness of contact with God as a power or treasury of life, not our own, upon which we can draw, and thereby grow in personality and in moral likeness to this God, with whom we have such communion. To this earlier discussion I wish at this point to add but a few further points regarding the conscious immediate or direct experience of God. I have no doubt, both from my own experience and from the testimonies of others upon whose honesty my judgment cannot but rely with confidence, that the experience of conscious communion with God, however it be defined or explained, is a real one, and that the content of that experience is one of the greatest things in life and will abide, when analysis and restatement have done their utmost for our vocabulary and for the scientific systematisation of all our experiences. But this communion is so direct and immediate an experience of the subject in us that it more or less defies definition. Nevertheless in some degree I believe the experience is available for all in the broadest human sense; but one must recognise, in the first place, that many have not had it, or rather (as I think more probable) have not associated such elements of it as they have had with the idea of God or of religion, and, in the second, that even in the highest and most intense religious experiences:, so far as we evaluate them and so far as they are recorded for us - in oral or written evidence - these moments of experience are intermittent. The vision fades, we long for the touch that is vanished and the voice that seems still, but their power abides, both in memory and in character. Not even the best of lives rises to these mountain-top experiences more than occasionally; these experiences are from God, not man, and all the sons of men, even Jesus of Nazareth (as being such), must hold to and work out their vision, when it is gone, in the hard and testing circumstances of commonplace everyday life (cf. Mark 1:12, Luke 9:37). There seems to be an economy of divine grace and power in such experiences; they have a purpose and an allotted place in life; and to those who would build tabernacles that they might stay and worship on the hill of vision and transfiguration comes still the same answer - the blessing of the abnormal is withdrawn and at once we have the problem of pain and sorrow on the plain below, calling for normal forms of service and helpfulness to which our new knowledge and new certainty must now be turned.

But these great moments of religious life do exist. In some measure they are probably experienced, however unrecognised, by all or most of our fellowmen; but few of the great creative souls of religious history have been without a succession of such great moments or crises of revelation, when God ceases to be an inference and becomes a fact of experience, when men no longer have to be content to know things about God, as we interpret our life, but when we know Him and see Him, in a sense as actual and effectual and formative as that in which they know or see anything. The experience may be extraordinarily hard to define in the language of everyday life, especially for a critical mind; but to those who have had it, it is the most real, the most powerful thing in life. Yet its form is so hard to fix in any except emotional tones that in later times of depression one may find it hard to believe in the reality or validity of such a past experience at all, even though its actual influence in life may remain nearly as strong as ever. This fluctuation of experience from exaltation to depression, and from certainty to doubt, is found in all the highest and most sensitive types very clearly marked, and not least in our Scriptures, Hebrew and Christian. But though one's sense of these immediate or mystical experiences may not remain uniform, as memory varies in emotional intensity, or as a wave of cynicism or pessimism floods our souls for a season, yet the true and original sense of the experiences may recur, the experiences themselves may be repeated in other contexts, and the ethical meaning of the experiences certainly abides in memory and will. Upon such moments, life is nourished and contact with the highest maintained; for such moments represent the coming of new powers, new ideals, and a new understanding of life, and not infrequently follow or precede great spiritual conflict.

It is absurd either to magnify or to minimise such times of direct experience; it is dangerous to take experience for other than it is, dangerous to seek either to deny it or to worship it. What is past is past, and its value lies in what it was in fact or what it remains in influence; our business is to accept it for what it is, and neither to boast of our possession nor to mourn over our lack. Men differ and their experiences must differ. We have no right to assume that it would be better for us if we had the experience of someone else, or for someone else if they had ours; we and they may be better as we are, for life has all sorts of types and levels of experience; and in any case sincerity is the high road to all that is best. Many of the creative souls in religious life have had vivid, ecstatic, mystical experience and violent conversions, but it is all important that, for all our admiration at such souls, we should be as natural as possible, taking life as it comes and trusting the great Gardener to treat his many plants individually as they need. These experiences that come direct from God are His gift; they are usually not to be won, but to be accepted both as a privilege and as a social responsibility. Of course, something of the kind may be induced by training, expectation, and preparation - and much has been written regarding the mystic way - for the artificial or organised has its place in life as well as the spontaneous, but it is rarely outstanding or creative. But, if such direct, immediate experiences of God are given to us, we are trustees rather than owners; they exist for the sake of God and men, not for our own isolated comfort and assurance. We must neither envy others nor undervalue what we receive, sincerely and unstintingly live the social life of receiving and contributing, as we have opportunity and riches, to the common life of our race. It is as we are true to what we have, that more is given to us. Let as then neither underrate the mystical experiences of others, as though they were the signs of a weak, morbid, sentimental mentality, nor so covet them that we cannot work nor escape depression as we compare ourselves with these others - God treats us all differently and has different purposes for each.

Now these moments of conscious communion are accompanied not seldom by the sense of complete surrender, as the individual, for a time at least is enveloped in the larger life of God and individual standards of measurement are lost sight of. They are usually marked by a sense of new power, especially power to love the good and the true, and to overcome evil habits and levels of conduct. As the vision fades, the struggle may seem to grow harder, but in some form the power abides, and, at first, at least, this power is felt to come from without, i.e. is felt as not being of or from the realised and conscious self, but from something behind or beyond it. In all ethical religion there is found this sense of transcendence, of contact with something greater than ourselves, farther along the path or direction of goodness, yet akin to us. And an essential element in this experience of God in its more definite forms is what we may call personality; we have a sense, not indeed of a mere individuality such as we see in ourselves and others, but of something not ourselves, though one with us, which completes our personality, builds it up, energises and satisfies it - a great super-personality if you will, which is the source and means and end of ours.

In this whole question it is of course possible for the critic to keep raising all along the unsolved problem of subjective and objective, and to be trying here, there, and everywhere, to resolve these experiences into fantasies, delusions, and the like; but in this chapter we are dealing with a problem of definition, even more than of fact, and with a type of experience which in its own measure is susceptible to the same social and practical tests as all other religious experience. The various tests of validity enumerated earlier apply as truly to mystical experience as to anything else in religion, and religion has little to fear from a test in this matter, as the mystical element has been so pronounced - so uniquely present indeed - in many of those very personalities who, on other grounds, are regarded as the greatest and most creative spirits of our race.

God, then, stands in religion as the great central fact, the source, life, explanation and goal of the whole activity of the universe as we know it, not a mere congeries of ideas and experiences, but a unity akin to man and making of all human experiences, other unities. Thus, God stands for the unity of man's seeking and for the unity of his finding, for the unity of the ideal and the actual in the real and the like. It is perhaps unusual to speak of religious experience without a reference to the idea of a special providence, but I imagine a few words on this point will suffice. If we believe in a personal God the claim of special providence, like a miracle, does not mean an isolated thing or violation of law, but the operation, through the laws and the system of life, of a personal intelligence and will, similar in kind to the operation of the human mind and will, yet the operation of a God big enough to care for the small, details of life - and the grasp of detail is a sure test of intelligence. I do not think anyone can read sacred or secular history without recognising the presence of events, especially deliverances, which seem providential, i.e., as being unexpected coincidences between historical events and the main formative purposes of aspiration and development in man. The history of Israel, the life of Christ and the experiences of most believers in God have had some content of happenings, large or small in kind or degree, which seem to us to presuppose a conscious adaptation of natural means, which were beyond human control, to actual human need, and that for a specific purpose of ethical or social value. Of course all written history is interpretation, and liable to be challenged at any point, and it is almost impossible to prove any interpretation of it to be necessarily true; but, granting a wide use of common sense and of the fitness of things as necessary to a fair understanding of the events of human life, I think we have good reason to believe that the purposes of God have again and again in history been shown in the moulding of events, and especially in the resolving of great individual or social crises, in a way which postulates intelligent direction by "a power not ourselves making for righteousness" not indeed by violations of the system of nature, but by its use.

Wonderful things, or miracles, have often happened (according to the evidence available) either in terms of nature as already known, or, presumably, in terms of nature as not yet understood by men; and it is hard to resist the impression, gained both from history and from one's own experiences, that God is controlling events, educating souls and societies and sometimes in abnormal or unexpected ways manifesting His purposes and His nature very evidently in the course of human affairs. Words may be inadequate and may lead us astray, but the facts seem to support such a view rather than a denial of it. In such ways we get an objective glimpse of a divine purpose which corroborates and strengthens the subjective sense of a divine purpose such as we seem to find in our own best thinking and feeling. I think this sense of divine providence is an element in all vivid religious experience - I have no intention of playing off special, as against general, providence, for, if God has unity and intelligence, I can see no particular meaning in the opposition, as human action has also its general and its special aspects - and this sense seems to have been strongest in some of the greatest religious personalities of the past. And a God who does not care for individual details is hardly credible to an intelligent man who does, and who does so more and more as he grows in intelligence. In any case the proof of all our interpretations and theories of experience must lie in the concrete happenings and results of our life and behaviour; and here, at least, the great souls of religious history have for the most part found a personal God of truth and beauty, goodness and power, one who acts towards us not merely through well-known natural laws, but in ways that seem particular and personal. Such was the experience of

Jesus, for example, and it was supported by the strongest and most vivid of mystical experiences.

In closing this chapter, I would refer to future sections on prayer, conversion, and mysticism, in particular as adding to and elaborating something of what has been said above, though in what remains of this book, I do not intend try to cover the forms and problems of religious experience in any but brief outline. To those general readers who are specially interested in the subject of mysticism I would here recommend the preface to Shaw's play "St Joan" as the work of an impartial and keen student of human nature with no axe to grind. For others who wish to go farther along that line I would mention the names of William James, J.B. Pratt, R.H. Thouless, Dean Inge and Evelyn Underhill, who have done much to popularise the important study of mysticism.

In concluding this discussion on communion with God (i.e., direct conscious contact with Him, which must therefore have, for the individual at least, emotional, intellectual and practical evidence and outcome) I would say that the forms of the experience vary greatly in degree of intensity or of moral content but that the experience itself, found in such primary forms as the thrill over a thing of beauty, or over a deed of heroism, and in such developed forms as the visions and communion with God of Jesus Himself, or of many of the greatest Christian and non-Christian saints, seems a thing of universal occurrence in some form or degree, often unrecognized for what it is; but at its highest, in forms like the Beatific Vision, it seems both the inspiration and completion of all that is best and most purposive and most divine in human life – "to glorify God and to enjoy Him,"

BOOK III

THE FORMS OF
RELIGIOUS EXPERIENCE

CHAPTER X

Prayer

In the two parts of this volume which remain, to be completed I wish to deal in an outline way, first with the shapes or forms of expression in which religious experience is chiefly to be observed, and then with some of the more serious of the problems which are associated with them or with religious experience generally. In this section I intend to deal in particular with prayer, conversion, mysticism and finally with the grace of God as expressed in human experience; and in the following section with the important problems of conscience and sin, freedom or free will, and the relation of doctrine to experience. These are not all the significant forms or problems of religious experience and religious ethics, but they are the more obvious and most frequently referred to, and therefore should, I think, get some notice in this book as making concrete the positions outlined in earlier chapters and as providing characteristic examples of the religious consciousness in various fields or aspects. The material with which this section of the book will be chiefly concerned consists of subjects on which much has been written - far more, relatively in recent times, than on the subjects considered in former chapters. The forms of religious experience such as conversion, prayer, mysticism, and the like have been most elaborately investigated in the last forty years, both in statistical and in philosophical ways, and the subject of the religious consciousness, considered in detail, has become a department of science, a young and still very imperfect science, but a science none the less. Elaborate questionnaires have been issued and the results collated with considerable success, as by Starbuck, Leuba, Pratt and others; indeed, literature on normal and abnormal religious development and its forms is already immense, and I do not wish here to challenge comparison with such books by attempting a detailed or exhaustive account of the psychological phenomena of religion, or a comprehensive discussion of the problems that arise. But in an outline, and, I hope, in a suggestive, way I wish to deal with the chief forms in which the religious consciousness is recognized, and, after that with the main problems, practical and` theoretical which are lit up by them. Those who wish a full and adequate treatment of the subject of religious psychology I would refer to the suggested list of reading given at the end of this book, or to other recognised handbooks on the psychology of religion.

The first subject to arise out of my recent discussion of communion with God is that of prayer, usually understood as conscious and deliberate communion with God, but with many varieties from that of a voiceless communion, to that of something like human conversation with a definite use of words; so, the rest of this chapter will be concerned with prayer. What is the meaning and value of the activity and the forms of prayer? Today the idea of suggestion is very prominent in all discussions of prayer; and, of course, in all deliberate or attempted communion with God - and the artificial or organised has its place in life, as well as the spontaneous - suggestion plays a large part, as we consciously tune ourselves in to Him, as He has been known to us in our own and others' best and most creative moments of religious life, i.e. as we reproduce the atmosphere of feeling and thought seemingly most conducive to the experience of communion. But real prayer is more than suggestion or an attempt to gain an experience; it is experience itself; it may be felt contact with power; and those who have been there knew it in a way which has changed life. In that intercourse of spirit, the potential in life is changed into the actual, and energy, is found for the tasks which life lays upon us day by day. Many are the questions asked today in this subject. What is prayer in itself? Is prayer of any value in an orderly universe with such a God as we today believe in? Does prayer get beyond the margins of our own personalities, and if so how? Does prayer change God, or life, or only ourselves? Such questions and others are heard today on every hand, asked, not by cynics and unbelievers, but by the rank and file of thinking and loyal Christians. Upon some of these questions I wish to touch, but I wish first to emphasise that the Christian conception of prayer corresponds to the Christian conception of God. i.e., God is our Father, we are His children; and prayer to God is on the basis of home relations, it is the speech, not of slaves to a despot, but of children to a father; and, in line with this ruling idea, prayer for Christians is a privilege, rather than a duty, a means of grace, not an essential condition of salvation or the like.

Coming then to the question of the meaning of prayer, we find here today a very vexed question, owing to the modern emphasis upon physical and psychical interests and systems, which compels men to ask, in criticism of earlier and naive, conceptions: Can prayer change things? Is prayer conversation with God or only with oneself? and so forth. There are certainly very wrong ideas of prayer prevalent in many quarters. Mr G.B. Shaw, speaking of the religious activities that man directs towards God has spoken of sacrifice as attempted bribery, and of prayer as attempted flattery, both alike low and commercial in their meaning and aim. Mr A.C. Benson in a very honest essay on prayer has deprecated the idea that God is pleased with our meeting together at certain times and in certain places to offer him a kind of complimentary effusion; no decent man, he says, would care for that, much less God. Again, we must distinguish clearly between public prayer and private prayer. Public prayer has many differing degrees of formality, approximating at one end to the *opus operandum* conception of a formal rite, and at the other to private prayer in its main essence. Speaking generally, public prayer is formal rather than spontaneous, it is thinking for others rather than expressing oneself; it is consciously aesthetic and liturgical to some considerable extent, because it is for others. That is, public prayer is only in a measure prayer to God at all - it is inevitably in part prayer "delivered to a congregation". This phrase has sometimes been used sarcastically but without justification; for public prayer, even if it is to God, is of its very nature to God via man. But, in dealing with the topic of prayer allied with the subject of religious experience, one is thinking, inevitably, of the more or less spontaneous exercise of private prayer. Public, or collective prayer, certainly has its place in religious life, but my present concern is with private or personal prayer.

I am inclined to believe that nearly all the theories of prayer, which have been held by men, have their measure of value and truth; but, when one looks at the phenomena of prayer as known to us, there are certain definite meanings and types of prayer which call for special mention, In the first place, prayer is self-expression in conscious weakness; it is the expression of creature-hood or dependence in the moment, or from the sense, of need. That is, it is the cry of a child to an unseen parent, perhaps in faith, but at least in hope. Again, prayer is probably in part telepathy, the contact with other minds by outgoing thought, touching God or influencing others. Indeed, one may not unreasonably, I think, conceive of God as a kind of wireless exchange tor the messages of human prayer and concern - I do not refer to the mere saying of prayers, but to prayer with the heart and will behind it, genuine aspiration and hunger. The true fact behind this seems to be that which, about fifty years ago, was suggested R. J. Campbell in his stimulating book, 'The New Theology' and sometimes repeated since, viz, that human souls are at root one in God; they are like coral islands, peaks of a great submerged continent, separated consciously from one another by the sea that lies around them; but, follow them downward below the sea and they are found united into a continent far below their normal levels of consciousness. In such ways one can explain Jung's conception of the "vague unconscious" into which flow the achievements of the human race as into a common pool from which men may draw who have the gift or have developed the capacity to do so - all may have the gift in some measure. It is a useful analogy and has, I think, a definite relevance to the operation of prayer and of other forms of serious thought or desire. The study of human, and especially Christian, biography seems to me to make it probable that prayer can touch both the universal mind and individual minds, and so have a very definite influence upon others; and I believe many of the answers to prayer of which we hear are due to this telepathic communication.

Prayer again is largely suggestion, i.e., the innervation of desire or motor centres by attention and directed thought. In this way prayer can influence oneself powerfully for the making of character. Perhaps this is the commonest and most fruitful form of prayer - putting oneself in line with God's will, as in the earlier petitions of the Lord's Prayer. Yet again, prayer may be real communion with God, of a mystical or ecstatic character in some degree, though in this form prayer tends to be largely voiceless, for it is so largely passive communion - things being done *in* rather than by us, c.f. Christ's secret retirements for prayer. Perhaps such true communion may seem rather purposeless to Western minds craving for activity and production; nevertheless, it is one of life's greatest things, the consciousness of an identity of life and desire with God, the beatific vision, or the enjoyment of God. But in this form prayer is rather more an atmosphere than a form of words or even of thoughts. Yet again, much private devotion is a discipline, a training of the mind to concentrate and feed upon certain thoughts and to defeat others, a forming of habits, an exercise of the will. This more articulate use of prayer is rather different from suggestion, and rather more dangerous, too, as it so easily tends to become formal and habitual, and so to oust the more real or spontaneous forms of prayer; but I doubt not it has its value and place in life, as discipline in general has, especially in relation to morbid conditions.

Later I hope to consider in some measure the relation of prayer to God and nature and the regular system of life under which we live. It has of course never been seriously contended that prayer can of itself accomplish things apart from God, therefore the conception of prayer as a force or lever, where it is not merely magical, really belongs to the earlier category of prayer as a telepathic kind of activity communicating directly with God and often, through Him, working upon other lives or circumstances. If miraculous results from prayer are claimed, yet these must be classed as the works of God in answer to prayer rather than the works of man or of prayer itself. Therefore, we cannot really claim that prayer changes God or changes things, but only that through prayer things are changed and perhaps even the action of God modified, (for example) He can trust us more. But of this point I hope to speak later.

Before I go further and pass from the more important theories of prayer, however, I wish to say one thing. As we have read of the Athenian altar to the unknown God, which some expositors take as an attempt to cover all the gods and to avoid leaving any out, by providing even for any of whom they might be ignorant, so in this spirit I should like to make a place here, among the theories I have discussed, for the meanings of prayer which I do not know, which perhaps I may feel in indefinite ways, or which others may knew and not I. Men have believed in prayer as being more than I have been able to state above; but why I cannot say, nor can they definitely say themselves, so far as my knowledge of the literature carries me. Their reasons for such further belief are probably good, even if they be not definite. Our analysis, our systematisation, our definitions, our theories are not exhaustive nor final; experience is greater than they. Prayer at any rate is a part of religious experience and therefore a part of creative evolution, and quite probably beyond accurate or adequate definition at every point. It has worked. We cannot easily believe that it changes God or compels Him to do what He would otherwise not do - that idea seems to be a relic from the primeval days of spells and incantations to compel or cajole the rather indifferent or malicious spirit world. But we may nevertheless believe that prayer can modify God's action by making it possible for Him to do through it what He could not otherwise do, for example, to trust men where He could not before; for prayer changes men, both ourselves and others and in such ways, it may render it possible for God to make effective to men gifts which He is offering them all the time. This may look like, a change in God, but it is not a change in His will or desire, but only in His action, so far as that is contingent on men's action. It may be somewhat open to objection to think of God thus in terms of time and change, but, if we are to think at all concretely and to relate God to experience as we know it, we must so or not at all. Even if one were to carry all God's actions back to a pre-cosmic foreknowledge, to divine decrees, the same elements must enter into the problem still, however they may be related to time and place. Such a change then, in God's action through human prayer, operating by suggestion or telepathy or receptive faith, or otherwise, is of course really a change, not in God, but in man and in the conditions of man's relation to God.

Prayer is often spoken of as a cause of miracles, just as faith is similarly referred to. But I think it is well that we should disabuse our minds of the idea of miracle as a necessary violation of an ordered system of life. The word implies nothing more than events at which we marvel or wonder because we do not understand; but, as the domain of our ignorance is greater than that of our knowledge, it is not remarkable that "miracle" has still a large place in life. Our knowledge of nature and its laws or systems is partial, and inexplicable things otter occur to us, and especially in connection with the psychological attitudes of faith or expectancy in thought. I think today the earlier scientific scepticism with regard to faith healing and other forms of "miracles", or abnormal events, has received some very severe blows, and that we are less inclined now to deny what we do not understand.

Thus, again, we are readier to believe that if prayer be the prayer of faith, it could and often does "change things" and even "work miracles", i.e., it enables God or nature to become operative in new and abnormal or little known ways. We cannot any longer with confidence circumscribe the sphere and power under God, of faith and of prayer. But however we are to view or to account for the power of prayer to effect the unexpected or seemingly impossible, for most of us, at any rate, prayer is an *instinct* in regard to the exercise of which naturalness, freedom, sincerity and expectancy will help us to the best results. And as regards the claim that prayer effects great things for men in ways other than those specifically mentioned above, as many still hold, and hold, I believe, with some basis in experience, thus, much falls to be said. Prayer is part of experience, that is, it is part of that chain of cause and effect which is somehow creating new things in the universe continually. Without it the effects might be other than they are with it; and as we look back, we may some-day see that it has had its influence in ways of which we knew nothing, that our prayer was part of the plan or organic unity of growth, and that in some respects it changed things for us or for others, either in ways enumerated above or in other; not yet known to us or perhaps to any men.

But there is a great danger in accepting the view of prayer as a kind of lever for doing or changing things, for influencing God and others in an automatic way. It is easy to believe that the spontaneous prayer which we cannot repress may have some such value, for it seems to well out of something greater than ourselves; but it is hard to believe that artificial prayer, the deliberate saying of forms of words of petition and intercession, in response to an idea of obligation rather than in response to desire, can have any such value. Prayer as directed thought issuing from a sense of obligation may have it or own value; but I do not think it is the prayer which works "miracles" and calls out superhuman power - it may help to make character, but it is not in the truest and most characteristic sense prayer.

The peculiar danger of the "lever" theory, if I may call it so, is that we come to think of prayer as a good deed, a thing, therefore, to be used to the utmost according to the obligations of worship or of love. So people come to make of prayer a ceremonial performance, demanded of us lest others should suffer, or lest we should fail of some blessing, a force which will induce God to do what He would not otherwise (!), and so they burden themselves with lengthy and detailed prayer lists, lists which they dare not reduce, but which ever grow in comprehensiveness; and so they have long and ever longer periods of intercession for all sorts and conditions of people and things, in which they feel they ought to be interested, and to which they are thus, as they believe, giving help. The whole thing is a legalistic and rather burdensome performance, especially for the more morbid consciences. If such do not feel the desire to pray, all the more fiercely they force themselves through the routine, as a medieval monk forced himself through a fast or a flagellation or a night on the cold stone, believing that their dryness of the spirit is of the devil. But it is often merely indigestion of spirt or of mind, or a sign that they are on the wrong road. As in physical indigestion diet has often to be reduced or regulated or even cut to the utmost minimum, so here drastic measures may often be necessary to rescue the spirit of man and the true ideal of prayer from this morbidity. What such persons are indulging in is not prayer but prayers – a very different thing which Jesus in the Greek calls "battalogia", much speaking. True private prayer must be predominantly spontaneous and natural; the only safeguard against formalism and asceticism in any shape is spontaneity. So, prayer most be linked up primarily with the desires and emotions of the heart; or, as we sing,

> *"Prayer is the soul's sincere desire, uttered or unexpressed; the motion of a hidden fire that trembles in the breast."*

In other words, we should mainly pray for such things as God lays upon us, not those which, under some theory of the efficacy of prayer, we lay upon ourselves; we should pray for definite objects as they engage our hearts and minds, not as slaves but as sons, not as a wearisome obligation but as a spontaneous privilege. Prayer undertaken as a discipline or remedial corrective is of course a definite thing with a place of its own; but all other prayer should, in my opinion, be as natural as it can be, as near to the instinct and the filial relationship as possible, not a good work laying up supposed merit for ourselves or others, but a free and unforced expression of our own highest desires and interests.

We must strive to be free and sincere in all our religion, using forms as we need them but with spirits independent of them at bottom. And our prayer should be, above all, an attitude or atmosphere of life, continual not intermittent - the practice of the presence of God. I have no sympathy with those who mock at the emergency use of prayer; that use is instinctive and right; but, along with the emergency use in time of need, should go a continual dwelling of spirit, heart, and mind, in the atmosphere of the thought and presence of God. For such prayer is our chief conscious means of contact with the unseen; it means the giving of attention and will to the fundamental realities of our life, it means the abiding purpose of a theocentric life, a life dwelling, in the presence, not of its petty individual interests, but of its own highest ideals and of its universal relations and meaning. Such a life of prayer is the chief goal of all true personal religion.

For practically all religions prayer in some form bas been a central activity, a normal means of communication with something beyond our known selves and of recharging our souls with vision and power); and, that it is such, is the belief of the majority of those who persist in it. For all civilised persons who use it, it is suggestion, in so far, at least, as it means a tuning in to God, or the best we know of life; but, for most who use it, it means also at least self-completion and contact with power. No doubt in many of its forms it still reflects the early prayers of the magical stage in religion when men sought to coerce and compel the divine by spells and incantations and offerings; and the recognition of that origin explains much of the strange prevalence even yet of the "lever" view of prayer - it is a force to compel God. But obviously this view of prayer does not work, and it is well, with our human limitations, that it does not. Public prayer, though more of an artificial thing than private, may nevertheless be the vehicle of definite religious experience and of felt communion of spirit with God and man. I have known those who found in corporate worship an experience of vision and power which they could not find elsewhere; such temperaments no doubt are usually of the "Catholic" or collectivist kind rather than the Protestant and individualist; yet even for Protestants the herd instinct has its place in prayer, and some religious experiences of value are probably to be found in most lives associated with corporate worship. But my main concern is with personal religion and experience and therefore more with private devotions or the prayer life; even though public prayers, as the attempt of one man to express and make articulate what others may not be able to do satisfactorily for themselves, has its place in this activity of private communion with God.

I have spoken of prayer as natural self-expression in need - even for the "irreligious" at crises prayer is released by a spontaneous impulse, whatever its explanation – e.g. the prayer of the drowning man; of prayer as telepathy - and many instances of the kinds, recorded in such biographies as that of George Muller of Bristol, seem to demand such an explanation of God as a kind of intelligent central exchange for human aspirations and needs (the analogy of wireless suggested above is probably to the point). Again, I have spoken of prayer as suggestion: "He who rises a better man, his prayer is answered." - and it is often so; by conscious attention and the innervation of the higher desire centres we have the creation of purpose, the finding of ideals, the feeding of the soul on its best aspirations, so the formation of character. Again, we have the more direct and immediate type of voiceless or passive communion with God, a type of prayer sometimes possible to attain by artificial means, but more usually not; a form of spiritual experience which is not very active, but which has great ethical and practical value, as all true mysticism has, in the permeation of life by great ideals and visions and by renewed confidence and power. The last view which I mentioned, that of prayer as a discipline of said prayers and set times for attempted communion, can have many of the above values, but its peculiar characteristic is in the ascetic attempt to help in the formation of habits, that are considered good, by concentration, to overcome laziness and lack of interest by application of will in the creation of purpose or intention for good or for the purging out of evil; in the training of the mind in order or self-control. It has a real value, as all serious attempts to bring purpose and order into life have, but it is peculiarly liable to abuse and to the development of a religion of good works by self-mortification. The Christian ethic is really positive, not negative; goodness is in the love of good, not in self-hate, and true salvation is in the release of the higher desires which automatically crowd out the lower elements in the soul, rather than in their conscious destruction - for they are not wholly evil. Grace not law, love not fear, is the true Christian way;

and to those who are seeking to face life as it comes, life usually offers sufficient material for discipline and self- education without any need on our part to create further ways of self-mortification or self-mastery. But temperaments differ, and the disciplinary use of prayer, for all its dangers, may have real and even great value – so many of the saints have declared, though it is not according to my own experience and outlook.

The truth about the efficacy of prayer is probably far beyond our power to systematise in theories; it is a matter of evidence, and the evidence is certainly in favour of prayer as a real activity of the soul with objective validity and relations; it is a living activity of the religious experience, both, desired and in a real measure successful. Even the facts of suggestion seem to demand an external reality, a power which the faith-state calls upon. At any rate men have believed in God and in prayer as communion with Him, and in that activity of faith have found power. But it is well to remember that the universe is on God's shoulders and not on ours, and that prayer should keep as near to its instinctive use as possible; that it should be natural, not legalistic, nor morbid, and, above all, that it be sought and maintained rather as an attitude or atmosphere permeating all life than as a series of acts - it should be prayer rather than prayers.

CHAPTER XI

Mysticism and related states

The word "mysticism" is often used very wrongly, as if stood for the obscure and mysterious, the irrational and occult. By its derivation the word "mystic" means one initiated into religious secrets and its correct use is of those who have entered directly, into the realities of the unseen world, those who have reached certainty and *immediate* conscious experience of the fundamental facts of religion. Such immediate experiences of vision and certain knowledge are practically always associated in some degree with a religion of feeling, more or less ecstatic, with states of mind which are characterised by keen pleasure, lucidity of understanding and aesthetic sensations of sound, colour or form, or others akin to them, less easily described by a human vocabulary. At its highest, mysticism stands for the beatific vision, the knowledge and sensation of communing with God directly, but from that peak down to the thrill one feels over a sunset or a well-run race, there are practically infinite varieties of form and intensity of the experience in life. The one uniform characteristic about the mystic experience in religion is its sense of directness or immediacy; religion ceases to be an inference of thought or a code of action and becomes a certainty with more or less of feeling-tone.

Perhaps the most striking form of communion with God is that which is thus described as mystic experience, historically so such bound up with sainthood, for the great saints have in large measure been also the great mystics, a company of men and women with some experience of direct knowledge of God or ultimate truth; a kind of salt of religion, it would seem, which has kept, it from becoming a theology or a morality, because of the certainty which the saints have experienced and which they have in some measure passed on as accepted truth to others who have had little or nothing of such experience. I think it is true to say that multitudes are more or less sure of God because Jesus or Paul or Francis were. For purposes of discussion mysticism is usually divided into two main classes, the lesser or milder and more normal mysticism, and the great or more striking and more abnormal. The great mysticism represents the experiences of ecstasy and other similar physical or psychical experiences of an unusual type, or at least such found in an abnormal degree. The lesser represents a less vivid but still real sense of God as directly known or felt, and the experiences of peace, harmony and certitude gained by many saints or others. The greater mysticism is by many writers regarded as pathological or dangerous, akin to dervishism, automatism and hallucination and not to be encouraged. It may indeed be a dangerous thing consciously to work for; but, in as much as nearly all the greater creative souls in the history of religion, like Jesus. and Paul, Buddha, Mohammed, Al Ghazali, Francis of Assisi, George Fox, Bunyan and others have known the greater mysticism, we cannot lay down the depreciatory law suggested above. Genius may be akin to, but it is not, madness; and to refuse it on that ground would be cowardice and folly and robbery of the race. We cannot say that the same results could have been secured apart from these greater mystical experiences; as with the phenomena of genius, it is practically certain that, apart from them, we should have no history or development to speak of. The genius and the mystic, who are kin, are the sensitive pioneer souls of the race. The mystical visions of Jesus and Paul, for example, were creative and essential to Christian history, though no doubt they were determined in form and to some extent even in content by the abnormally sensitive minds concerned, as well as by the material gained from training and environment; poets, musicians and artists in their own way share in these creative experiences through their unique sensitiveness to reality, as for example, William Blake. What the mystic sees no doubt is cast in the mould of his actual mentality and his former experiences, which furnish the material for the visualisation or translation of the reality offered to him; but the content of the vision in a greater or less degree is often new and creative. As mentioned above, in Shaw's "St Joan" the author on the whole deals (and especially in the Preface) very fairly and lucidly with the mystical experience as a method or way for creative minds of appropriating new and valuable truth. We are not in a position to class such mystical experiences and the lack of them as morbid and healthy, but only as abnormal and normal, knowing that the abnormal may in some cases be subnormal and in other cases supernormal; and that the question, in any particular case, which it is, has to be decided by the tests of practical meaning and outcome, i.e. by an evaluation of the content of the vision and by its actual results.

The lesser mysticism is common in some measure to all men, though often not recognised as such, and it carries us back to some of the primary elements of religion, to revelation and worship, the sense of value and awareness of reality. Revelation, worship, aspiration, awe, the sense of beauty, satisfaction, peace, glory, and assurance all have an enormous value for our lives. A lady friend of mine told me that the greatest experience of her life was associated with a white flowering bush in an English garden; it was to her revelation. Moses met his, though racially a more important creative experience, in a flaming bush in the Midianite or Kenite desert; but both experiences were mystical, and in both, nature became God's vehicle. We find the same clear claim in H.G. Wells' remarkable confession in "First and Last Things", pp. 43-46, 66, 67, and 150. In a measure, then, mysticism or an immediate felt knowledge of value and reality is normal in life; but the more dangerous, the more profound and the more ecstatic experiences are abnormal. There are pathological parallels to the greater mysticism which have often been pointed out as found in nervous troubles, especially in epilepsy, or as induced by alcohol or other drugs - a point I discussed earlier - but these are largely irrelevant to a discussion of the validity of the experiences of Jesus and the saints. Life is full of such imitations and caricatures, just as the experience of a dream can be as vivid as those of waking life, and yet be absurd and valueless except as symptoms; and the most we can truthfully say here is that alcohol or epilepsy can in some degree effect the same brain centres as religious experiences, the one in a morbid, the other in a healthy way. The real test not the vividness of an experience but its value for life in thought, action, and influence.

Not all the results or phenomena of the greater mysticism as historically recorded are good; yet, for all that has worth in life, there is a cost to be paid; and spiritual leadership with its intuitions, like aesthetic genius with its visions, has had its cost. Keats dead at twenty-seven, Mozart and Raphael at thirty-five surely have some such meaning; and they hardly prove that poetry, music, and painting are morbid things, or genius in those fields a pathological condition of mind! If so, morbidity might well be proved to be above health and all our values inverted. No; rather it is true that the sensitiveness which makes genius, and creative or pioneer service of the race possible, has a heavy price to pay, and that the nervous system, which is seeking to accommodate itself to an abnormal gift, may not always be successful in its quest. Religious genius, requires a sensitive type of mind, greatly tortured by the thought currents and morbid suggestions of its environment; a focus of human thoughts in which the viruses are neutralised at a price and life integrated in a new measure. Such souls are usually lonely and experimentalist, abnormally cut off from the herd and shut into abnormal risks or ventures of faith through their keen perception of the un-ideality of society and its codes, greatly tried by their own vivid emotions and desires, capable both of tragedy and of glory in a peculiar degree.

And it is not for us to deny the ladders by which religion has climbed to its present content through the visions and experiences of great souls. Subtract from Christianity the visions of the baptism in Jordan, of the Transfiguration, of the Resurrection of Christ, of Pentecost, Peter's vision on the roof, Paul's visions on the Damascus road, in the Temple, of the man from Macedonia at Troas, John's vision in Patmos, and others of the like kind, and I doubt if, historically speaking, we should have very much left to our faith of either content or power – probably it would not have been preached, nor accepted. In these experiences, abnormal and mystic, if ever experiences were such, there came into human life and history the moving and motivating power of God for a new creation and a new epoch in the human story.

The lesser or more normal mysticism has its own universe sense or reaction, its sense of God, however it be described in detail, or from time to time - as awe, reverence, worship, harmony, satisfaction, or what you will - a universe perspective, a universe emotion and an active relation to them. Such an experience, common at least in some degree to all religious minds, which are not content to follow the codes and opinions of others at second hand, stands for human significance, though with humility; it stands for faith and hope and love; and, to the glory of the vision granted, surrender and homage are our native response, and the issue thereof is in the moral fruit of enthusiasm and courage and service. We have therein felt a relation to One greater than ourselves, yet akin, and, in to far as that relation is felt, not inferred, it is mystic in the truest sense. Such moments have an enormous value for ourselves and the race.

But such experiences vary greatly in intensity and form, and they are intermittent and usually infrequent, even in the best and most sensitive of types; doubt and conflict return even after the moments of transfiguration - "Oh that it were as it hath been" - the touch, the voice, the sound of many waters, the colours of the throne of God, or merely the new understanding that came to us have gone and left us with but a memory, creative and stimulating indeed, but a thing of the past. Paul's light from heaven, Pascal's fire, Joan's voices, the temple vision of Isaiah, the living creatures of Ezekiel, the opened heavens of Jesus - they pass, and life becomes perhaps harder than ever, though a new inward peace may abide at the core of our life, where fear and torment and discord reigned before; but power remains, if the vision has been a real one, in memory and in character, and often in a new social life built upon a great personality, as the Christian Church was built upon Jesus. For all true vision has its social as well as its individual meaning, just as all true artistic or musical perception is a social possession. A Welsh friend of mine, a man of great intellectual gifts and a leader of men, told me of his great time of perplexity and crisis, when, as he walked along the seashore, he heard a voice behind him telling him precisely what to do. There was no one there to be seen, but he did what he had been advised and found peace and power for good in his community. Call it unconscious activity, or what you will, judged by its fruit it was real and vital revelation. Even for Jesus Himself the vision fades, and the routine of work has to be faced on the plain below. There is an economy of divine grace, and from the mystic vision one is driven forth by the Spirit, it may be to the wilderness for the work of thought, or into the heart of the waiting below for the work of service; but we go now with a new love and certainty and sense of vocation.

Few of the creative souls of religious history have been without a succession of such times when God, or the unseen and eternal world, passes from inference or hypothesis to experience or certainty. It is hard to interpret so personal and so subjective an experience to others; in measure it can be done, but in measure no experience can be fully transmitted to others; yet at least these moments add a new quality to life, the quality of God and the enjoyment of Him, and in the sequel, they have worthy ethical fruits to show, in proportion as the vision had ethical content and value. The greater moments of such a kind usually come unsought, and often when we are most in need; but they are usually dangerous to seek for their own sake or to attempt to reproduce. All mystical experiences have fluctuations, and, in so far as they depend on the material of our past experience for their form, there are probably better and worse elements in them all. But such experience of God, felt or seen, of life really known and understood for what it is "at its roots," are not mere individual possessions, but have a social meaning; and most of our human religions are built upon loyalty to some who had such vision and certainty of the unseen world, the spirit or quality of which so permeated them that they could become effective symbols of God, or the unseen, even to those who had little or no personal experience of the kind. The mystics are the trustees of their experience, rather than its owners. The true life of man or of the Church is a common social life in which different types with different gifts make differing contributions, and so became truly one as being co-essential to the whole, mutually necessary. Aristotle, Francis of Assisi, Hildebrand, Harvey, Marconi, Einstein – all are different, and all are in their own ways essential to the race. So, let us not covet the experiences of others, but be faithful with our own; and neither underrate or overrate any part of life. Life is sacred, and each soul has its own conflict and purpose; but in some measure mystic elements are found in every life, even if it be labelled agnostic or atheist. There is for all men the reality of beauty, the sense and meaning of nature, a world of ideals, a universe sense of some sort; together with all kinds and perceptions of values which uplift and bless, releasing desire and energy for the harder task of working out one's vision in actual life. But the testimony of the mystics to a wider self is clear, and to its contribution of inspiration and of individual and social influence. On this subject of mysticism, I recommend especially James and Thouless.

A few miscellaneous points before I leave the general question of mysticism. Music offers us an interesting parallel. There are those with "no ear," as there are those with no mystical experience that can be clearly recognised - though everyone who is not completely deaf has some power of discrimination in sounds, and everyone has some sense of immediate value. There are those who can appreciate music - the great majority - and a smaller number who can interpret it as players, and finally there are those who can compose - creative musicians. This last category presents a parallel to the greater mystics; the appreciators and the interpreters present a parallel to the lesser mysticism with its different degrees. In our life of today we have men who believe completely in free thought, living in a society that only partially believes in it; we have pacifists who believe in the power and ultimate reality of love, in a society which is still largely governed by valuations of physical force and of control by fear. In both cases they are men living in one world yet belonging to another, men with the conviction of a world which is not actual, yet real, and with which they have fellowship; so with the mystics. The true mystic can stand loosely to human forms, which are the crutches of so many, because they are independent, in a real sense, of the seen. They must often cry "Stand thou on that side, for on this am I." Yet the mystical experience is reasonably common in one main event of the religious life (i.e., apart from its everyday existence in the experience of value), viz, in conversion. Conversion by crisis. must, I think, when genuine, always contain a mystic element, an element of direct contact with the divine, the eternal; and even when the conversion is a gradual one by process rather than crisis, the elements of revelation and valuation in the experience represent a knowledge of God. Indeed (apart from insanity) I doubt if there is any real conviction without mystic experience – religious conviction is an awareness of reality when it is sane and not a trick of the morbid mind (as when a man asserts with confidence that he is Napoleon or a machine of glass, or the like). Science itself has something akin to mysticism in the creative leap that the great scientist makes by intuition.

Before I leave this topic, I wish to make a passing reference to the allied question of automatism in religious experience, and especially in the history of revivalism. The two subjects of mysticism and automatism, though in many respects far apart, the one belonging chiefly to individual experience and to creative or supranormal moments, and the other to crowd or mass psychology and to somewhat subhuman levels, nevertheless have features in common, in particular the strong emotion which accompanies them and the striking physical phenomena of a more or less pathological kind which may follow or be associated with them. Automatisms, or involuntary physical movements, are found outside religion as well as within its field, but perhaps nowhere in the modern world so strikingly as in some of the phenomena of crowd evangelism and conversions. The story of revivals is full of such cases - clapping of hands, uncontrolled laughter, shouting, gesticulation, falling, jerking, jumping, rolling, barking, trances, and the gibbering of uncouth sounds, commonly dignified as "speaking with tongues." These automatisms are matters of temperament and have no religious values in themselves; they represent emotional storms, which might indeed occur in many connections, but which are most powerfully felt in the crowded revivalistic atmosphere with its suggestion and mass technique, its expectancy and its temporary reduction of man from the rational human plane to the irrational level of the pack, and with the coming of impulses which are too strong for the habitual nerve channels. As far as true religion goes, these phenomena are really irrelevant, but their occurrence is evidence of the presence of a great emotional stimulus, sometimes real and creative as at Pentecost, but often at root artificially induced and imitative. I have spoken earlier in the book of dervishism and orgiastic religion, which in primitive human history approved these states of "possession" or abnormality, even as they reverenced madmen; and the primitive instinct to work for such orgiastic and nervous excitement persists strongly even yet, so that men often still value the abnormal as peculiarly religious. In the Old Testament we read of such prophets and such excitement in Israel, in the stories of Moses and Saul and David and the priests of Baal; and to the present-day revivals may present similar features, which are often a real problem to earnest souls. In the year 1859 in the North of Ireland there was a great revival of which two notable local accounts were published by differing interpreters, the one called "The year of grace" and the other "The year of delusion." Each writer had his justification, for the revival did both good and harm. It has left a deep and permanent impress for good on the community, and yet it did produce much that today we can only call pathological, ranging from hysteria, through all forms of automatism and the loss of inhibition or self-control to insanity; and more recent cases have also occurred, though in lesser degree.

The fact is that such automatisms of body, limb or voice represented the weakness of human nature to receive and coordinate the strong impulse received, whatever its inherent value. All through known history such experiences are chronicled, come with considerable, and others with little, meaning. At Pentecost a great new life force, was felt and human nature unused to its management, could but show itself, in its weakness, as uncontrolled and as if "full of new wine"; but in the course of the years such impulses came to be more normal and more organised and so to be directed into the true lines of service such as Paul recommended. Some sects however still prize these pathological evidences of human physical and psychical impotence or derangement as specially spiritual, in the manner of early savages, They are often marked by some great emotional excitement, of fear or joy or aspiration; the emotion may in itself be good, but, to be effective in the truest sense, it should be assimilable by the life as a whole; and modern religious education aims at such a gradual and controlled and balanced development, where unfortunately some revivalists still aim at shock and crisis and the overthrow of the individual judgement by artificially heightened emotion. I have no time to speak here of such work, its pros and cons; but I think it is today realised that the quieter the process and the more organic the development the better, and that the truest evangelism lies in a continual education producing a persistent and healthy self-adjustment to life as it moves on. That is, the truest evangelism is the feeding of the soul with its right food, and the teaching of control, balance, and growth and of the true integration of life under the religious impulse and purpose. Therefore, today we aim at conserving the good and eliminating the evil in the methods which we have inherited of influencing the growth of souls. This whole question is most interesting, and, for an adequate discussion of revivalism, evangelism, education, crowd psychology and normal growth, a great deal more of ink and paper would be necessary than I can afford in this place; but it is not a main issue in my present discussion. I would refer readers who wish to go farther into the subject to the books by Coe, Ames and others cited in the list at the end of the book.

CHAPTER XII

Conversion and normal development

The word "conversion" itself means nothing more than a turning or readjustment of heart and life, as in Isaiah 6:10, or in Acts 15:19, or Matthew 18:3; it represents the change of direction which is associated with a new beginning of ethical or spiritual life and endeavour; but in some sections of the Church it has come to stand only for a more or less cataclysmic experience associated with strong emotions of terror and joy, an experience in which the subject is usually conscious of an unfathomable chasm between the old life and the new. There is no doubt that such conversions are frequent among Christians, especially in communities which value them and aim at producing them; but even in such communities other quieter forms of change also are not infrequent, and I have known some of the strongest advocates of sudden conversion completely silenced by the testimony of the life of someone they knew and loved, such as a son, who had never tasted such cataclysmic experiences, but who they recognised as living at least as near to God as they were. Education and nurture of a Christian home are the normal means of religious development.

At any rate there seem to be present with us various types of conversion - the sudden, the gradual, and all variety of stages between the two. Conversion is a thing we all know by experience or observation, and, it we have kept our eyes open, we know too, that every true conversion, like every true marriage, stands by itself; that no two are wholly alike, that there are great varieties, and that no hard and fast rule can be found to cover them all. Perhaps the nearest parallel to conversion in human experience outside the specific realm of religion is the experience of love and marriage - each case stands upon its own feet; each is a law to itself. Indeed, the truest Christian conversion is falling in love with God or with Jesus, but conversion, like love, is a thing of infinite varieties and types and, like love, it is one of the most real and creative things in life. It is therefore worthy of our best efforts to understand its nature end how it should be worked for.

In the first place then, let me point out that religious conversion is not a specifically Christian thing. Christianity has no monopoly of the form of the experience. That which makes Christian conversion unique is not its form but its content - the fact that is a conversion to Christianity, to Christ, with all that implies. And modern psychology treats conversion as belonging to the normal religions experience of most seriously minded men in some form and in some degree. That which we are dealing with, fundamentally, in conversion is a change of mind or heart, a change of attitude in the relation of a man to the life around him, a change which in a healthy spiritual life should accompany adolescence - it is the readjustment which the adolescent makes, or should make in passing from the egoism of the child to the social life of the full grown man who, to be truly man, must think and act socially, not selfishly, i.e. with kindness, courage, humility, sincerity and the like. No doubt a man cannot truly get into the best relations to life without an experience and doctrine of God, for God is the true social environment of our souls, the All of good life; but men may experience a conversion of sorts even apart from a formal belief in God, and such conversions may even be sudden and cataclysmic, as modern investigation has shown; see Pratt, "The Religious Consciousness". The characteristic thing in true conversion is the repudiation of the life in which self is the centre, and the affirmation of a wider self, it is metanoia or repentance, a turning from sin with dedication of life to the highest; it is acceptance of a worthy life purpose, for true life is unselfish and purposeful. All change to a better life is a conversion of a kind, but only that which involves the life of union, in heart and mind and purpose, with Christ is true Christian conversion.

The natural time for conversion is adolescence; it is then that life is broken up from its foundations, the egoism of children sloughed off, and the wider social challenge felt which comes, with the emergence of sex and a new self-consciousness, in the form of social cravings and ideals. Unfortunately, many people never grow up but remain children for years or for life; and how hateful is the egoism and purposeless of the child in a grown or growing man or woman! Modern psychology tells us that it is natural for conversions to occur between nine and twenty-five, especially between fourteen and nineteen for men or thirteen to eighteen for women, which is the period at which the social challenge of ideals is keenly felt for the first time and most conversions do occur at that time. Conversion is readjustment of life, and readjustment may occur at any age, though early childhood and advanced age offer few examples for obvious reasons; but in actual fact the great majority of conversions occur between thirteen and nineteen or very close to that period. Starbuck in his famous book gives elaborate statistical tables, carefully compiled, showing the association between conversion and such important incidents in the life as puberty, with a rapid increase in weight or height, or other such changes of a physical or psychical kind. As William James wrote in 1899 of Dr Starbuck, the whole tendency of his patient labour is to bring compromise and conciliation into the long-standing feud of science and religion. Your evangelical extremist will have it that conversion is an absolutely supernatural event with nothing cognate to it in ordinary psychology; your scientist sectary on the other hand sees nothing in it but hysterics and emotionalism, an absolutely pernicious pathological disturbance. For Dr Starbuck it is not necessarily either of these things. It may in countless cases be a perfectly normal psychological crisis marking the transition from the child's world to the wider world of youth, or from that of youth to that of maturity - a crisis which the evangelical machinery only methodically emphasises, abridges, and regulates.

Sixteen then is the year par excellence for conversion both for males and females, and sixteen is the end of the anti-social, and the beginning of the social, adolescent stage, when boys and girls, who have kept apart, begin to draw together, and when the rebellion or mischief of early adolescence and its gang life tends to decrease. I might add that Dr Starbuck's figures are drawn from Americans, and Protestant Americans for the most part. It is probable that in this more temperate zone the ages would be a little later than those given in his statistics, It is also worth mentioning that, while the male cases showed a wonderfully uniform emphasis upon the age of sixteen as the normal age of conversion, the female cases, while placing the same age at the head of the list, showed very nearly as numerically important a crisis at the age of thirteen, and another of lesser numerical importance at eighteen. Both male and female graphs then agree upon the age of sixteen in the States as the most important for conversion, which in this climate might be seventeen or eighteen. I do not know of any actual tables for Great Britain of a similar kind. Most of this important scientific work has been done in America, and perhaps in nothing has America contributed more to human progress than in the spheres of religious and educational psychology. Now these scientific observations of psychologists are borne out in substance in the work of our Churches; and the statistics of most revivalists or revivalistic campaigns will also give them clear support. Of course, the question of revivalism raises many problems of its own into which I have no time here to enter, though I have touched on some earlier in the book. But it is well to think hard and clearly about things which matter so much as our methods of doing God's work, and to seek to purify them from all that is dangerous or unsatisfactory. One very relevant truth is that human nature is very diverse and that what helps one injures another; methods of personal contact are certainly best, and especially methods which are educational which seek results, not by stimulants and excitement, but by food and nurture - in other words, the historical methods of Christ Himself.

To return to the predominantly adolescent experience of conversion (also found frequently in undeveloped adults who, mentally at least, have not grown up), this essential experience of adjustment appears in a variety of forms; between the two poles of an absolutely gradual change and an absolutely sudden one appear all kinds of intermediate stages, but, speaking generally, there are the two main types, the sudden and the gradual, and the sudden is itself divided into two main varieties, that in which the crisis is passed by *effort*, and that in which the crisis is passed by the *cessation* of effort. The latter is the more startling type and gives rise to the impression that the conversion has been almost entirely supernatural. Many psychological writers treat gradual readjustment as the normal line of development - and certainly sudden conversions are not quite so frequent as they are often assumed to be - and the word "conversion" is by many writers restricted to the two main types of change by crisis, a crisis passed either by an effort of the will, or by the relaxation of effort. This latter is peculiarly associated with neurotic types in whom Baudouin's "law of reversed effort" seems to operate; and the probabilities are that in this case long sustained effort and emotion have already so tired the mind that only by rest can progress be made. In all cases we have the working of God, but the former case he works obviously in cooperation with the man's will, while in the latter the operation always seems more miraculous. There is no doubt that a certain type of conversion has become a kind of standard in the Church, though it is not at all certain that it is such a common type after all, the type represented by the great names of Paul, Augustine, and Luther, who were men of much the same kind of temperament and of theological outlook. In their cases "grace" rather than effort. seems to have been the deciding factor - a supernatural interference as it seemed; but, to one who reads their stories with any care, it is obvious that in each case there had been a very sustained effort of will after goodness and truth, without which their later experience would probably have been impossible; the grace of God, like many of His best gifts, is conditioned by human effort, and if, at the moment of crisis, the soul finds it necessary to rest rather than strive, that does not imply that effort has contributed nothing to the change, or that other types of mind will find the same road to peace. If the mind is tired, it may need to find God by relaxation, but for most of us Christ's word stands, "Strive to enter in." Even those, who seem to pass in by ceasing from effort, appear to have earned by effort a right to do so.

But most sudden conversions are only seemingly so; the crisis may be cataclysmic, like the explosion of a powder magazine, or the production of water from oxygen and hydrogen, but the elements are all there before the crisis, the preparation is complete. Paul heard a voice saying, "It is hard for thee to kick against the goad." Assuredly his conscience had had a long struggle and preparation, and, by his efforts after righteousness according to the law, and by zeal in his Jewish orthodoxy, he had already laid a good character basis for the coming of truth and power through Christ. Augustine's conversion seems either a definite miracle or a marvellous coincidence, but for year before it he has sought for truth and moral victory, and for days before the crisis in the garden he had said over and over to himself: "It is decided. I will do it now!" But his will had refused to obey. So, with Luther; painfully in thought and deed he had sought holiness and truth and his own conversion was the culmination of a long journey. Thus, the sudden conversions that last and which have value for the world are usually the end, however sudden, of a long process. Mere sudden conversion, though it occurs, can have little root or depth; and most sudden conversions of this order are superficial emotional blazes reached in a crowd. All things are possible with God ad one cannot lay down rules, but on the whole we are bidden to work, not for the quick returns of the seed which found no depth of earth and so sprang up quickly without real roots, but for the slow-growing corn of the true harvest.

Two facts have emerged clearly from the study of religious experience, viz., its reality and its varieties. Whether it have in it elements of illusion or not, it is certainly not a delusion, for it is creative of good life and bears worthy social fruits; but its varieties are many, and what is one's meat may be another's poison. It is well to remember this fact as against a facile standardisation of certain types in certain communities as necessary or as peculiarly valuable. There are well meaning but narrow people who will not accept anyone as converted who cannot give the place and date of the change. One of the best known of modern evangelists finding himself thus doubted and in great distress of mind, went to his father to ask if his inability to give the date meant that he was still unconverted. His father with great common sense asked him, "Do you need a birth certificate to prove that you are born"; and thereafter he found rest in the fact that he was spiritually alive, because he had really come to love Jesus and the Kingdom of God.

William James in his classic Gifford lectures divides religious experience into two types, the normal, which he calls the religion of

healthy mindedness, and the abnormal, which he calls the religion of
the sick soul, with which he more or less classes sainthood. I imagine
that today psychologists would be content to speak of extravert
and introvert, or of stable and unstable types. But two interesting
admissions of leading psychologists fall to be chronicled here, one
that of Dr Rivers who has pointed out that mental power is associated
with a considerable measure of instability, and the other that of James
himself, who admits that the "sick soul" seems to get farther and
deeper into life and the truth of life than the "healthy minded."
It is no doubt another proof of the value of suffering and of that
sensitiveness of soul which makes for suffering. The creative souls
have tor the most part been introverts, often unstable and always
sensitive to life, men of sorrows and acquainted with grief. The
creative souls of religious history have been men for the most part
who grew by crisis, and even Jesus Himself seems to have grown by
crisis, if we can trust the accounts of our gospels - at the age of twelve,
at His baptism and temptation, in Gethsemane, and at various other
points of His ministry less obvious on the surface, Christ passed
through sudden crises of supreme importance for the history of the
world. Such a spirit too was Paul's, though he never attained the
wholeness of Jesus; to the end, like Augustine, he remained somewhat
of a divided soul, an ascetic seeking to be free. Luther seems to have
travelled farther than most in his wholeness of spirit, and I do not
think the greatness of Luther in his power for the accepting of life,
like Jesus, has yet been fully appreciated. He is called coarse, but I am
not sure that it is not in measure part of his greatness and spontaneity
as it was with Abraham Lincoln; for Luther, with all his weaknesses
and social blunders, stands for a full and balanced life.

We may indeed criticise many elements in conversion by crisis, as
we know it, but the fact remains that such has been the way in which
the great souls of religious history - lonely souls - have developed for
the most part; by crisis, not by slow invisible growth, but by seemingly

morbid tension and conflict. The probability is that the great souls feel life too vividly in all its contrasts, and with all its conflicts of values, to have an easy time or a healthy mind on any plane but the highest. One other fact of importance calls for notice, the fact that the readjustment of life may be effected, not by one supreme crisis of sudden conversion, nor by a gradual process without perceptible crisis, but by a number of crises of greater or less importance. For many people the crises of readjustment are two, or three, or more. It has been customary to call the first of these, conversion; but in actual fact that crisis may be the least important of the series. The so-called "Keswick blessing" is one well known example of a common second crisis of this kind; it is admitted that one may receive that blessing at conversion, but that many do not. Again, the awakening of the social conscience in a definite sense may constitute a still later crisis. At two points in particular is a crisis natural, at the passage from child to adolescent and at the passage from adolescent to adult. At either or both of these points a crisis may easily arise; and there are many other events which readily provoke crises in those who tend to grow in that way. Thus, some lives seem to show no crisis, some to have one supreme crisis, and some to make their religious readjustment by two or three or many crises. What is important is not the way we grow, but the degree of spiritual life and vision and power which we attain.

But is conversion necessary? Let me discuss for a few moments this often asked question. The first thing to answer is that it depends on what is meant by conversion. The redirection of life is necessary, is essential to a true religion; and using the word "conversion" in this broad sense our answer must be "yes". The inevitable egoism of the child mind, with its self-centredness and lack of moral purpose, must go if life is to be what it should. In spiritual things many seem not to grow up, and a definite conversion is necessary if life is to be what God meant. But in the narrower use of conversion to denote a sudden crisis successfully passed, one cannot answer a general "yes", for everything here depends upon the individual life and temperament. Change there must be, but how far it will be gradual and how far sudden will depend on the individual. Perhaps the clearest parallel is physical growth; one child may grow fairly gradually in height, and another may shoot up three or four inches in a short time. Neither is wrong in our present state of knowledge, though the day may come when we shall be able to control growth and make it more uniform. There is no doubt that, the more gradual and organic the physical growth, the healthier it is; and in the psychical world I believe the same thing is true – sudden change is dangerous and involves the same kind of strain as a sudden increase in height. When we come to consider the disadvantages of sudden conversion, this is the first to note - that in living organisms, whether bodies or minds, sudden growth is less healthy than systematic and gradual development. Again, sudden conversion usually involves an abnormal division of personality, and so tends to prevent the finding of that true wholeness or integration of personality which is the Christian ideal as shown by Jesus. This failure involves loss of balance and a greater danger of the pendulum swinging back under temptation. A sudden break with the old life also tends to make a gulf between the old and the new, such that even the useful or harmless things of the old life are regarded as "the world" and consequently evil, and life becomes like that of the Pharisee, very zealous, very narrow, and very unattractive, with a great temptation to, or tendency towards, priggishness, hypocrisy, narrowness of sympathy and unreality. What we truly need is not so much renunciation of parts of life as consecration of the whole of it.

But the sudden conversion certainly tends to the ascetic rather than to the full Christian point of view. The argument of one well known evangelist, who used the illustration of a heavy sack on a man's back being emptied by a small hole (gradual conversion) or by a large rent (sudden conversion) - the argument that the latter gives a greater joy and sense of relief - means nothing of importance if what we are seeking is not pleasurable sensations, but health. Alcohol may give more pleasurable sensations than bread, but I prefer the bread; and all psychologists are in favour of the healthier, sounder, and more systematic growth where possible. Where possible! That is important. For in many cases, it may not be possible to get the same results in any other way than by crisis. And certainly, the great creative and saintly souls have usually passed by this way of sudden conversion; therefore, it behoves us to be reverent and cautious in our criticisms. Sudden conversions, where natural, are probably, like possession of red hair, unavoidable for many in the present of our knowledge, but none the less we should control growth, physical and psychical, as far as we can; for, the more systematic the growth, the better. But for some there is probably no other way than change by crisis, and especially for two types, for the creative saintly soul with its abnormally sensitive nervous organisation and its vivid sense of life and its tensions, and for the old chronic sinner hardened in evil habits. But for the most normal young people the element of suddenness and shock should be reduced to the minimum and educational methods followed as far as is possible.

There is no doubt that shock tactics and crowd exploitation are both mentally dangerous; and, in addition, the emphasis upon sudden conversion in revivalistic communities, where psychological studies are very little known, tends to an emphasis upon seemingly supernatural ways of change. To those who do not know much about the workings of the mind, a sudden conversion seems like a direct act of God, while education seems a purely natural and human method on a lower level. Revivalistic communities often undervalue or ignore education. Yet the Spirit of God is given rather to those who do, in this and in other ways, prepare the way of the Lord and make His paths straight; and it is interesting to note how many modern movements in the Christian Church are developing more and more the educational method. Education is of the essence of our Church life and of any true religion which has depth and strength of root. We cannot cut out sudden crisis, but we can eliminate it as far as possible, so that it shall only occur when in God's purposes it is necessary. Our chief business is not to provide drugs, stimulant, or narcotic, for the soul, but food; and that is best found in education. And, if education is truly used with individual attention, the time of change will normally come of itself, and a crisis of some kind and in some degree probably develop naturally. And it is to be noted that most long-established Churches have put the time of confirmation or first communion down for about that period of natural awakening; a practical knowledge of psychology has again preceded its scientific formulation. We must therefore endeavour to see God in normal healthy life so far as we can, we must learn the truth of the varieties of religious experience, and we must try to keep our religion, in the fresh air as Jesus did.

At this point let me speak of the importance of what is the vital thing in conversion, however attained - decision, decision for God and His Christ, and the things that belong to His Kingdom. It is not the type of experience or the type of doctrine that we shall lay our emphasis upon, if like Christ, we would know them by their fruits; we must look at the results, the outcome, and find what produces the type of man who is a "good Samaritan"; the type who will, pass the tests of Matthew 25 in the Great Assize, i.e., the truly social type of life which Christ inculcated and exemplified. If we standardise experience or doctrine, we create hypocrisy or despair, as men find themselves unable to reproduce the experience or accept the doctrine; but if we standardise a spirit or attitude of soul, the spirit of the life and of the parables of Christ, then we are at least on the right road, for such a spirit must express itself naturally in Christian deeds. In Matthew 25, the King tests faith by its works, which is not to deny faith, but to test it in the only certain way - by its fruits. And, judged by fruits, many men today, who do not call themselves Christians, or who call themselves Christians in a non-ecclesiastical sense, are certainly converted men, men who have made their decision and passed from the side of self to that of God - and that is the supreme thing in conversion, the acceptance of a worthy dominating purpose in life; the identification of oneself in heart and vision and purpose with Jesus of Nazareth, and the mind of God. Christ's own test is not whether men call Him "Lord, Lord," not profession or theological systems, but whether they do the will of God, whether in their hearts and lives they are at one with Him.

There may be such a thing as the saving of one's soul in solitary conversation with God, but if that is the end, the child, of that new birth may be still-born, for man is a social animal, and no true life is possible for him which is not social; true salvation is the saving of man in his social relations, in his relation to God and man, i.e., to God in the aspect of principles – "God is truth," "God is love", and so forth - and to God as found in man – "For inasmuch as you do it to one of the least of these ye do it to Me." The social temperature of a man's soul is a good index to his spiritual health; an individualistic salvation may be Pharisaism, but it is not the religion of Christ. What we need is real decision, dedicated life, i.e., life with a purpose of service and with joy in service; and any man who, under God, can initiate or feed such lives is the true evangelist.

The difference between Christian conversion and non-Christian conversion, where found, is simply that. Christian conversion is a conversion to Christ; and only in Christ is to be found that true freedom and joy in goodness which the world really needs. Here at the focus of man's attention today stands a figure, not that of a philosopher or statesman, but that of a carpenter, and all eyes are being turned to Him. His is the focal life of our race; His is its creative life, the life productive of that new creation which is sonship to God, and which is characterised, where it is true, by peace, and power and love, by integration or balance of personality, and by the social direction of all its activities for the glory of God and the good of men.

Conversion is the coming of that life, the life of consecration and loyalty to all that is best. Loyalty to God, not opinions about God, is the prime consideration; men may differ in philosophy and theory, but they can agree on a purpose, the purpose of self-dedication to God and the best they know. Conversion is the acceptance of that purpose, the consecration of life to the will of God. Christian conversion defines that will of God as having been seen in and taught by Jesus; and the work of the Christian Church is the furtherance of such conversion by all such means as seem really sound and effective.

It may be objected that. in the above discussion of conversion, it is inconsistent to say that sudden conversion is on the whole the less healthy and more morbid line of development and yet that most of the great creative souls passed through it. But in actual fact, as I have said earlier, the creative souls in religion are pioneers, very sensitive to the conflicts of life, foci of morbid thought currents which they seek to neutralise and to integrate for mankind. It is because the social organism is unhealthy that the great souls must perforce bear its diseases and conflicts; by their very nature the social problem will reach its most critical temperature in them, and almost inevitably they learn and develop by crisis; but by crisis which is pioneer and creative and of social value. None the less it is our duty to reduce to the minimum all that is morbid and disruptive in soul growth, and so far as possible to effect a more gradual and controlled change. I have no time here to spend upon the elaboration of the subject of conversion and its varieties as illustrated in the documents of personal experience - for that I would refer renders to Ames op. cit., and to such Sunday school handbooks (now a large literature) as

Archibald's "The Modern Sunday School". The literature on religious psychology has devoted more space to conversion, or normal and abnormal development of the religious consciousness, than to any other single topic; and I have no wish to compete with the experts in that subject) some of whose books will be found mentioned in the note of literature at the end of this volume.

A word much used in connection with such experiences as that of conversion is the word "grace", a word which has had not a little prejudice raised against it because of its excessive use in certain quarters, but nevertheless a valuable term which we ought not to surrender. The word normally represents, in theological use, the divine impulse felt in human experience, the touch and power of a greater life than that of the individual, a power recognised in the challenge it makes, or the peace it, brings after storm, or in other less striking ways. The Greek word translated as "grace", has a variety of meanings e.g., beauty, charm, favour (both objective and subjective) and gift. It is this later meaning which its predominant in theology, where grace stands for the unmerited or free gift of God, even God's self-giving. Thus, the term may be taken generally as covering two main ideas, the influence of God found in some or all of the experiences of human life, and the further associated idea of God as giving Himself in these experiences. A divine influence tending to move men and a free or unearned divine benevolence towards men are then the main ideas of the term "grace" in theological use. This influence and giving of God may be regarded as outward or inward, as coming through environment without, or through the spirit of man within; it may be considered as going before and preparing the way for man, or, again, as assisting and influencing man in his problems and circumstances, i.e., as prevenient or as co-operant; it may be treated, as effective or merely as seeking to persuade or encourage him. But the one word "grace" can cover all these varieties of meaning. This is not the place to go into the many serious problems of grace, that are more or less the same as those of freedom and free will, which will be referred to in the following section; indeed, the problems of grace and freedom cover all the fundamental difficulties of our ethical faith.

The grace of God can he found in all life and in any experience, for God is everywhere and His touch may be felt anywhere; even in relation to sin and ugliness and ignorance we may find truth and progress if, and in proportion as, we react aright to these experiences and by experience learn to know them for what they are. Even in matters of our evil and shame we can see His grace ceaselessly at work; we can see that His curse is always a blessing; we can see the transmutation of evil into good by a divine alchemy of His redemptive purpose; we can see discipline and meaning in all things from His hand. It is not my purpose to discuss further here the problems of grace, such as the question of its resistibility, which has arisen largely out of a mistaken mechanical psychology; my purpose has merely been to show the universal meaning and value of the term, a term so much used of such experiences as conversion, which is certainly a striking example of the operation of divine grace in the individual life. To many persons in this land the year 1859 is "the year of grace", and the use is a justifiable one, though grace cannot be denied to any of the experiences of our life if properly viewed. It is a word which I think we should not lightly surrender, for, like the word "God", it has a universal content and usefulness as standing for the consciousness of divine power or influence in the outward or inward elements of our religious life.

But as "conversion" can be applied to the process of readjustment, whatever its form, but is more commonly applied to adjustment by crisis or cataclysm, so grace, though applicable to every influence of God, is more, usually found as referring to a divine working in the human heart of such a sort that the obedience following is *spontaneous* and not compulsory - freedom not bondage. The reclaimed drunkard who no longer desires to drink is an oft-quoted and fair example of "grace", i.e., God's working in harmony with the laws and values of our being so that His wishes are our wishes. The truest independence in life is through realised dependence, the truest freedom through a conscious and voluntary bondage. I would refer the reader here to the section on "freedom" in the section of this book that follows. If conversion is an outstanding case of a work of grace, the supreme example of such a work of grace is the regeneration of the spiritual life by the release of the higher, better, more social, more integrating and more conceptual desires so that men freely desire that which is according to the will of God and best for them and for the race. This conquest of lower desire by higher desire, "desire exalting in desire's defeat", this release of the diviner nature which is a man's truest self, is the most characteristic of the works of grace, and is the supremely Christian method of redemption - by love or positive passion, not by fear; by real values, not by codes of men, by grace and not by law - it is the true evangelical experience and the supremest form of Christian conversion; it knows no backsliding, it has the true perseverance of the saints involved in it, for "we needs must love the highest when we see it". The mission of the true evangelist is to release in men the love of God, the love of Jesus, the love of goodness, by making this love so real that it draws by an inherent power which is akin to our deepest nature. Such conversion is a regeneration of nature, by the growing destruction, not so much of sins or acts of the past, but of sin as the lower principle in the nature of man, and by the release and development of man's desire life on the side of God. The deepest things in our nature *are* on the side of God, of love and truth and beauty. and all goodness; for ultimately no man can desire the defeat of God. Sin springs from fear and hate and doubt, and the like; but at least all men wish to trust and to be trusted to love and to be loved, to find true life and to grow in it. Thus grace operates, not against the grain of our natures, but in harmony with what is best and most powerful and most integrating in them, if only that divine thing can be released by an effectual vision of reality or by the infection of personality. Thus, the experience of grace is truly the completion and fulfilment and integration of human personality as well as the self-giving of God.

There are some who would draw a distinction between conversion and regeneration, regarding regeneration as a prior divine act and conversion as the human response. Such stories as that of John Bunyan would seem to lend some sort of countenance to such a view, for, as recorded in "Grace Abounding" Bunyan spent two or three years after his wakening before he found peace, in which time he seemed to reach the conversion experience again and again, only to lose his new-found peace in a fresh conflict, though at last he attained stability and a more or less permanent peace of soul. One might say from this account that by an act of regeneration God had wakened him, but that the achievement of his conversion was a long, definite and distinct process of human effort, till he found peace in a consciousness of complete surrender of the self in his final acceptance of the Puritan doctrine of justification by faith alone. Such a twofold description is not unreasonable, but in view of recent research it does not really add anything to our comprehension. For one might describe his awakening as a work of prevenient grace, his conversion as a work of human effort and co-operating grace; not even the latter can be made purely human. Some conversions or readjustments involve many crises, and it seems arbitrary to single out any one as peculiarly divine. And, if we look at the matter from the modern psychological point of view, we see readjustment never truly as an act, but always as a process and a life-long process, too; some periods may seem more critical than others, but no one without omniscience can say what points in the process are really the most important; even the point of beginning can be a matter of dispute, for all life and experience is continuous and interwoven. It is of course a harmless refinement to use the word "regeneration" of the divine and the word "conversion" of the human aspect of the change in direction of life and purpose, the former throwing the emphasis on divine grace and the latter on human effort; but in life the two aspects, human and divine, cannot be separated out even in thought; and, if one recognises that life is kinetic and organic, and that grace co-operates as well as precedes in our experiences, the distinction comes to have little meaning.

Conversion is not an item of abnormal psychology, though some of its forms may be less normal than others. The fact that the modern study of psychology began with abnormal rather than normal experiences, experiences of disassociation, neurosis, hysteria, psychosis and the like, has been seen also in the study of religious experiences, and has given undue prominence to the idea of morbidity, so that the normal has tended to be overlooked and even undervalued. Some among us today would still insist that conversion is an absolutely necessary experience for the development of a spiritual life, others assure us that conversion is not at all necessary, and that it is at the best a rather morbid and jerky way of finding one's path into a life of religious and moral purpose. Here we have the two extremes, those who make a clear-cut conversion a condition of their recognition of spiritual status and those who deprecate or even condemn it. Well, people differ and so do their experiences; for some a typical conversion is probably natural and for others, unnatural, just like the possession of red hair. You may dye your hair red if you wish, but others have red hair by nature, and it is so with conversion so-called; for some it is seemingly the natural and genuine method of development, for others it can, in the old sense of the word, have no meaning; they may admire it, and even try to imitate it, but they cannot produce it naturally. But the root question is one of definition. If we use "conversion", not of the sudden and striking change, but of self-adjustment generally, sudden or gradual, many of these questions cease to be important; and it is in this wider sense that I have used the term generally in this book. How cataclysmic the change in personality must be to qualify for the word "conversion", used in the older sense, was never settled, and 1 think we no longer need to ask; the essential fact is change, moral and spiritual development or self-adjustment. If life is to be healthy at all, there must be such, mortification, and re-adaption and especially round about the period of puberty, which is one of the main organic changes in human life.

Personally, I value the word "conversion", and I cannot see my way to join the ranks of those who would depreciate or surrender it. To many, like myself, growth has naturally been by crises and jumps, which may recur at different stages. But conversion is not in itself morbid. Perhaps most of our life could be classed as morbid from some ideal standpoint; but, if sudden conversion has been the one and only means to readjustment for certain personalities, as seems to have been true in the past - whatever may be true of the future when we know more about the subject - then it is relatively not morbid and evil, but natural and good, There are elements of morbidity about all sudden readjustments of life, no doubt; the ideal would probably be a gradual, harmonious and proportionate development *pari passu* of body, mind and spirit; but, as things are, the experience of sudden conversion will be relatively healthy and good till we know enough - if we ever do - to secure the same results in other ways. The grace of God is not to be found only in the abnormal; it ought to be everywhere in this normal; but in the abnormal, at any rate, we can often recognise its presence and be thankful. Yet the more gradual forms of change are on the increase, with the increase among us of education which is psychologically sound, alert and continually better informed; and, where the normal is also natural for the individual case, it is to be encouraged and never despised.

For conversion or religious development, of whichever type it be, is a process of right self-adjustment to God and man; its course may vary enormously in all kinds of ways. What matters is that it should occur and that, so far as possible, in a healthy and organic form, so that life has its maximum of integration and power and meaning.

CHAPTER XIII

The grace of God

I wish now to speak in some detail, though briefly, of the theological conception of grace and the vital experience or experiences it stands for. I have dealt with conversion, so often referred to as the supreme work of grace, and I shall not speak further of that except occasionally by reference. The word "grace" has perhaps lost lustre by its excessive use in certain circles with narrow horizons, but it is too valuable a word to surrender; rather we must retain it for the religion of the ordinary man. The word represents the divine impulse in human experience, the touch and power of a greater life than that of the human individual; and for this idea there is no other word which is really suitable, as the Greek term "enthusiasm" has largely changed its meaning and, in any case, represents for us a rather boisterous or emotional type of experience. The Greek word "charis" has various native meanings, but the essential one here is that of gift, free gift; and so the word comes to mean the self-giving of God to human souls. Speaking generally, the experiences of human life, and with that the further thought of God as giving Himself in these experiences - divine influence and divine benevolence. This influence may, as I have said before, be regarded as outward or inward, as coming through environment without or through man's own spirit within;

it may be considered as going before and preparing the way for man in his environment or as preparing the man to meet his problems – prevenient grace - or again, it may be considered as assisting and influencing him in the solving of his problems – co-operant grace; it may be treated as effective or merely as suggestive, as moving the man or merely as seeking to persuade or encourage him; but the one word "grace" is, I think, sufficient to cover these varieties and intensities of the divine self and influence and to do duty for the complex idea in all these associations or senses. The fundamental problems of grace are exactly the same as the fundamental psychological problems of freedom; granting human freedom and divine influence on man as real co-existent things, we are faced by problems regarding which we have no complete solution to offer in the present state of our knowledge: Can God persuade without compelling? Is there exercise of divine power through a man's mind or circumstances not the application of a divine force to his life which will automatically move it? Can we find the grace of God in sin and error as well as in righteousness and beauty and truth? Indeed, in the problems of grace and freedom lie most of the fundamental difficulties of our ethical religious faith.

Now I think that if we analyse our experiences carefully, of joy and pain, satisfaction and strain, passion and fear, and the like, we must come to the conclusion that there is nothing in life in which the grace of God may not be discovered; even human sin teaches man the true values of life and its meaning, and much of our social learning in life is by our mistakes. Even in relation to sin and ugliness and deceit we find truth and progress as we react aright to these experiences and by living learn to know them for what they are. In the whole of life's experiences, the pure in heart see God; and if we cannot see God anywhere in some context, it is not because He is not there, but because our eyes are not yet open to see Him in all things. Even in relationship to our sin and shame we can see His grace ceaselessly at work; we can see that His curse is always in intention a blessing; we can see the continual transmutation of evil into good, as we find out the evil we have done is taken up into His pattern and made to teach lessons and cause results of value to ourselves and others; we can see discipline and purpose in everything, and that all things, to the God-centred mind, work together for good under the persistent influence of a good, wise and powerful will.

All life, then, is full of God, i.e., to the understanding mind all is grace; for at no point does God cease His work of education, persuading, limiting, and directing us by His laws, physical and psychic, and by the inward operation of our own best selves in revelation, rebuke, and aspiration. In these inward experiences, as in the strains and reactions of our outer environment, we find God; and spiritual growth is a growing in the sense of God, a growth in the seeing of God in life, i.e., in seeing life as a unity in His purposes and against the background of His being and character. God is teaching and influencing us all the time in our growing sense, appreciation, and co-ordination of values, in our thrills or ecstasies, our desires, our sense of lower and higher moral experience, and the like.

But in the whole of our discussion of these fundamental elements of religious and moral experience we must be careful to think in terms of a personal, not a mechanical, psychology, a psychology derived, not from our knowledge of inanimate things and their ways and conditions of movement, but from our knowledge of conscious personal beings, moved and acting as we move and act. Modern psychology has done us a great service in repudiating a mechanical static psychology, based on a science of things, in favour of a dynamic understanding of the living processes of subjects or human minds. And one chief point, in which modern psychology has modified the older views of human action, has been in its new emphasis upon, and appreciation of, the factors of desire and judgment. Now desire and judgement are things unknown to inanimate objects; and therefore, when one thinks of such a term as "motive", one must not think in terms of mechanical or automatic force, but in terms of human desires and judgements which operate with very different laws, as we are moved not from without as things are, but from within, as persons are. Judgement has indeed played a part in all the great philosophical and ethical systems of the past; the great watchword of the modern psychoanalyst is libido, or desire plus energy; and, in view of what I have said earlier, I think we may affirm that perhaps the chief form in which we know God's grace, or the divine influence, is in desire, while judgment appears to-day peculiarly in the discrimination of desire.

As opposed to legalism, to external codes, to a concern with what is done rather than why it is done, we have the clear Christian emphasis on grace, faith, and spontaneity, which are all allied with desire. Of course, grace operates in all kinds of circumstances and in all forms of experience - hopes, fears, limitations, compulsions, and the like; but in nothing is its place so clear and so important as in relation to desire. A converted drunkard confessed to me that, since his conversion years before, he no longer had the desire to touch intoxicants; here we have a very clear and obvious case of what is normally spoken of as grace, and it had to do with a regeneration of wishes, with a release of higher and better desires. It is not every reclaimed drunkard who has this experience of sudden change in desire; in many cases the fight is long and stern; but behind both the sudden transformation and the prolonged fight stands a new and growing desire for a better and worthier life, a love of nobler things released by God within the heart and working along the lines of the individual personality.

God may exercise His grace in our external circumstance by changes in fortune or health, by bereavement, by encouragement or failure; but it is chiefly through our desires that divine grace operates. Even the lower desires which lead us to sin are usually not wrong in themselves but only in our discrimination, application and control

- sin is action at the wrong time and place; they are essential elements in life, which, for the most part, cannot be destroyed nor ignored. They many simply be redirected aright, or they may be sublimated, but they cannot be swept aside; for they are not mere temptations to evil, they are creative factors of racial or personal life, through which the grace of god can still operate. And if God is to be found in the "lower" desires, as we call them, He is obviously present in the higher. The child playing with soldiers or engines or dolls is dealing with fundamental instinctive impulses which, for a variety of reasons, may not in fact issue in soldiering or engineering or motherhood yet the impulses are at bottom from God and must somehow be fitted into the scheme of life, perhaps in warfare for truth or in the constructive work of medicine or music or the like or in the mothering of the sick or helpless. Sin is not in the desire but in its expression in life; in the desire we are dealing directly with the creative activity or grace of God and with the divine self-expression in man. Our ethical problem is not to choke desire, even so-called lower desire, but to find for it its proper place and function in the true harmony of a good life. And at bottom all the desires, if only we can see and use them in the light of knowledge and of their racial or universal meaning, are on the side of God. It is the fact which is the best basis for an eternal hope in the final victory of God.

The old question whether the grace of God is irresistible or not is really a carrying over into psychology of the language of mechanics, as science which has nothing to do with desire and motion from within, but with motion through externally applied force, i.e., force of a different order and quality from that of many psychically conditioned and controlled. In the case of grace God and man are akin, and His grace in our desires cannot conflict with our natures because our desires come from Him. Of course, in our experience we are often conscious of a conflict of desires, but they all come ultimately from God the Creator, and so we cannot fairly divide them into divine and human; all are both human and divine. It is our desires above all, our wishes and aspiration, that we are chiefly conscious of the creative activity of God, of the ferment or urge forward into new experiences or towards the finding of peace or fulfilment or new power. These wishes of ours, however, are motives for us only when our judgment, such as it is, has found and approved a means of applying them to life, for we do not act on mere impulses - we are men; they must have found conscious direction, means, and ends before they really become motives. And as psychological motives they move us, not by compulsion from without, but by persuasion from within, i.e., we are moved not by others but by ourselves (just as hetero-suggestion must normally become auto-suggestion to be effective or enduring.)

Power in psychological matters means nothing apart from desire, for we cannot do what we do not wish, though we may at times have to resolve a conflict of desires. "Irresistible grace" as used by some seems to imply that we might wish to resist, but the essence of grace as operating within us is that *desires* are used or released in us in such wise that we do what we wish, even in doing new or unaccustomed things, in such wise that we love the things that God loves. For desire is the love of value, and love is the one force which draws and does not drive, which changes us with our will and not against it, and so respects our personalities. We cannot help loving God when we see Him any more than He, being what He is, can help loving us. Because love is the foundation of the universe, our willing service of love is a necessity or law of our very nature when, by the grace of God, our love is drawn forth by experiences which awaken it as it sleeps within us.

Here, then, is the secret of grace; it is God's working in harmony with the laws and values of our own being so that our obedience to God is not servile but free. The true violinist who fingers lovingly the strings of his instrument is obedient to the laws of sound, mechanics, and aesthetics, but the obedience is of a master, not a slave. All our human mastery is through obedience to that which is greater than ourselves, yet which, in us and with us shares the mastery we have found. So, we come to the paradox that independence is ours through dependence, freedom through subjection in knowledge and use to a divine system which is objective to ourselves.

The idea of grace as "free gift" emphasizes this aspect of grace very clearly. God has made us at all points partially dependent on others and altogether dependent on Himself; and it is through the perfection of our dependence that we win the highest relative independence or freedom. It is when our dependence on others becomes a hindrance to our ultimate and more vital dependence on God or the universe, that we have to deny the former and throw ourselves utterly on the latter. Even the most bigoted atheist is aware of his dependence upon the universe - the Stoics only achieved a measure of independence by their attempted sacrifice of the emotional side of life, and their boasted independence was little more than a partial hypocrisy, very noble in some respects, yet unreal and untrue to life; and many of them, like their disciples today, did accept an ultimate doctrine of trust in the universe as the only possible escape from insanity. Dependence is one of the essential notes of religion and one of the most important secrets of character.

Mystics in particular have stressed the central idea of grace in human life; and, looking at life in this way, we come to understand more fully the meaning of Christ, when, according to our best tradition, He said "Why callest thou me good? There is none good save one, that is God." All that a human life has of worth, it has from God; in the last analysis it is the expression of His life in us. If we are good, our goodness is only the indwelling of His nature released in us as we have dared to desire and achieve it by His gift. Thus, all our goodness is God acting through us as His channels of self-expression (cf. Matthew 5:16), and we grow in character as we are brought more and more into vital contact with this real life of the living universe, of which we form a part, or focal points. Our goodness, thus, is not really ours but God's. Therefore, our business, as those aspiring to the heights, is to be our best selves by letting God function in and through us. So, our need is to keep that contact with God which means power as the current of His life flows through us. Thus, through the grace of God, given in our aspirations and in the characters, we love and admire, we come to know the character of God; through our environment and God's dealing with our souls we come to know the laws of His working; and by dependence on Him we grow like Him from day to day.

The importance of this fundamental idea of grace is to-day enormous in most of the concrete and practical concerns of life. In our economic, political, and social life we are growing to realize the importance both of the theology and of the ethic of grace as free giving. Christ's parable of the penny a day has a new relevance with more communistic ideas of society abroad which would consider as primary, not man's work, but man's need. Not justice but free gift offered in faith and love and demanding no return, though hoping for one, is coming to be recognized in a growing measure as the better and more Christian expression both of the life of God and of the duty of man, though it still meets its own problems in human ingratitude and laziness. Yet such is the philosophy of the Cross, and, in dealing with human offences to-day we are realizing slowly that our treatment of our fellows should be based, not on their deserving our gifts, any more than we deserve God's, but on a faith that our giving so without grudge will help to make them more deserving. Hope, anticipating and faith in the unseen in men is a better method of persuasion than compulsion or punishment, because it is in tune with their deepest natures, their divine potential. We make responsible citizens by giving them responsibility and letting it draw them out. Such is Christ's teaching in His parables and in the Sermon on the Mount regarding our human relationships - need, not want, is the basis. Now, this is radically opposed to the older viewpoint, the ethic of rights and justice and recompense still so strong among us. But men will never agree about their rights, though they many someday agree to a way of life, already experimented in with success, in which love and this vital dependence are not the way to insecurity but the only true security. Justice is a poor word in view of its history and misuse; the true Scriptural and better word is righteousness; justice tends to be thought of in a neutral way to be associated with a law of retaliation, and is even elevated to a supreme position in the Eastern and theosophical yet unmoral law of Karma (standing though it does for the reality of sin and evil as foes to be beaten by an impersonal ethical system); while righteousness stands for a positive conception and for a moral passion which aims, not at punishment, but at redemption, not at payment for wrong done but at regeneration of the wrong doer at whatever legitimate cost. Our business, then, as followers of Christ is to treat men, as we would treat God, with reverence, expectancy and ready service, and to believe that, as we approximate to the character of God, and as we keep our contact with Him, He will in fact work through us by grace in the hearts and desires of our fellows and conform us together to His image.

The new emphasis upon desire has thrown a fresh flood of light upon the old controversy over asceticism. In earlier periods of religious history sacrifice had been valued as something which *per se* conferred religious standing on its giver, as something which had merit with God or gods. Hence it was often held that the doing of unpleasant things, the hurting or injuring of oneself, the mortification or suppression of desire, and the like, made a man or woman more acceptable to God and more developed in character and holiness. Of course, the idea of self-denial and self-mortification as a discipline, necessary at times, at least, as a remedial practice, and parallel to a strict diet in digestive and other troubles, also operated to strengthen this view; but it can hardly be denied that, throughout the greater part of Christian history, desire has been, officially and theoretically at least, at a discount and holiness measured largely by the suppression of desire and the extent of self-mortification. The morbid death wish overcame the positive zest for life, and living became narrow and its virtues military, though the many breaches of the demands in question could be not only too easily by confession and absolution, yet still labelled sins. To-day we all recognize that self-control has its place among the Christian virtues as representing the subordination of lower desires to higher; and we recognize, too, that asceticism, or the starvation of desires has its place as a remedial measure for morbid conditions, personal or collective; but, as such a therapeutic measure for cases of disproportionate growth and unbalanced activity, it is a witness to *weakness*, not to strength, and it is for the sick, not for the normal. Its place was further secured in history by the theology of human depravity, which denied all moral normality to men and treated the whole race as sick. It is true that in all men there are abnormal, diseased and irrational elements, but this means often, not the presence of essentially evil things so much as a disproportion or faulty relation in things actually good; and, in a growing dynamic view of life as being trial and error and learning thereby, some such disproportion, or imperfection of harmony, must be seen as normal at times, paradoxical as that may sound. The imperfection of the bud is relative to the flower; the bud itself may be perfect, but it is unfinished. According to the views of the newer psychology desire is usually looked at as essentially good and creative, or it may be construed as neutral; but on the whole it needs discrimination rather than destruction or repression. Repression may be necessary for a clamant case of morbidity; and the inner censor does naturally act so, even in sleep; but, for the normal man, education the full and sincere use of his faculties in judgement and consequent action is the true way.

The strangling of desire is the strangling of the creative impulses of life; and, if persisted in as a general duty, it can only lead to diseased, imitative, and secondary forms of life and to the historical supersession of "civilized" peoples by some more vital stock. We see this in racial ways as the less mature and less sophisticated actually come to the front in political power (cf. the rise and fall of empires); and in personal life we see the frustration of those, who have denied desire, leading to bitterness, pessimism and narrowness of sympathy. The true life is the life which is proportionately developed to the fullest possible extent, in which desire as fully comprehended, organised and interrelated as it can be, has the freest available play, and in which spontaneity, harmony, and generosity of impulse go hand in hand. Puritanism and asceticism in all their forms are basically wrong as positive principles of life; their own justification in history is as reactions against moral morbidity; though a wise and approved control of impulse is a necessary part of that sublimation which (largely out of sex energy) has produced all our culture; but the aim and way of culture is always enjoyment, and positive use, not fear and denial. The pormocracy of the Dark Ages produced a Hildebrand, the suffocations of the official Jewish Sadducean religion made the Pharisees, the corruption of particular Christian societies has again and again made Montanists, Donatists, Waldensians, Franciscans, Lollards and the like, with a smaller or greater message of renunciation and unworldliness in a crisis; but ascetic religion has never appealed to the normal man as a permanent way of life; and, though the names of those, who have been able to hurt themselves and deny themselves pleasures to a remarkable degree, have been canonized and reverenced as not of this world, their example has never been regarded as generally obligatory; they have been called holy, but their morality has not been accepted by the ordinary decent and intelligent man as a standard for normal life.

And the ordinary man, with all his mistakes and his escape-valves, has been right. St Paul, puzzled by the speaking with tongues of the early Church, did not dare to reject it, but he put it low in the scale of spiritual gifts; had he known more of it, as we do, he probably would have denounced it more definitely with explanations of its nature. And the ordinary man of a more or less healthy outlook has not dared to deny the spiritual value of self-sacrifice, even though he knows that the best sacrifice must be reasonable and useful, and that desire is not such an evil guide as the "holy" have told him. The ordinary man believes in both desire and sacrifice, and as yet the Church has given him no synthesis of the two, because it has stressed self-denial rather than love, a negative rather than a positive ethic. But to-day we see that sacrifice or renunciation *per se* is of no value - it is throwing God's gifts away, or back in His face - it must be conceptual and teleological to be of value; if its true end be not useful and its content reasonable, it is an evil thing, an enfeeblement of life, no cause for pride but for shame; and often it has fear at its root, the fear of life or God, and is then no way to strength. Strength, joy, energy, peace, love, and the other positive goods of life, lie along the line of desire, interest, emotion, not along the line of their negation. The ascetic, knowing that a capacity for almost anything can be dangerous, may take the line of seeming safety by refusing to employ it and by wrapping his talent in a napkin. His action is usually motivated by fear, fear of emotion, fear of instinct, fear of pleasure, fear of the snares of beauty or of hunger. But emotion, instinct, impulse, beauty, hunger and thirst all have a positive meaning; and the policy of fear both fails in accomplishment and raises up an earnest school of more "pagan" men who believe in their desires and emotions, and who profess to seek to live a fuller life beneath their sway.

The artists are perhaps the last class to turn to Christianity because Christianity, false to the spirit of its Founder, has shut them out more resolutely than any other class in fear of their Hellenizing and hedonistic influence and philosophy. Of course, limitation is essential in life - proportion and self-control with self-respect - and the doctrine of the Incarnation shows this even in the activity of God - to reveal Himself God must limit Himself in time and place, in language and sex, in education and ethnic stock and so forth. The artists have their peculiar weaknesses or temptations in relation to proportion and control and definite and objective ends of action; but the lovers of beauty and the champions of emotion and impulse have their measure of truth, and neither Church nor Gospel can ever wholly win the world till the truth in the pagan revolt has been recognized, and with it the vital place of desire and grace in the religious life. For asceticism and the morality of the codes are legalism, but, for the true Christianity of grace and freedom, desire is of God rather than the devil, though it can be misinterpreted and misapplied. Faith, not fear, must govern our treatment of desire, and nothing has done more to rehabilitate desire and faith - and incidentally the Creator - than the newer psychology. Christianity is not a code of prohibitions, nor even of commands; it is not a system of virtues; but it is a spirit, an attitude or point of view, to which we are committed, consisting in faith, hope and love, which seeks to live and learn by experiment and social contacts, and which sees in life a unity, not a duality of God and the Devil, according to which part of life is the good gift of God and part the baleful gift of the Devil. For us as Christians, life is one and good; the forces of life are basically on the side of God, and evil consists in fear, division, distrust, ignorance, malice, and selfishness - disruptive tendencies which are contrary to our own best desires but fastened on us by evolution, environment, habit, undue self-regard, and by the propaganda of sectional loyalties and diseased mentalities.

"By grace we are saved, and that not of ourselves, it is the gift of God." But we have a certain response to make to His divine grace which is somehow within our power - for salvation, though it is not earned, *is* conditioned, as the getting of the electric light is conditioned by the pressing of a switch, which does not make but conditions the light - the response of faith as trust or committal, as expectancy, as a venture. And such human response to the divine grace is followed by new revelation, new achievements, and, in measure, by a new world. Life develops through our conscious responding to the continual and ever-present influence or grace of God, found especially by those who have eyes to see and hearts to feel His presence in this urgent and colourful experiment of living, which is ours by God's gift as both task and opportunity, and as the way to glory.

BOOK IV

PROBLEMS OF RELIGIOUS EXPERIENCE

CHAPTER XIV

Sin and conscience

When we come to a consideration of the problems associated with religious experience, of which the two most obvious are sin and freedom, we come to questions of great difficulty of which there is as yet little solid agreement among the experts; so, in place of a full dress discussion of these two topics, which would tend to be endless and very much in the air, I propose to state the main factors, conditions and attempted solutions of the topics to be faced, and then to state the more or less central elements in the Christian conceptions of sin or freedom as they have been reasonably expressed according to my judgment. The first and more obvious difficulty is that here we pass beyond science in any attempt at explanation, for science has to objectify in order to study, while here we are dealing with the subject of experience, in both sin and freedom, and this cannot be done with success in definition, though we may reach some satisfying elements of a practical faith which may seem, if not logical, at least reasonable.

Sin is probably the most difficult conception of all in our list to handle for it has so many aspects that defy accurate definition in view of our ignorance of the facts about personality, freedom and evil. Some, however, think that it presents no difficulty at all; that sin is just a deliberate free choice of evil; but this seemingly simple formula raises the questions of choice, its nature, method, ground and aim, of deliberation and what that means in personal action (on which philosophers do not agree), and what evil itself is - is something that may be chosen for its own sake as evil, or, when it is chosen, is it chosen only as a good because of its apparent advantages, or, again, is it a form of atavism or regression, or is it insanity - i.e., unorganized action? For many people the determining and overriding conception is that of responsibility, and some would deny any view, however probable or strongly championed, that seemed at all likely to reduce the sense of moral responsibility. Now it is always difficult to define ethical and religious notions adequately, but an honest man will find it peculiarly so in the sphere of sin, for sin is not merely moral evil, it involves a relation to God of disobedience or refusal or failure; but where the true standard of right conduct is to be found, is a matter of dispute – is it in a code of divine laws, is it in intuitions of values of the inner man, is it in human intuitions, or in prudential or utilitarian dispositions towards other men which seem to make sin the doing of anti-social things? And so forth.

A picture of our difficulties regarding sin can be gained if we face one or two orthodox or modern statements on the subject of sin. For example, I heard this summer a continental scholar dealing with the subject, who regarded the sense of sin as a form of Christian revelation, a mystical experience in which a man in the presence of God (cf. Isaiah 6) felt himself unclean and needy and therefore received cleansing and redemption and mission. In other words, a sense of sin, like salvation is impossible without faith. And there is no doubt that sin in the Christian sense is different from mere wrong doing; it is against, not men, but God. If, on the other hand, we look at the ordinary orthodox views of sin we find it as individual transgression and as a present racial deficit. If we take individual sin we have the theological judgment, not drawn from a scientific induction of cases but from an a priori principle regarded as revealed, that all except Jesus Christ have sinned and are sinners. This universal negative at once raises the problem that, if a man cannot avoid being a sinner, he is not free in the matter and therefore is not guilty - he is shut in to sin by his nature. And, if we take the racial end of the subject, all men (Jesus Christ being an exception for some theologians but not for others) are stained and enfeebled by derived or original sin, so that temptation, evil and, some would say, guilt are present before a man has made his first moral choice. Thus, it looks as though man has really no choice in relation to sin; he may avoid sins here and there, but he is under bondage and under condemnation as a sinner from the beginning of his life.

These things may seem difficult to believe but, before I pass on to a more positive discussion, I wish to say two things:

1) As regards individual sin it is well to distinguish between sin and guilt (see later) and between sin and immoral, or anti-social, acts or attitudes, offences against men. The essential thing about sin is that it is against God, an offence against God directly, or against a kind of divine blueprint of one's individual life.

2) And as regards sin considered as racial, we recognize to-day firstly that heredity in us gives us a bias towards the patterns of the past; we have all in us the pull of the days that are gone making for moral regression and sub-human behaviour. In addition, we recognize that we are all caught in institutional forms which are imperfect, but which maintain and at times compel action on lower levels - "moral man and immoral society." Before we can think for ourselves, we are caught and hypnotized by the moral crystallizations of the past in the social, political, economic, and other human forms, which affect us all and tie us to levels of life which many now

feel outworn and retrograde. Thus, we have in us by both
heredity and nurture what we can call original or derivative
sin in pulls that are backward - we have as moral men to
move continually up and forward.

The fact is that the modern world is, in many matters that have
moral significance, so far removed in thought from the older world
of a few centuries ago that it is hard to find bridges between them at
all on some issues. The older Christian philosophy believed clearly in
a personal devil, in evil as absolute and almost as a positive principle;
it believed in "sin with a high hand" or the deliberate choice by
men of what was evil, knowing it to be so; it believed in conscience
simply as the voice of God, and in goodness as the keeping of a fairly
definite code of rules relating to desires, opinions and institutions,
and, speaking generally, in a static view of life and conduct; while the
modern world believes in values as morally ultimate, in evil as mainly
relative and negative, in the devil and temptation as predominantly
the pull of the past backwards, in the moral conflict as a conflict
of values presided over by a judgment still very immature and
uneducated at the best in questions of real worth, in conscience as
a very mixed and complex possession, sometimes fairly healthy and
sometimes morbid but usually needing education; it has little place
for codes or institutions, except as things that minister more or less
effectively to the value and happiness and efficiency of life; and,
speaking generally, it believes in a dynamic, progressive, organic, and
often relative, view of life and conduct.

Life is kinetic, yet many of our moral judgments are static even
yet; it is extremely difficult to express in a philosophical form the new
comprehension of ethical realities. James, Freud, Einstein, and others
have completely transformed the problems of conduct and of personal
or social relations; and a new philosophy of movement and relativity
and growth is needed to replace the old philosophy of the static, the

absolute and the final. What is absolute is a direction for man, and this is ultimately that of the character and nature of God; but this needs interpretation for action. And as for the relative view of morals, one of the clearest and most interesting statements, far ahead of its time is the word of Jesus preserved for us in the Western text of Luke 6:5 as spoken to the man seen by Jesus working on the Sabbath: "If thou knowest what thou does, thou are blest, but if thou knowest not, thou are accursed and a breaker of the law" - a case of the relativity of morals and of the importance of thinking down to foundations in relation to goodness. It is not what we do that matter so much as why we do it – not works but faith, as the Protestant Reformers said.

We have, then, discovered today the truth, which is a truism, that life is living, i.e., that it moves and grows, and no definition of life, on the religious or any other side, can be adequate which is fundamentally static, or which deals with life as a series of fixed points at rest; yes, life is dynamic, kinetic. This modern view of life as moving and growing, not by addition from without but by assimilation from within, i.e., an organic growth, is of very profound importance when we come to study morality, for here, more even than elsewhere, men have tended in the past to static judgments. Human action was judged by fixed rules, or in reference to a fixed standard, and goodness was conformity with rule or imitation of the standard example. To-day we see that morality must be considered relatively to its circumstances and, to be of real value, must be spontaneous rather than imitative, growing from within rather than imposed from without.

In the book of Genesis, Adam and Eve are credited with "sinning" *before* they had eaten of the tree of the knowledge of good and evil i.e., before they actually knew good and evil. All of us, trained in static methods of ratiocination, according to which motion is a fact but irrational, have had the same experience of reading back our later knowledge.

Looking back upon an act with the judgment which has been won through the act, we often condemn or approve our act as if we stood at the beginning of it but already with the knowledge which has come to us through it. A past "sin" may have been the record or expression of what we were, but through it our judgment, by the observation of effects, by the release of shame, by mental anguish, remorse or repentance and a truer analysis of our mind than we could have made earlier, and by the reactions to our act of the universe generally, has so grown morally that to repeat the action would be sin in quite a different sense and degree.

Of course, there are very different types of sin, sins of impulse, sins of habit, sins of confusion or uncertainty, sins of experiment, sins of choice of the lesser of two or more evils, and the like; and I do not propose at this point to discuss their relative standings and meanings. I suppose the beginning of this new movement in thinking, which has reached its chief expression in the pragmatism of William James, the relativity which followed Einstein, and the psychoanalysis of Freud, is to be found in the critical work of Kant who set aside the static Greek conception of knowledge - *theoria* - and substituted a philosophy with emphasis upon the will and practice. But in every sphere of knowledge the new idea has won its way, and tardily it is creeping at last even into theology - the last citadel always to fall, perhaps because the most important. It is important, however, to distinguish between sin and guilt. Sin implies evil on the moral side as an offence against God, and even apart from any consciousness of the individual, as in the concept of original sin; i.e., sin stands for the more social and more objective point of view which conceives of actions, words and thoughts as evil in relation either to some final or objective standard such as God's will or nature or to practical results for evil as effecting our lives and those of our fellow countrymen, and so has much to do with a level of living which may actually be unconscious - sin rather than sins. Guilt implies responsibility and individual consciousness of evil (the obligation to have done otherwise than we did) and is therefore relative to the stage of development which the individual has reached and implies a conscious acceptance in some sense of what is known to be a lower level of life. Sin we may take then as referring to moral evil in a racial or social way, but guilt as referring to the individual mind and will. Thus, it is possible to speak of a past action as sin, without necessarily implying either that those committed it were guilty or that anything else could have been done at that time and in those circumstance by those same people. Questions of guilt however, if the word has any meaning at all, must be relative throughout. Now, in religious experience it is not questions of sin which matter so much as questions of guilt, for we have very little consciousness of personal sin apart from our consciousness of guilt. Neither a low social code nor unfortunate results necessarily prove sin to us and produce a sense of guilt. We cannot as individual persons accept the opinions of others as final; and, as to the proof from results, we many feel that even the results, unpleasant as they may be, do not make our action wrong - e.g. unpleasant results following the telling of the truth do not necessarily convince us that it would be better to have told a lie - but in some cases we may recognize that, while we were not wrong in acting as we did, we should be wrong if we did so again, i.e., we may recognize evil or sin without recognizing guilt.

But this type of impersonal judgment is unfortunately very hard to attain to, however right it be, because in many a case the suggestions of others are so strong that, even in a perfectly defensible moral experiment, we have some sense of guilt due to our violation of a code which has been imposed upon us, perhaps by continual suggestion from the dawn of our earthly consciousness. We do not start our moral judgments any more than our behaviour, unbiased; if in behaviour we are drawn primarily by our wishes, in our moral judgment we are often dominated by suggestion or the herd complex,

and the two factors are in ceaseless conflict. We are continually
doing, for good and evil, what we think or say we ought not - and
the idea of "ought" or obligation is frequent social suggestion, i.e., our
actions are contrary to inculcated rules regarded by our surrounding
fellowmen as authoritative, whether observed or not. Our conscience,
so-called, operates in part with a sense of proportion, in part with
ordinary reason and judgment, in part with a genuine immediate
awareness of moral values, but chiefly, I think, with ideas implanted
by continual social suggestion and based in some measure on past
moral experiments by men. These codes ought to be a help to us,
but they ought not to be a final authority, otherwise moral progress
becomes impossible - and it is always difficult enough to act in a
progressive way with herd suggestions of the past against us without
adding the quality of infallibility to those suggestions. In the early
stages of our religious development the reading of a story, not religious,
on Sunday, or the going for a walk, not to church, on the same day,
or the dropping of a religious service or of devotional reading when
very tired - these and the like actions, perhaps not wrong in the eyes
of God or of our own truest self, may have been attended with a sense
of failure and shame, social no doubt in measure, but to us often
unconsciously so. It is very hard in this experience of right and wrong
to know just where we are, as we are always being torn between
the two poles, the spontaneous and the organized, the individual
and the social; and a true full life must do justice to both. But, in
any case, a true morality is not imitation but spontaneous goodness;
it is the harnessing of the mind and the wishes in a personal and
independent activity or judgment of behaviour, not the following
of rules or regulations made by others however exalted, for the true
morality is written on the heart. The morality, like the art, which
Is not true self-expression, is doomed because its foundations are
insecure and artificial; grace is the Christian key to a true ethic.

But this sense of moral freedom and private judgment is comparatively recent in the world, especially as applied to ethical questions, or socially important questions of conduct or belief. If we examine the growth of the idea of sin historically, we shall find much to explain our own mental confusion. For sin began as a social rather than an individual conception, it was not a judgement of the individual consciousness, it was a violation of an external standard of action imposed by a group on supposedly divine sanctions. A violation of this standard, which was no doubt believed to represent the line of action most conducive to social well-being, and which did rest to some extent on earlier experiments, was held to imply an anti-social state of life or mind in the violator which we may call transgression or sin, whether the description was always valid or not. The original moral code consisted of customs and tabus, and the violation of these ceremonial laws was sin. This early "sin", more or less external and ceremonial, i.e., physical, in its meaning, was regarded as a kind of physical infection, dangerous to the group life, which later was supposed to be bound up with the correct observance of these customs and tabus; and so, as the idea of personality had not yet developed and thinking was almost purely social, we find that Achan's sin, in the book of Joshua, of breaking the ban laid upon Jericho, is followed by the stoning to death of his whole family - as we might to-day effectively isolate a household in which plague had broken out. In the development of Old Testament religion, it is not till we come to the days of Jeremiah and Ezekiel that we can be sure to have reached the ethical or personal stage of morality; "The soul that sinneth, it shall die; the son shall not bear the iniquity of the father." In such words we see the swing of the pendulum away even from the truth inherent in the social idea of original (i.e., derived) sin, viz. the backward pull of the past; for they mark clearly the new realization of the individual as a conscious moral agent with a sense of responsibility and of inward approval or disapproval, i.e., a sense not only of sin but of guilt.

Our sense of guilt usually arises from a comparison of what we did and what we thought, or now think, would have been the better thing to do; and it has in it, pain – a purifying pain. For this sense of contrast involves pain to spirits that are emotionally and intellectually keen, and their mental pain, like the physical pain which continually saves us from disease and death, is an angel of benevolence, warning us and impelling us to the painful process of change. Moral experiment may involve such a retrospective and painful judgment, even if we thought we had sufficient motives for our action at the time; and owing to the lack of moral clarity in all our minds there is still much moral experiment on the part of independent vital souls who seek, through curiosity and action, new knowledge or enlargement of life or new experiences, and who do not always class as evil the urges of their own desires - this is one type of activity which may lead to new truth or life, or, again, may, in the light of fuller and later knowledge, come through fault to be adjudged sin. But, of course, there are many other types of sin than that of the moral experiment, more deliberate or less deliberate, in particular the sin of habit or bondage, which it is peculiarly hard to break; yet even here it is the sense of moral contrast or guilt, inducing shame, which is the chief power to release our best nature and win the victory for good. Even sinful habits may have been contracted innocently enough, and, if we are content to take the sense of guilt and shame as God's surgery, a help to rouse us, not a depressant to case us down, we shall seek to condemn less and love more, and to think more positively about the whole question of goodness.

True morality must be spontaneous and autonomous, not imposed from without, i.e., it must be self-imposed according to a man's own moral light, values and wishes, the formative elements of his moral being. And in life there is no power for right decision and action like the power of love or positive passion i.e., the love or worship of some good or value. Even in the pursuit of evil so called we recognize today that men do not choose the wrong because it is wrong, but because it has for them a positive quality of value, the quality of something loved or desired. All human action follows values, and values are our fundamental moral category; the problem is to discriminate and harness and direct them aright. Most true moral life is the education and readjustment of our sense of value by experience, rather than the doing of praiseworthy or blameworthy things by a morally neutral will, liable to reward or punishment according as it moves to one side or the other.

Nietzsche has expressed in an exaggerated form the modern psychological emphasis upon action as good and upon values as worthy in themselves in his doctrine of the weakness of the "moral" man i.e., the man who dare not be himself and follow his own sense of value. All the great saints have seen the same truth in some degree; "the same force as make a great sinner, makes a great saint," Augustine's "love God and do what you like, " and so forth, all represent the realization by the pioneer souls of moral development that action and values are positive things and good in themselves, however dangerous at times, and that suppression and imitation are never quite true to ethical realities, because ethically such foundations of action are inadequate or wrong - "I would thou wert cold or hot" (Revelation 3:15-16) says God to the lukewarm!

Guilt then represents our sense of moral failure in the conflict between opposing desires, regarded as higher and lower, and, in particular, failure in overcoming or controlling those less worthy desires which have established a power of habit over the mind. The bondage of habit is the constant moral problem for the race and for the individual - the low levels of our living – though habit has its value and power for goodness as well as for evil. Habits mean easy channels in mind and brain for the passage of energy, and our habits are the crystallisations of our past - in social life we call them institutions. But there are higher desires continually arising within us as we grow, challenging our habits and breaking through our mental systems of organized impulses and ideas; and so, arise conflicts between the new and better elements of our mind on the one hand and the old and more consolidated on the other. What the actual relations of habits and desires is we do not know, we cannot compute their respective forces in any common unit of measurement, and only in experience and by experiment and effort, can we find in what ways they are associated and how old habits may be overcome, or new habits formed. Much of the study of modern psychology on its practical side has been devoted to the laws of the mind by which impulses and aspirations may be organized or changed into habits and to the investigation of how older habits may be broken up or modified by the release or stimulation of new desires. But the word guilt covers the consciousness of the conflict and of our failures in it.

We cannot say that the conflict in itself is evil; it is inevitable and common to man; even at its highest levels in Jesus Christ, or in other great leaders of the spirit, the conflict is obviously acute; for there is difficulty and strain in moral growth as in all growth. Three times in Gethsemane Christ must pray before He can achieve a unity in His own mind, and it would be a fatuous theology which regarded this struggle as a mark of failure; it may be a mark of a true human nature, as it grows and seeks to grow stronger, but no one can dare to impute blame in the matter. And indeed, it is doubtful if our current idea of blame is ever really justified; Christ's dictum is "Judge not." The moral pain which blame represents or translates, is a spur to us to avoid the failures of the past; it stands for a suffering of the spirit aspiring to new things yet struggling against the old and at times failing; but the common use of blame is probably not truly ethical or Christian at all. "Neither do I condemn thee" said Christ in another context, and His reference to moral judgement; "By their fruits ye shall know them," does not carry us beyond the need of making provisional personal decisions on moral questions for our own use, i.e., of using our judgments for positive ends. The true spirit of Christianity, I think, forbids us the luxury of condemnation, or contempt, which always involved the making of ourselves a standard for the measurement of others - our desires, our values, our systems, and our codes; but judgment in that moral sense is not ours, it is the attribute only of omniscience.

Thus, sin is primarily racial or corporate, guilt is personal, and blame is something beyond our power to assess in any real sense; it is a piece of social mechanism for influencing men. In speaking of these terms, sin and fault, I have tried to show that they correspond in a real measure to facts of experience, but that those facts have frequently been greatly misinterpreted and so have given rise to moral snobbery and to a depreciation of the individual's spontaneous self-expression in the interests of an organized and imitative morality, which is probably often quite unjustified.

I wish now to turn back to the duality of moral experience expressed in the idea of the conflict between good and evil. We all have in us, as it were, a brute and an angel living in the same house and sharing the same life, by that alternation which makes all our experience; and the moral conflict is the strife between the preterist brute and the futurist angel - the illustration is from Tolstoy. Sanity and power require that the two be somehow made to live in peace and that no element be lost, since both contain essentials of the full life, for man as we know him needs the brute as well as the angel. The destruction of either element would be fatal; yet the angel must maintain some sort of control, as only the higher is fit to appreciate and integrate both elements. Human experience functions between two foci or poles, however they may be defined, the one belonging obviously to the past and the other as obviously to the future. The same conception is also found in the orthodox Augustinian doctrine of the will which regards it as in itself essentially good, with its freedom only in goodness, and which treats evil as bondage. It is in virtue of our higher diviner nature that we are personal and free, and differentiated from the animals, and it is this higher self which alone can integrate and control our whole nature so that we become truly one and truly free and grow towards that Personality which is the God of our Christian faith.

It is important to discriminate clearly in thought between freedom as a kind of arbitrary choice between good and evil - as if we were unbiased and so free to pick either - and freedom as a positive power making for goodness and the control of circumstances and evil; and moral goodness is certainly no case of indeterminacy as the latter is today discussed by philosophers. To that point I shall come later, but I wish here to point out the meaning for our doctrine of sin of the question just discussed. All action is motivated by values and is therefore not arbitrary but according to desire and the discrimination of desire by reason; that is, free choice does not mean arbitrary choice but a choice which is truly our own and so expresses us. But if our actions be motivated be desire, the way to improve our action is by the improvement of our desire life in its relations to the rest of life, which must be accomplished in part by divine grace and in part by hard work in suggestion, education, discrimination, control, and a better understanding of means and ends. But the real problem of human progress in morality is the problem not of the head but of the heart, the problem of the release of desire and the overcoming of disintegrating, by integrated and conceptual forms of desire, so that men desire not merely to do but to be, not action but character, i.e., an integrated life; and this is the problem of regeneration, as theology calls the event or process. Real morality is not obedience to a code, nor imitation of a person, it is the love of goodness, and no other morality can endure the tests of life and reality, for all worthy action must proceed from a genuine and sincere emotional basis. This love of goodness is implied as existing in all by the doctrine of man as in the divine image, and I think experience proves that at bottom the embers of such a love and worship of goodness are to be found still aglow in every human heart; but they need to be kindled into flame, and in no other way can they be so well kindled as by other hearts which are on fire. The real redemption of man is not by preaching nor legislation but by the infection of goodness, the spontaneous kindling of soul from soul in the contracts and fellowships of social life; and this is the real meaning of the Incarnation - the regenerative or creative act of God in history, the infection of goodness in Jesus. Thus, our real need for moral development is not example nor a code of precepts nor a fear of consequences but a spirit of goodness; it is that the love of the higher, dormant in our hearts, should awake, or be awakened to life, and sweep all the evil and irrelevant elements of our lives aside in its spontaneous power, the power of God within us - for moral growth is by the opening of the door to God, especially as He is found in Christ.

Authoritarian systems tend to consider the outward act and to stress sins rather than sin, but where, as in Protestantism, personal responsibility is accepted in an adult faith or mode of life, the emphasis tends to fall on sin and on regeneration rather than on sins and forgiveness, except that forgiveness remains in experience and in memory as the restoration after fall to conscious communion with God. Our moral experience is one of value and of pain; and our own sense of value and of pain rests ultimately (including our conflicts of value or temptations) not on any choice of our own, but on the work of our Creator; our generation is becoming conscious of the imputations of the older views against the character or the power of God, and therefore concerned to restate the situation in the light of what we are sure of. The facts as we see them are that men have grown up with two pulls operating upon them, the pull of the past or habit, which may be evil, and the pull of the future or of foreseeing purpose, which is usually good; and the relative strength of the two pulls is largely a matter of circumstances. All men tend at times to regress to habits which now are evil, by virtue of their historical derivation, and all men feel in some measure the call of a better world and a better life beyond them. Here is the real conflict adequately accounted for by the two elements in man as we know him; his past, subhuman, and human, and the divine in him, which in some sense is present all the way through his development as the seed of progress and as the challenge or power of God. If man's wishes lead him to sin it is his wishes also which lead him from sin; the more integrated and personal his life becomes, the more purposive and conceptual becomes his wishing, and the lower state of the immediate gratification of wishes gives way to the higher state of facing, inhibiting, controlling, and sublimating his desires to attain a greater fulfilment of his whole nature both as an individual and as a social being. The difference between the truly moral man and the ordinary man is the same as that between the ordinary man and the child, only at a different stage of growth, and integration, of purpose and understanding. The evil man is the man who merely wishes to do so and so, the good man wishes to be so and so; and this usually means to be such a man as would not engage in an otherwise desirable course of action, till at least it can be engaged in without inquiry to society or principles.

Blame, however - to return that topic - is a depreciatory judgment of disapproval or condemnation which presupposes deliberate choice and a recognized moral responsibility in relation so a certain action, or activity, but usually without adequate knowledge of the facts; and it is exceedingly difficult at this stage in our knowledge, if not indeed impossible, to set forth any adequate moral theories of responsibility and of praise and blame - the first is a necessary faith, the others are techniques of social pressure, like reward and punishment. We are only really at the beginning of moral inquiry, and conscious of many of the mistakes of the past. The whole problem may be shortly but cogently stated by the illustration of one point alone, on a kinetic and not static view of conduct, viz., the question, is there a sin of ignorance? If we be ignorant, can we sin, or at least can we be guilty? And if you answer "No," may we not be guilty for our ignorance, if we have not taken every advantage to change it into knowledge? But who could ever know if he had done so in every case? Would anyone, however, ever seek knowledge unless he wished it? Can we, with our limited powers of attention and amount of energy, wish for more than a few things out of all possible things - are our wishes here not determined in general by the circumstances of our environment and the needs of our lives? And is not God in a real sense primarily responsible for our circumstances and for our needs or wishes? One might ask an infinite number of such difficult questions. At least they show the utter impossibility of reaching a stable position and leave us with our moral theory, whatever it is, largely as a confession of faith, which we may attempt to keep true to life as it teaches us more, but which in different minds may take very different shapes. Blame at least is often a form of moral snobbery and an injury to the spirit of love. Yet by their elaborative systems of praise and blame churches and states have sought to mould and influence men by the pain and pleasure attached, whether mental or physical. This however is the voice of the crowd, not necessarily of God, though God may occasionally speak through the crowd; but it is, however, commonly the pressure of the herd instinct and quantitatively the chief element in conscience.

It is a challenging fact that in many important moral problems people to-day go more readily to a doctor as father confessor than to a minister of religion. They feel that the minister stands for a code and will probably automatically condemn, but that the doctor stands for science and will not be so ready to pass moral judgments.

And I cannot avoid the judgment that parts of our experiences are scientific experiments of the 'trial and error' sort, the learning of the values of life by living; this may at times seem a callous or dangerous view, but God certainly permits such experiments. Psychotherapists at any rate take and heal moral weakness and moral bondage to-day in a scientific spirit and atmosphere. There is a new attitude to human sin, a new setting of helpfulness above moral judgements as the way of treatment, a new humility of mind as to our right to condemn. A book like "The Problem Child" by A.S Neill which deals almost entirely with what is normally called sin - thieving, lying, immorality, cruelty, and the like - seems to me, non-Christian as it is in profession, to represent very fairly the true Christian attitude to sin, i.e., by regarding it as nature warped in growth, and by seeking not so much to argue as to help. Whether the sin in question is the person's own fault, in part or not, is largely a speculative question, in view of our abysmal ignorance of human nature and motives, means and ends. What is important is the question: Can we change it? Can we heal it? Mr Neill's work has proved conclusively that, even with such knowledge as he has, he can often do so with his difficult children; and so could we in our measure, I believe, if we approached the matter in the right way, in the spirit of Christ, in faith and love, not in condemnation and fear. Love, not sin, is the Christian faith and preoccupation and gospel; and it works.

The problem of goodness is not so easily solved by authority as it was. Do we know goodness immediately, or have we to find it out? Is goodness intuitively known, or has it to be built slowly out of values and facts and results? For most of us life is education in value i.e., in goodness. True goodness is founded on spontaneity of desire, it is our own, loved and chosen and willed by us; and the modern emphasis on "libido" has changed the whole outlook except for those who think in terms of traditional formulae. Inaction tends to atrophy and stagnation, action of all kinds to learning by experience.

Inaction tends to morbidity; action, risky as it is, to the reactions of life being felt and known, i.e., to a discovery of the true laws of life. The "glutton and winebibber," as men called Jesus, believed in life and life more abundant, and He regarded the sins of desire, real though they were, as far less serious than those of fear and pretence, the sins of the hypocrites, by which a man shielded himself from life. After all the way of Christian Salvation is by faith, and faith among other things means venture or the taking of risks. Innocence is not purity, and goodness is no negative thing, but a positive passion or love of that which is for the good of ourselves and the world and God. The Church is at a long remove on many points even yet from its Master. It is preoccupied with sin rather than, as He was, with God. Self-depreciation, self-hate, timidity, and a negative morality are what Christianity has so far brought to many instead of self-respect, love, venture, and social living.

Most human sin comes from the fear of losing something of value, and this appears in many forms. Sin is regression in fear to past habits or levels of life, racial or personal; goodness is progressive. Sin is a shortcut in haste or panic to something which may in itself be good but which we are afraid of losing; goodness takes the long view and is content to wait till our end can be gained in ways that are not socially or universally injurious. Sin is anti-social and short-sighted; goodness is social and long-sighted. Sin is egoism, the part caring, not for the whole, but for itself alone; goodness is a true self-respect which seeks the good of the whole, knowing that we are social beings and that our true life is the life in God and in fellowship with men. Sin is disruptive of the soul and of sincerity; goodness is integrating, making for peace and unity, for sanity and well-being. Sin is an infantile acting from impulse; goodness passes its impulse through mind and will into a deliberate positive activity. Perhaps the most characteristic note and activity of goodness is integration, the integration of the mind in sanity, the integration of the nations, in peace and co-operation, of industry, art, education - of society in all its aspects; and a common modern word for personal goodness is "integrity." As morality is a progressive thing, a keeping up-to-date with the facts and needs of our situation and environment, and real function of normal growth is often paradoxically the turning of good into evil by putting the good of one age out of date for the next; it is the discovery of how truly to adjust life to the present stimuli and strains and requirements of life, so as to keep it healthy, and to advance and enrich it for man and God. In this conflict and search one of the chief elements referred to is conscience, sometimes regarded as a faculty of the mind, or the voice of God in the soul, but really a complex phenomenon containing diverse elements of varying value. In modern psychology the chief process which lies between desire and action is that of discrimination, and the soundness of the action following upon desire depends largely upon the health and thoroughness of mental discrimination. This discrimination is the activity of judgement which leads to choice or judgement-in-action, and conscience is little more than the conscious demand and facing of judgment in moral matters by the individual man. The characteristic tone of conscience is "I ought" or "I ought not"; it is personal, it is moral, it recognises responsibility for results and the contrast between different possible courses of action, recognized as higher or lower. But in the activity of conscience various elements are involved as entering into the complex process of moral judgment.

Of these the most obvious is that of herd suggestion which is the main ingredient in the thought "I ought", quantitatively considered at least, for there are in conscience also other more personal and more immediate factors. The sense of "ought" or obligation usually represents the pressure of one's herd with a long history of suggestion, example, and the social education behind it. All social animals have a conscience in this primary sense; thus, a dog has a social conscience, a cat has none, for a dog will come however reluctantly to his master to be punished - he recognises a pack morality and puts his master in the place of his pack leader; a cat will run away with no qualms. Social life implies a recognized group authority and group pressure in the individual mind, a racial instinct of law and order and submission to a larger unit than oneself. And the greater part of our morality, as felt in conscience, is the work of suggestions implanted by mother, relatives, teachers, ministers, and public opinion - a felt social pressure which not only claims our assent but gains it to some extent with our own will. Thus, there is a real meaning and real value, for a social being like man, in prestige, authority, and even prejudice, as belonging to a herd complex and representing a real past with its achievements, experience and lessons, but yet not final when it crosses other elements, such as the even more immediate and more creative element of desire in either its primary and perceptual or its later and more conceptual form.

In the second place there are in conscience the ordinary processes of judgment by reason, by the consideration of means and consequences, of antecedents and aims, a process both logical and teleological. This is the meaning of conscience stressed for example by Dean Inge, and, if only we make the sphere of reason large enough, it can be taken as covering all the processes of judgment, not merely logical but intuitive and aesthetic or other. Here however I am using it of the logical powers of deduction and induction, of the syllogism and the estimation of results.

In the third place we have in conscience the very important sense of proportion or congruity; a more or less aesthetic element, which recognises and estimates what is fitting and what unfitting in a certain situation. This aesthetic element of proportion or balance is the chief element in common sense, as distinguishing it from logic; and the so-called morbid conscience is usually a conscience oversensitive in certain directions and so unbalanced or lacking proportion - though, strictly speaking, an under-sensitive conscience is also morbid. The ordinary use of "morbid" in relation to conscience however refers to such an over-scrupulousness, which is logical but not reasonable, intellectual but not under the guidance of the more aesthetic judgments of unity, proportion and fitness, or congruity. Of a healthy sense of fitness humour is a very important element, for a capacity to appreciate the incongruous involves the power to perceive the congruous.

In the fourth place a very real element in conscience, and indeed its most valuable component, as being the vital and creative core of progressive morality, is an element of consciousness or intuition or knowledge, an immediate awareness of reality and of values, whether we describe it as instinctive or intuitive or as acquired. It is in virtue of this element that conscience may truly be called the eye of God or voice of God in the soul. This is the basic element in conscience qualitatively, though not quantitatively the more important ingredient. To the same category of intuitive or immediate awareness probably belongs the aesthetic sense of proportion spoken of above, though it is useful to speak of the two apart - values and proportion. But it is well to note that this immediate element of conscience appears rather as desire than as obligation. The sense of obligation - I ought - is rather the sense of herd pressure; for what we really value, what we see as real good, we desire by a sort of necessity of our being. Reason and the herd exert pressures which we feel as obligation; values and the sense of proportion make a more immediate appeal to our desires; and conscience is thus often clearly divided where independence of judgment has been developed. But for most men still the voice of the herd seems to be the code of obligation. Conscience is certainly not as a whole the vox Dei; it is still more frequently the vox populi; and education of conscience, especially in proportion, discrimination, and independence, is often very necessary.

Few of us can or wish to combat more than a few of the countless suggestions of the herd which make our moral codes, however undeveloped morally they may be, for life is short and energy limited, and the pressure of the herd is strong and continuous on normal men; so for most of us conscience is still predominantly suggestion, education and public opinion. But in operation conscience represents the judgment of the whole personality, however made, the judgment of both heart and head as these are influenced by the diverse elements of suggestion, proportion, logic and awareness of value. It takes stock of both inward and external authorities, so far as these are recognised either as imposed or chosen. As children we are compelled or conditioned to value the imposed authority more than we tend to do as adults, but even adults recognise both sources of authority, society, and the soul; though when the inevitable clash comes, the true adult must regard the inward as the more final or authoritative, for only so can we ever become free or morally responsible. Even the adult who chooses to regard as final some external authority does choose to do so - the responsibility is still on his judgment, even when he has played for fancied safety. The moral life is moulded by the great universal instincts of the herd, sex, and the ego, and the specific instincts which evolution has produced; but in the truly moral man the ego and the herd have come to terms, and self-respect for himself as a social being has become the centre of the individual's moral life. The truly conscientious or moral man is the ideal spectator of his own life, he is his own incorruptible judge, i.e., God or his best self is his final court of appeal; and so, he seeks to live as an autonomous or independent soul, and yet as a part of the great whole for which he feels and thinks and plans, i.e., he lives for God and not for self, contributing as he can to the universe life from which he comes and to which he goes.

CHAPTER XV

The problem of freedom

What a trumpet call in human history has been the idea of "freedom" or "liberty" and what a part it has played in national life and individual aspiration: How we all long to be free, and yet how few of us know what is the meaning for our minds of a word that means so much for our hearts. Some tell us that liberty is not license, that freedom is limited; others that, if it be limited, it is not freedom. Some say that freedom means "doing what you like," oblivious of the fact that in the deepest sense we always do. When a man acts sullenly under the compulsion of a revolver, he prefers to avoid a bullet at the moment rather than to follow his inward inclinations; he is choosing to do what he likes in the circumstances, but he is not free, he is in bondage. Other men have chosen the bullet; and the history of mankind, and especially of religion, is full of the stories of these stronger men, who have also done what they liked, but who have liked better things - men who, if they were not free, were at least freer. Others again, tell us that freedom is in being determined by nothing outside oneself; but, inasmuch as all our actions and states of mind are largely determined by the external stimuli of environment in one form or another, this is no very great help, though, like the other solutions suggested, it has its value as a half-truth. Even the most satisfying statement of this last position, which defines freedom as self-determination, leaves us two serious problems - first, whether self-determination implies that we are self-determined or self-determining; and second, what the self is; and on these questions we are still far from any real agreement among thinkers.

What then is freedom? If we consult our feelings, we know fairly well what we really mean, but, when we try to put the thing into the black and white of language, it is a different matter. It is certainly a difficult word to define, like all great words that have moving power and immediate value for life; but it is not so difficult to describe by the method of comparison. If we approach the question by comparing man and lower forms of life, we discover that freedom in actual fact is a growing thing and depends upon knowledge. Man is freer than the animals; that, at least, is true as a general statement, even if there are points regarding which one might be inclined to make exceptions; but, speaking generally, man *has* a greater freedom than the lower animals. His mind has a better control over physical nature, and he is better able to do what he wished, or rather he is able to satisfy a greater number of his desires, and often simultaneously, because he knows himself and his environment better, and thus is better able to adjust himself to that environment or to adjust that environment to himself, and so to devise means for a satisfaction of his instincts and cravings out of all comparison with the satisfaction possible to the animals. The mind always works for satisfaction of desires, whether higher or lower, for the release of tension, for the resolution of stress or discontent; and in man this satisfaction is a growing thing, dependent on his growth in the knowledge of life and nature. Bondage is the frustration, the thwarting of desire, and freedom is its satisfaction, in spontaneity of life or self-expression; and, when we appeal to our feelings, we know that this is the truth - the bondage of frustration and impotence is what we chafe at, power and spontaneity are what we yearn for.

Thus, freedom is seen to be conditioned by the facts of our life and environment and our knowledge of them; and of these facts one of the chief is society - man is a social animal, social in fact and social in inclination; so man's freedom can only be achieved by adjustment to society, and perfect freedom only by a perfect adjustment to that full environment which we call God, in Whom all the essential elements of life find their focus and unity. Mr Bertrand Russell in his book, "What I Believe", has very ably described the good life, the ideal of life, as a life inspired by love - i.e., by benevolence and delight - and guided by knowledge, in which the maximum possible number of desires find satisfaction. Most sins are simply shortcuts to satisfaction which men take in their impatience and selfish egoism, shortcuts that fail through ignorance of the true laws of life, which are the laws of God. They are not prepared to "play the game", to wait till they can have that satisfaction on the terms that it is open also to their fellowmen, to society as a whole. True freedom depends on the knowledge of facts, it is possible only on a basis of love, or true and kindly and satisfying relationships, and consists in the unhindered expression and satisfaction of man's hungers and aspirations, i.e., complete freedom is unimpeded self-expression, and so akin to a spontaneity, art, and beauty, and it is conditioned by the moral factor of social life and the intellectual factor of knowledge.

But knowledge in making us free convinces us of a knew bondage, the sense of which grows with our knowledge, bondage to the system of nature, the laws of God. It is here that we come to the strange paradox of the well-known phrase which describes the service of God as perfect freedom. Freedom is bound up with the true knowledge of our essential bondage to nature and to God, and by that knowledge we grow freer as we submit – self-emancipation is by self-surrender; and, when we remember that God is love and God is truth, we have here merely Lord Russell's argument in a new dress. Man is able to turn his knowledge of his bondage to the service of his freedom; by obeying nature he learns to control nature. Thus, by knowledge man is growing free, and his freedom is no arbitrary thing, no *deus ex machina* in a world otherwise systematically regulated, but a thing true in and through the system of life. But such bondage is a voluntary thing - it is freely chosen. We submit gladly to the mathematical and other natural laws of music that we may create beauty; we submit willingly to the rules of football or chess that we may enjoy the rigour of the game; we submit voluntarily to the conditions of a great common experience in one form or another in order that we may have the thrill of experiencing it together, as, for example, when we observe the one beat in the united singing of a noble hymn, or accept the fixed hour of a great commemoration gathering. Voluntary or self-chosen obedience is not bondage; it is the highest form of freedom for a social being. And once a man has seen the living universe of God with a true and pure heart, he delights in the rhythm, and he finds joy in sharing its orderly life and in the beauty of concerted activity.

This line of thought is also supported by the work of modern psychologists who find in "libido", or desire, the creative element in life, and who have shown us how bound up the healthy expression of desire is with knowledge and a conscious discrimination and direction of the fundamental instincts and their energizing libido. Unimpeded functioning of the individual or society is the ideal of freedom, and it is only obtainable by obedience to love and knowledge, or, in the words of John's Gospel, by abiding in the word of Christ and His disciples and by knowing the truth (John 8:31-32). A true satisfaction of desire which does not involve injury or frustration to oneself or others - and either will hurt the sensitive spirit of a true man - depends upon the spirit of Christ being accepted and facts being known, upon love and truth; but desire itself is the creative activity of God in man, by which history is made and the universe progressively created toward an ever more glorious future. This modern gospel of the psychologists is the gospel of the New Testament, the gospel of grace as opposed to law; but, like most of the things which Christ brought, it requires courage to face it. The past has too often shrunk from the implications of Christ's teaching both as regards society and as regards the soul, and Puritanism, or asceticism in one form or another, has too often been the religion of professed believers, the religion of fear in place of the religion of faith, the religion of the repression instead of that of expression. Yet the old words stand - "unto the pure all things are pure. Every creature of God is good, and nothing is to be refused, if it be received with thanksgiving. For all things are yours, and ye are Christ's and Christ is God's"! Puritanism can never be more than a temporary expedient to correct a morbid hypertrophy of the soul, by a re-education in purity and simplicity. Desire cannot for ever be denied, for in itself desire is from God and at its foundation essentially good and creative of better life. In her cheering and suggestive parable of the house crickets called "Waiting", founded upon the Scriptural words, "It is good that a man should both hope and quietly wait", Mrs. Getty has expressed for us her own faith in the words, "Everything will fit in at last; no cravings are given in vain". Is not this our true Christian faith, that "nothing walks with aimless feet" which God has made, and that all things, and not least our desire, are shot through with meaning and purpose?

He who was called "a glutton and a winebibber" by His critics was no ascetic, though He recognized the place of self-discipline as a medicine for sick souls. His free faith is ours. Puritanism can never give us a freedom, though at times it has been, like a restricted diet in physical illness, a necessary measure of social and moral hygiene. True freedom is in doing what you like and liking the right things, i.e., by love and truth. As in the New Testament we are bidden to speak the truth in love, so freedom also must be founded upon and used in love and truth. Therefore, as knowledge grows and the spirit of Jesus spreads, freedom grows too – and this is a fact of historical observation; an informed Christianity is the greatest of liberating agencies. But many are afraid of freedom, they prefer bondage; like the Jews of New Testament times, they prefer law to grace, a code of negations and safety to a personal religion of love and venture upon God. It takes courage even yet to face freedom and to desire it truly, as it takes courage to face truth (cf. Fromm, The Fear of Freedom), because each is an adventure of the spirit, and men have too often still the souls of slaves, clinging to their chains, and shunning the rules of the open road where the free children of God make their journey. Freedom is good, truth is good, desire or passion is good, as love is good. All God's gifts may be abused, and we must learn to use them aright; but a life of free self-expression, in which God's creative element of desire can find full satisfaction, in harmony with love and truth, is surely the aim of life. It is certainly the end of morbidity, the beginning of complete sanity and wholeness of personality, the full discovery of power and beauty, for so to live is to share the life of God Himself. Such a life is man's chief end, "to glorify God and to enjoy Him forever". We speak of the freedom of God and only in such a sense is God free; and only so, too, can man be truly free.

Freedom then - the sharing of the unfettered unimpeded life of God - is the great end of life, not a means but an end; the means thereto is truth. And truth has both its outward and inward meaning; it is the willing of sincerity and it is the finding of facts. God is truth, truth in the inward parts and the truth of things without. It is our business to hear His call and obey, to follow truth with humble hearts in the spirit of our Master. There is too much arrogance in our lives often, even in our religion, and too much sham. If we would find truth, we must look at things about us, and at questions of evidence, with open minds - and that means open hearts. History has proved that Christ's spirit of reality and consecration is the way to truth and liberty, for both society and the soul. The great scientific movement of our time, of which we are so proud, is the Christian product of a Christian environment. As Mr Bernard Lucas has said, Christ's lesson of "Deny thyself", is the first lesson of modern science. Jesus called man by word and example to be honest and real, and to face even the morbid and evil in their hearts and the world with faith, not indeed in themselves but in God. Scientific method, or the discovery of truth by observation and experiment, is an essential of progress, and it may involve for many of us a waiting in the land of negation and denial till the light shall come, as befell the hunter in Olive Schreiner's profound and bracing parable of man's search for truth. We cannot bargain with God as to what our experience shall be, or what the price of knowledge shall amount to, though history shows at least that everything of value has its cost and that nothing great is cheap.

Freedom then, can only be obtained by the right adjustment of the soul to its environment; and to make that adjustment we must know our environment and ourselves; we must discover the real facts of potential life, for religion, the greatest of the interests of the human spirit, is largely concerned with the realizing of the potential in man, with the drawing out of that which is not and yet is; that which is reliable by the creative activity of faith.

In one form or another we are all seeking happiness, satisfaction, joys, and they can only be found in achievement of freedom of soul, in the unimpeded activity of our best selves, which are made in the image of God; and this freedom will be found in the company of love and truth, or in social and intellectual healthiness of soul. To look upon beauty without cease, to share in God's life of free goodness, to enjoy Him for ever, that is the end of all our striving, whether as social animals or as lonely souls to pass from bondage into the life of joy and beauty and freedom and all delight, in the unity of love and the bond of truth. And the way thither is the way trodden by our Lord Jesus Christ, the way of sincerity, humility, love, and wisdom. The way for us may pass into the darkness and wind through the haunts of suffering - indeed it must at times - but it leads into the light and love and life of God himself. If we would reach that blessed home, that beatific vision, we must walk in the steps of Jesus, and of His Spirit we must drink; we must be His followers, not by slavish imitation of outward act, but by unity with Him in passion and purpose and desire. In His spirit we have the key to every door that baffles us, for in discipleship to Him, as we abide in His word or message, we shall know the truth, and the truth shall lead us into freedom, into perfect communion with God Himself, into the satisfaction and attainment of all that our souls truly desire.

So far I have dealt with freedom as an ideal or end, an aim or goal in life, but there is another sense in which the word is also used, when moral freedom is being considered i.e., as a power or means, a use of the word which is common in the form "free will", i.e., a power of moral choice, a faculty of the spirit of man for moral growth. This more dynamic use of the word or idea is associated with most discussions of the moral conflict, for it is a normal persuasion of man that they are not mere puppets but have it in some sense in their power to change or modify or determine their character or actions by an independent voluntary activity. This idea I now wish to consider briefly, and there is probably no more difficult problem presented for classification by religious experience, for this sense of freedom, however difficult to define or to visualize clearly remains a kind of intuitive certainty, expressing itself no doubt legitimately in the conceptions of moral responsibility and less legitimately in judgments of praise and blame. I have not time nor space for a full and adequate discussion of this question, which would call for a large volume; but at least a good deal can be said briefly which may illuminate the issues or at least suggest lines of fruitful thought.

We are dealing here with freedom as a creative element of means to life in the sphere of moral values and the moral conflict. I am prepared to believe that many common ideas of this free will or moral freedom are innocent and yet, if moral judgments are to have any valid significance for us, we must find some meaning in the words, even if we find them to be in part illusion, for, as I said before, illusion is not delusion. Thus, the problem of freedom is raised acutely by the discussion of sin from the modern standpoint, which emphasises the wish; for if we sin, we sin because we wish it, if we do good, we do it because we wish it. In what sense, then, are we free? Can we choose or change our wishes? Must we not wish to do so before we could? And, if so, is not the wish ultimate? And if the wish is ultimate, are we responsible for the wishes we have? Or, to put the question back to a further point - are we responsible for the wishes with which we were born and which have moulded everything since, both in thought and action? Can we still assert responsibility, or is it the Creator alone who is responsible for all things good and evil? It is important, then, that we should seek to find out what meaning lies in the idea of moral responsibility; how, if at all, we can change morally for the better (which is our practical moral problem), and in what sense our belief that we are free represents truth.

Here we come to an extraordinarily difficult problem - but let us remember throughout that the subject of experience cannot adequately define himself. If we think clearly regarding our wishes, we cannot think ourselves *logically* out of sheer determinism, or into any true meaning for responsibility, except as a mental counter of social and other pressures. Any moral action which we perform we do because we wish to do it - it may be to please ourselves directly or to please ourselves by pleasing others, or to please ourselves by escaping fear or punishment, or to please ourselves by our own heroism and venture, but all moral or self-conscious and purposive action is done ultimately to *satisfy* ourselves as wishing creatures, it springs out of one or more wishes - usually a *complex* mass of wishes for and against, which can give a kind of resultant of wish forces. Ours is no unemotional life determined by logic, but an emotional life determined by desire. Now, we did not create our original wishes, which were present before self-consciousness or morality emerged; as children we were not free to choose the wishes which moulded our infancy or our adolescence, and nowhere is the causation of the chain of wishes broken. We are not free, if free means being determined *apart* from our wishes. If no one from without is compelling us, we are still incapable of acting independently of our wishes, which we did not create and which we cannot control, decrease, or increase, without at least the wish to do so. Of course, wishes are very varied things, but all are bound up with our values and our values are immediate possessions, not chosen but inevitable, yet growing in clarity, relations, and conceptual forms. If we choose to believe a lie it is because we wish it, and this is only possible by identifying it with the truth in some sense; for truth compels our recognition as a self-regarding value of our lives, and we can never feel satisfied nor content if we think our "truth" is a lie, but a necessity of our own natures, as psychoanalysis shows clearly. We are under real moral compulsion to recognise our values, and to act in accordance with our wishes. Our moral experience consists primarily in the discrimination and growing coordination of our wishes and values, of aspiration and knowledge.

But moral estimates may be of two kinds, induced and suggested, or spontaneous and real. The ordinary idea of responsibility - "I ought" - when it does not correspond with "I wish", is due to social suggestion for the most part, active probably for years and stamping upon the mind a code of moral duties or standards with all the social pressure which results from our desire to please others, and to avoid eccentricity or abnormality with its suggestion of insanity. Social influence no doubt has its place and its rights as representing reality in a supra-individual form; but the codes of society are so manifestly the production of a past, which in science and other forms of thought is no longer regarded as infallible, that even in morality they must be questioned and brought to correspond with reality. Moral codes are only the crystallization of past experiments to adapt life to environment; and their only real moral authority lies in their being recognised by individuals as true or valid by virtue of that in them which corresponds to the individual's own values. Society may have the right, or at least the might, to suppress individuals who differ from the common practice, but social codes have no final moral right over the individual, beyond that which he himself recognises as binding by virtue of the response of his own nature to the social standards in question. These have perhaps the right to demand consideration, but not the right to demand obedience. One meaning of moral freedom, then, is the right to be yourself, even if all men stand against you i.e., independence. If you do not approve of social arrangements, you may yet wish to follow them and avoid unpleasant consequences - that is bondage, for the determining wish is negative fear and registers dependence on men - or you may refuse to follow them and perhaps suffer - that is freedom, for the determining wish is positive and registers independence.

The sense of responsibility is no doubt misinterpreted by the majority of men, who still think in terms of moral codes rather than of personality, in terms of an arbitrary idea of free will, long ago exploded and usually incoherent, rather than in terms of behaviour and motives, organised personality and the newer psychology of desire and discrimination. But I do not think any sane person doubts that the conceptions of responsibility and freedom have a real meaning for personality; in some sense we may claim them as intuitions, facts which we all assume and act upon; and, even if they were to be classed as illusions, they must still be regarded as necessary and socially valuable illusions. But I cannot see why our logical difficulties should ever lead us to class their beliefs as delusions simply because we cannot systematise them in our present schemes of thought. I believe they have positive and real content, and that they are matters, not of inference, but of immediate knowledge, foundations, or conditions of our personal consciousness, though very seriously misstated and misunderstood, as our logic and science are both sufficient to show. Life is a dynamic and living thing; not a static dead thing which can be dissected, analysed, and defined, but something which defies analysis and definition till it has already become past and dead. We may, as I have said, analyse the object of experience, but not in any adequate way as yet its subject. Where we are conscious of choice, i.e., where action is self-conscious and deliberate or fully personal, we are conscious also of freedom; where action is subconscious or automatic by habit or instinct, we are not conscious of freedom, i.e., the sense of freedom and responsibility appears to belong to our highest personal life in self-conscious and deliberate thought and behaviour. Thus, freedom seems to be part of that in us, which is not static and habitual but progressive and creative; it is related to the positive and noblest sides of personal life. I have already pointed out that it represents personal independence or the dignity of personality. I wish now to carry further the thought suggested above that moral freedom belongs to the highest elements in our consciousness, to the positive and creative side of our being, and so is eventually akin to the divine.

This hypothesis would naturally lead us to the conclusion that freedom is a positive and not a negative force, i.e., that man is in some creative sense free to do good, to progress and become better; that is, that freedom is one clear expression of the divine in man. And at this point we find in our theological thinking two supports for such a view which are of importance, one from our thought of God and one from our knowledge of man. In the first place only in such a sense can freedom be predicted of God. God is not free to do evil, because He can have no desire or temptation to do so; a true good and powerful and wise being could not in any real sense be free to sin. But he is not compelled to do good; He does good freely. Thus, God must be conceived of as free to do good, and His freedom as consisting in His activity in goodness i.e., in a perfect or unimpeded expression of a nature which is good. Along this line we should expect freedom in man also to be a freedom to do good, and this, as there is in him certainly a lower pull to evil, freedom would seem to be a power to rise above evil and do good. We should also expect to find in man the same kind of freedom as in God, so that freedom in man, as in God, should be, not an arbitrary or neutral ability of will, to do either good or evil, but a power to express his truest nature, the image of God in which he was created, a power to realise as actual the divinity which is potential in him.

At this point, in the second place, we find that Augustine, the greatest and most reverenced of the early church writers on moral questions and the relations of God and man in sin and grace, has defined human free will in much that way. He treats of freedom of will as positive and good, and his teaching is that the doing of evil is the bondage of a will which is essentially good, while the doing of the will of God is the only true freedom.

Some may think that these distinctions do not matter much, and that the old idea of a free or neutral choice between good and evil remains, but in actual fact the whole position is altered by our attitude on this one point. In my personal crisis one line of action is good, that is according to the mind of God, but anything else is evil; and thus, good and evil are not on equal terms in relation to the will. To do evil one does not need to do anything; if a man does not positively determine himself for good, he is determined by environment, circumstances, and his own past, automatically. Choice of good is a real thing; choice of evil as evil is probably unknown - all men even in sin are following values or positive things however obscurely or foolishly - and the doing of evil is simply the inaction of this free will, or power to rise, which we possess. The evil action does not necessarily involve a choice of evil, but merely a failure to choose the good; yet to fail in choosing the good is not, strictly speaking, to choose the evil, for it is not deliberate, as choosing the good always is. To do right we must make up our minds, in doing evil men do not, speaking generally, make up their minds or exercise moral judgment in any real sense; rather they suspend judgment till after action (though they may then, when they see that they have not done right, accuse themselves of actual evil choice retrospectively), and so allow desire and circumstances, not their true personalities, not their own best selves, to determine the issue. Stop men after an evil act and they will admit often that they were wrong; stop them before it and you find often that they are refusing to face the issues, refusing, or suspending judgment in the heat of the strong impulse.

I have not time to analyse this matter in more detail, and this short statement of goodness as a swimming upstream with conscious effort, and of evil as a being carried downstream by the current of life as it is, may be challenged by many, yet original sin means in fact that the current is against us; we cannot be neutral but must go up or down. But, however we may state the problem, I think it is obvious that goodness requires a different kind of choice from evil, more deliberate, more satisfying and more difficult, or attained with greater conscious effort - it is the use of power in a different sense, in a more personal way (by choice or organised will), than the doing of evil; and it is positive and creative and in line with God and the highest we know - yet how very short the distance sometimes is between anti-social and social has been shown again and again (cf. A.S. Neill). Evil is static, goodness is dynamic; for life is moving, and even the goodness of yesterday is not sufficient for today. Sin then appears as bondage, passive forms being often worse than active, because the bondage then is greater and there is less of independence and less of value and of education (by reaction and experience); while righteousness, or harmony with God and our own best self, is the only true freedom. And this freedom is as God's freedom and is the shadow in man of the divine Personality, free and good and with power to express itself in activity.

Thus, if one meaning of moral freedom is independence, another is power. There are in life many things which our hearts, made in God's image, aspire to do and everywhere we are met by the suggestion of, or belief in, our inability, that we cannot do these things, that we are haunted by our past, determined, or damned by our circumstances, environment, and character. Yet our character is not a fixed thing, but a thing with power of modification and growth under the control, especially of the ego complex, while our circumstances and environment are under the control of God and of ourselves as personal agents of divine power. Therefore, as we realise our independence of things and of others and our communion and co-operation with God, we can rise to the further realisation: "I can." This, it seems to me, is one chief moral meaning of freedom - "I can" (I am not bound) - the power to accomplish the *real* desires of our hearts, which are essentially and fundamentally good and social and from God, created not by us, but by Him, as means to life and progress according to the teaching both of the theology of yesterday and the psychology of to-day. Moral freedom, then, is a consciousness of moral ability to grapple with circumstances, it is the power to accomplish, however slowly, the moral ends which of necessity we aspire after (cf. Kant on immortality). And it is from sin itself that we usually learn most effectively to hate it and to correct our values; and to cast out fear by faith is the means to new life and goodness and to that satisfaction of personality which is the presence of God with us.

Thus, we see that the investigation of morality, in sin and freedom, leads us to the great ultimate paradox of religion referred to earlier, that true independence consists in dependence upon God, that true freedom is in obedience to, or harmony with, the universe. And these things are true and reasonable because God is our own best self, and in satisfying Him we satisfy ourselves and so attain the goal of harmony within and consistent and unhindered self-expression without, which is the aim of all our moral striving, as it is of art and the pursuit of beauty. It is very important to grasp these facts, for they reconcile the apparent opposition of the coherent system of causation, to which science seems to lead us, and the sense of freedom to which intuition seems to shut us up, the opposition between the psychic determinism of psychology and the immediate consciousness of responsibility. In experience we find that freedom is not something outside the system of physical and psychic law, but something operating within the system, which the system does not invalidate but to which on the other hand it contributes. System as we know it is necessarily a stumbling block in the way of an arbitrary theory of will, but not in the way of the theory of a positive and creative will to which the system offers the material and conditions of progress. As the doctrines of Immanence and Incarnation both imply power for man, as a soul or as a race, comes to him from within the mental or social cosmos in which he lives. I think we must all admit that man is freer than the lower animals, and that, not because his life is less systematised and ordered - both live in substantially the same universe, and the life of man is the more complex and elaborate in its arrangements - but rather because he knows more about the system. It is the coherence of nature and man's knowledge of nature which make him free - truth makes free. We know that the animals are in bondage to nature as we are not, yet not because we can violate the laws of nature, but because, knowing more of those laws, we can consciously use them to help ourselves and to cause re-combinations of natural circumstances which lead to new and better conditions and better things, and so our wishes find freer and larger scope.

Thus, freedom is a comparative thing in human experience and is found and enhanced, not as a rival of system or law, but in and through them; the growth of knowledge and the growth of freedom go hand in hand and depend upon the consistency and rationality of physical and psychical life, i.e., freedom is essentially bound up with order and causation, and thus a philosophy of determinism is no foe but an ally. The service of God or reality means a growing freedom, a growing independence of man and circumstances, and a growing power to choose and create the best; and it is through a growing knowledge of, and obedience to, facts and ultimate values that this freedom is progressively won, a freedom which, like the freedom of God, is a freedom to express oneself, to do good, and to enjoy cosmos rather than chaos. It is a knowledge of his "necessity" which makes man free; and lack of knowledge, in the form of error or of consequent fear, makes for sin and bondage. Thus, the greater our knowledge that life is a system, and the greater our obedience to that system of natural law, the greater our freedom, our independence, and our power. On the physical and mental side power comes through limitation and acknowledgment of limitation; but, on the spiritual or progressive side of the creative imagination, obedience must never become subservience to limitation, potentially life, though systematic, is unlimited and the faith which keeps our spirits free must always be ready when the call comes, to break through limitations with the affirmative "I can." It is through this belief, tenaciously held, that the necessarily slow progress upward in physical and psychical development is securely accomplished. Limitation is only true as a relative thing in the adjusting of system to aspiration, but the rate and extent of possible progress we do not know and therefore, till we do, we must cling to a general faith in the power of growth and infinite development which can make progress possible and actual; we must refuse to be tied statically by the limits of our past or present.

It is upon this systematic, yet creative conception, of freedom that the orthodox doctrine of the perseverance of the saints is experimentally founded, i.e., the belief that the saints cannot fall away from goodness but must continue upon the path they have chosen, because good is now the conscious choice and free expression of their own natures. Their moral advance, where genuine, has been won by the release of desire and its creative achievements through will, and they cannot ultimately go back because they can never again wish to do so, having once seen and known the truth - only a mad man can wish to be blind, once he has seen. To follow out this very important, though sometimes problematic line of thought is not my business here; but I wish at least to point out that it implies that moral gain is real gain, because it is desire and knowledge in and at one, and because one can never basically *wish* to ignore either desire or knowledge. Both love and knowledge or reality are in their very nature permanent possessions which we cannot will to surrender; I do not mean that a good man has no further struggles - his struggle may become ever greater; but victories won are, in some respects at least, permanent gains of the spirit, and, just as "we needs must love the highest when we see it," so too we cannot desire evil for its own sake. It is only as value, as good, that we can desire evil at all. All the forces of our deepest nature are on the side of God, and His victory, be it soon or late, cannot fail, because in the last analysis we cannot desire that He should fail, and life lose its unity and beauty and meaning. But in all our discussions regarding sin and freedom we must beware of negatives; it is our positives, as known and tested in experience, which are true, and negatives are frequently wrong. And we must recognise the place of two truths side by side which seem in measure to conflict in the present state of our knowledge, the truth of system, causation, or determinism on the one side, and the truth of responsibility, independence, or freedom on the other. We can see lines along which the two are congruous in measure, we can experience their interrelations and co-operation for good; but we cannot logically synthesise them as yet, if indeed we ever shall. In that future or practicable synthesis by a necessity of our nature we must believe, for all intelligent rationalisation is the reduction of our varied life to a unity in which it is seen as coherent and becomes manageable; yet we cannot now see how this synthesis is to be made. We must believe in both the conflicting elements, and perhaps the most convenient illustration, which makes the position clear or tolerable, is that of two intersecting planes.

If we suppose that determinism or system is one plane of experience, and voluntarism or creative freedom another, and that life is lived along the line of their intersection, we obtain a more or less reasonable picture of the probable position of our moral consciousness. According to this analogy every point in life lies in the plane of system and also in the plane of freedom, i.e., is found in both planes, the planes of law and grace, of order and spontaneity, of object and subject, of mind and spirit. Neither plans of experience can be neglected with safety - that is obvious from experience - both must enter into our calculations; and our moral problem is the problem of this duality of experience, as we speak to make two different sets of conceptions or values commensurable in action, and so find our true way along the one and only line of intersection in other words, to discover the will of God. But if every point be in the deterministic plane, which is to us the one reducible to our logic, then we can act upon determinism as true. And in fact, psychical determinism does work; in the hands of psychotherapists and educationalists it produces marvellous results, and there is no other theory which is thus systematic and available; in its own way it may be claimed as gospel. But let it be clear that determinism is not fatalism, nor does it deny freedom. Freedom is the creative quality of life found in and through the deterministic stuff of mind and nature, while fatalism is not a belief in order and system merely, but a belief in the course of events as fixed *apart* from us. "Let us sit still and wait for destruction, for it may be fated that we are to perish, and, if so, we shall perish" is a fatalistic argument. But determinism regards ourselves and our actions as being, with all their qualities of necessity and freedom of laws and wishes, part of the cause of whatever happens, and will always insist that we must do our utmost to avert destruction, for, if our destruction is contingent upon many things over which we have no control, it is also contingent in measure upon that which we do control, our own thoughts and actions and influence on history; and no man can say how great these are or may become by intention and effort.

Ethical freedom is bound up with a true self-respect, with the acceptance of an inward, as opposed to an outward, authority as final, with the freeing of the self from the compulsions of the herd or from physical limitations.

It is a growing thing, but its centre, as McDougall points out, is the complex, or sentiment, of the ego, based on the self-regarding instinct or impulse. True self-love is self-respect, and true freedom is to follow one's own judgment, to seek under God, one's own approval and the direction of one's own life. It is the ego complex which gives will its power of free action, but the ego can only have power where self-consciousness exists, i.e., where contrasts between different courses of action are possible; and this brings in the creative power of imagination as the effective force in moral freedom. In or by the imagination we can create what does not yet exist, and so free ourselves from the bondage of what does, and, by true self-respecting action following our vision, we can make our freedom actual and practical. Now, goodness and moral freedom for man are bound up with conceptual thinking, with aiming not at carrying out certain types of action primarily, but at being a certain type of character, one who will not do some of the things he is tempted to do. Self-hate is the enemy of life, true self-regard is the foundation of a really creative or free life, and therefore Christ bade us to love our neighbour as we love ourselves. All true love of others is self-enlargement and self-projection, and the truest self-sacrifice springs from a self-love which loves our truest self best. For true self-regard, or self-respect, or self-love is a social thing, since man's nature is social. If a man loses his self-respect and comes to self-hate he destroys himself, often by suicide; and even a measure of such self-hate is sufficient to paralyse his life.

It is important to get views about this subject of freedom, i.e., views which will work; for our active faith and our action will depend on them. A fatalist may be paralysed, a pure voluntarist helpless to heal, while a true determinist has in his hand a great weapon for the healing and improvement of himself and others. There is no certain philosophy or psychology as yet of will and of the interrelations of desire, judgment and effort; but some points have become clear in the course of the historical consideration of the problem and especially of recent years. The old voluntarism is dead, and today it is best represented by those who are against an automatic view of determinism and claim that, in creative or emergent evolution, there are factors making for growth and progress which correspond to the more or less intuitive feelings of freedom and responsibility which we all share, as in all creation there are found factors and moments of "newness". These factors are hard to describe, as they are at present impossible to define; but we can apprehend what we cannot comprehend, and modern developments are in the direction of admitting them, factors which we may call unpredictable or contingent, though both words are foolish. It is hard to believe that, if we knew all, anything would be "unpredictable", and still harder to believe that, if it were so, it would be moral; and contingent must either mean arbitrary, which is not moral at all, or conditional, which means causally related to its environment or basis, and so systematic or deterministic. Only in a moral sense is freedom of will of any urgency for human thought.

Chance is perhaps free but not moral, and its freedom, if it exists, is of no value to us ethically; and an arbitrary or unpredictable action is not thereby moral. True freedom requires systematic life, but be it noted, "systematic" does not mean "automatic". Freedom can only be brought into the sphere of necessity by claiming that all things are necessary, i.e., the word "necessary" here has in fact no opposing category of "free" for comparison and therefore has no relevant meaning at all. Rather is freedom the growing transmission of God, the growing activity of our best self, moulding life in new and better ways; or it is a power of creation, not indeed out of nothing in our circle of experience, but out of our environment as it exists, spiritual and physical.

Moral freedom is bound up, not with a stray good action without adequate motives, but with adequately motivated action and with the development of character by the formation of habits or systems of good. God could not do evil because *ex hypothesi* He could not desire it; and a limited being can only desire evil as value i.e., as in some sense good. Freedom of the will, then, can stand only for the experience of a vital option, a choice between two real opposing alternatives, both of which are valued or desired - for we may be considered free to do what we desire, but certainly not to do what we do not desire. The man who says he is free to cross the road, if he likes, usually forgets the importance of the condition "if I like". If he does not like, he will not. There is no way of choosing morally between likes or desires without a reference to some determining motive, and this for McDougall is, I think, rightly, the motive of self-regard or self-respect i.e., moral choice between two desired alternatives is made by the self in its own felt interests oneself (whether the self be but a conception or idea, or a central and substantial focus of life), and such choice is called free because it is determined by the self. Moral freedom, then, is found when a man throws himself into the scale alongside the desire which has truest meaning for himself. Of course, the self-regarding impulse is in action still a form of desire; but all action can and must be so stated, for there could be no choice at all, if there was not somewhere a reduction to the same terms. But desires differ as more perceptual and more conceptual, and moral freedom is found at the conceptual end of the scale. The ego is certainly attached to certain parts of our experience more than to others, and when, by its interposition, it wins a conflict of desires, the choice is felt as self-determination, a victory of the higher or self-team. The thwarting of the self is moral bondage, the victory of the self is moral freedom. McDougall however does not in my opinion give enough place in his analysis to the imagination as the creative power by which the self is enabled to judge an action, i.e., by the visualized contrast of other lines of conduct and by the vivid realisation of consequences; and decision by imagination, or by non-actual elements of our thought, will certainly be felt to be a release from the system of the actual, and so be felt as freedom in a real sense.

One matter, however, which causes great complication in the whole discussion, and which weakens the element of system in choice, arises from the conception of the organised self (see McDougall, Social Psychology). The moral will is more or less identified with the organised self, i.e., with the memories, impulses, desires and conceptions built round the self, and so largely a moral complex. But in all men in some degree there are elements which are not, or which are inadequately, organised with this central self-regard, especially elements of the sub-human brute, which, on the occasion of a rare and powerful excitement of primitive impulses, e.g., of lust or cruelty or of a disgust with sophistication and moral discipline, may break through, in a kind of insanity, and defy the carefully built-up character and its controls. Few are immune from occasional impulses of the sort, when circumstances conspire to weaken the appeal to the normal standards of life, and when some specifics desire, not adequately systematised in character, runs amok for a time, to leave behind a sense of shame or frustration or remorse. The only safeguard in facing such rebellion against the organised self is a complete and honest facing of the facts of our nature, and as thorough a psychoanalytical discrimination of desire as possible in relation to these rebel elements, which lurk in the unconscious all the time and may sometimes, like an earthquake, shake our lives and the lives of others to their foundations. Only light can expel the darkness, and only love can meet and conquer such savage challenges. In some men this insanity of inner chaos, usually due to faulty education or treatment by others, may be serious and near the surface, but in most men the organised self is adequate to deal with most of life on its moral side. But it is well to recognise that there are such concealed rocks, which psychoanalysis alone, whether religious or scientific, may be able to handle; to fail to mention these chaotic or insane elements would be unfair to the reader; even if we can do little to prepare for such crises. But these outbreaks bring such impulses into the open, out of the unconscious, and therefore they can be more easily dealt with, and then organised in character and will, when they have been truly and consciously discriminated.

No theory of moral freedom as far propounded is both logically sound and satisfying to our sense of its meaning and value; but, by aiming at synthesis rather than analysis, one can at least make a reasonable statement of some of the practical meanings of such freedom. So far as a theory of its nature is concerned one must, I think, adopt as a basis a more or less deterministic view, because such a view both explains much and works out normally in practice; but such a view need not be taken as denying the reality of freedom as something creative or emergent in our experience, nor as denying the existence of terrifying and unorganised hidden elements of danger in most minds. The tendency of modern biology and psychology is to a greater humility and to the recognition that our views, however true they may be, are but part of the truth and fail at many points, because there are factors of which we know little or nothing, as being subjects not objects of our own experience. Until we have eliminated, if ever, static methods of measuring and defining life, we shall not be able to solve adequately the problem of defining creative freedom, which belongs to a world which is not static and rational but personal and psychic.

The older problem of freedom was metaphysical, concerned with the will of God and all the questions it involved, and its chief difficulty was the harmonising of predestination with human free will; and even over this problem many minds are still greatly exercised. But our chief problem today is the psychological one of maintaining rationally a felt freedom in a world where practically all conscious action seems to have its adequate motives; and our problem is, how can action, caused by desires which a man does little or nothing to make, yet be free? So much, as I have said, depends on the meaning of the word "free". Psychical determinism is sometimes stated as the view that mental states and behaviour are determined and explained wholly by their antecedent mental states, i.e., that a man's actions flow from the prior elements of his mind as logical necessary consequences. But modern science, like more recent philosophy, is not so sure about causation as it was, and in any case a reasonable determinism must omit the word "wholly" from the sentence above; all we can claim is that determinism helps us and explains much, not that it accounts for all - for example it does not easily explain the universal sense (or illusion) of freedom itself, which seems to be morally and socially as important as the belief in God, and is in fact part of that same belief - a thing may be, not illogical but absurd, and such, I think, is the denial of either God or freedom. But we can get no scientific description of moral freedom which does not presuppose system as that within which moral freedom lives and works, i.e., the systematic is true, yet it is not automatic. Fatalism is automatic, but the fatalism which argues that inaction will make no difference to what is to happen is a static absurdity; for inaction itself is a determining element, as surely as action, and will have very different results. And we certainly have it in our power, according to our knowledge, to modify the antecedents or conditions of all kinds of action and so to affect results (see later on "thresholds"). At no point perhaps can we modify much, but the power itself is of enormous importance, and over a long space of time can have tremendous effects.

How our desires, again, are measured by our judgment we do not know, but we know that action proceeds from desire, for desire supplies both the initiating motive and the energy, and we know that desires are of two kinds, immediate or perceptual or spontaneous, and mediated or conceptual or teleological; and that personality and freedom are bound up with an affirmation of the latter, but, to be healthy, with such a form of them as is no real denial of the more immediate desires. Moral freedom represents the power of the conceptual and teleological desires (i.e., the personal and ethical or purposive elements of our conation) to win the conflict of wishes. Such a victory is possible up to a point; but in moral life resistance is truly a bedrock fact as in the passage of an electrical current. The universe could not afford to give full rein to our partial understandings and theories; it must frequently bring us back to the primary elements of our natures, physical and psychic, and their wise checks upon development. Not all regression is wrong, for life may grow too artificial otherwise.

Some believe that true moral freedom or choice is only rarely known and exercised, as at crises of the moral life; others hold that it is a quality or accompaniment of personality interpenetrating all our conscious life; and the latter seems to me to be the more probable i.e., that freedom and necessity, like divine and human, are two poles or conflicting pulls in our moral development. Even free choice must have its motives; we can cross the road, if we wish; but our wishing to do it determines us at least as much as we determine it. And, as action apart from the springs of action in instincts and values is impossible, some form of deterministic theory is inevitable, but a true theory will, I think, make place, both for the systematic determinism of action by its antecedents, and also for the voluntary creative element that belongs, not to antecedents, but to the present, to God and a spiritual world which makes for progress and is ever creating new things. More determinism does not adequately explain either the fact of advance and newness in the upward climb of life nor the sense of responsibility and urgency. In practice moreover, determinism can only be appropriate as a method, for we never know all the antecedents of action - indeed seldom more than a few - and our knowledge of the immediate present factors of creative life is almost nil - we live, but we do not know how.

It is well, on the other hand, to remember that words like responsibility, guilt, freedom, praise, and blame are not experience in themselves, but interpretations of experience, and our views of them may be illusion or partial truth only. The actual experiences concerned are experiences of stress, pressure, pain, discomfort, and the like; and a truly Christian philosophy will no doubt reinterpret and restate these terms very differently in days to come. We need more interest in life and social love, less in death and condemnation; more respect for personality and less for codes of behaviour. But by fairly general consent the old neutral idea of the will is gone for ever, vis. that man stood, blessed or unbiased, between good and evil, and that his will could freely choose either. The truth is that moral freedom is bound up with growth, it is an ideal and it is a power belonging to the creative side of life, an ideal and a power making for progressive integration of life under the only possible dominant factor in moral man, the ethical self, which is the child of God and in His image. Evil action is action which fails to satisfy the demands of life, individual or social, for peace, harmony, well-being, and unity. Only good action, social action, really solves in any lasting way the problems of desire and of tension. But we are still far from understanding how our mind judges between values of goods, how for example we can choose in given circumstances between a dinner and a symphony. Yet such choices, in things at present incommensurable to our thought, are being made continually by our judgments - this fact alone shows how impossible it is to have a closed theory. At the most our modern deterministic theory only explains "How" not "Why", and freedom remains a faith and today, at least, with its still static and non-creative philosophies and sciences, a very necessary faith, as the foundation of character. "I must" and "I can" are both the voices of that moral sense which for us involves both freedom and responsibility.

If our actions are determined by our wishes, it may well be asked Can we change our wishes or choose them? Must we not wish to do so before we could? None of our life is in a vacuum, we are pressed on all sides by wishes of all sorts. It is impossible, seriously, to argue ourselves into the belief today that we can so choose our wishes, for our temperaments and dispositions are largely laid down before birth and before self-consciousness, and we are certainly in large measure controlled by our innate tendencies, specific or general. But as the ego complex develops and our moral life begins with a consciousness of our solidarity with, and yet difference from, others, and of the various pulls of our nature, which are no longer dealt with automatically, but passed before our self-conscious judgment and our developing conceptual values, we can definitely modify our desire life, in any direction which our personal judgment chooses, by the process known to practical psychologists as "raising or lowering the thresholds". By persistent effort, attention, repression and suggestion we can develop a resistance to certain types of thought and a susceptibility to others, and so change the whole ratio of our minds on any moral issue, as e.g., by refusing consistently when we feel it arise to feed our minds on certain sexually exciting types of picture or literature, i.e., exciting then not as evil but as inexpedient. It is in such ways that character is formed, bad habits broken, and good habits formed. It is in such ways that the direction or tendency of our lives is changed, and character modified. We can feed or starve certain sentiments or groups of interests, giving attention or refusing attention, according to a dominant self-chosen purpose, and so remould our conscious and fore-conscious life, decreasing the stimuli of evil, increasing those of the good, and so, however slowly, altering the tone and proportion of our minds. It is practically impossible for a man to give such sustained purposive effort to evil; only goodness has the power over our minds to demand such consistent and patient and courageous efforts of the will. This avoidance or increase of occasions of stimulation, in one or other direction is greatly enhanced by the use of religious exercises, especially prayer. But in such ways, we can change our index of receptivity towards goodness. Such activity is teleological, involving patience and cost; but it is an achievement which brings us the joy of the approval of God in the approval of our best self. All truly moral purpose aims at the fulfilling of desire and the higher integration of life, but that, not on the individual, but on the social or truly personal plane.

Thus, both freedom and determinism are gospels of hope. Freedom says, "I must, and I can" and determinism says, "I know how". The way of advance is by obedience, for we are living in a world of law and system; but it is obvious today that we are using it already more than it is using us, i.e., that we are by now in a very real measure free and are achieving more and more of freedom, both physically, psychically, morally, and socially, every year. Upon an incalculable freedom nothing can be built, and no programme laid down; but in fact, life is being classified and systematised for our understanding in an increasing measure and so becoming less incalculable. At one time the weather was regarded as unpredictable; today it is forecast with reasonable success every day. And it may be so with human behaviour some day when we have achieved a better philosophy and a better psychology of motive and growth; at any rate a scientific view of our life of a deterministic kind is being progressively verified by its results in practice. Voluntarism on the other hand is not a theory - there is no logically systematic statement of it available anywhere - it is a *protest* in favour of a certain apprehension and interpretation of experience, and in the opinions of most thinkers it is, as such, eminently justifiable and necessary.

Freedom, then, to sum up, stands for the idea of unimpeded self-expression, and again it stands for the universe as creative, new every day and vital; it represents the consciousness in the human mind of a creative and urgent present fact of newness or divinity. It stands for independence, or the being determined ultimately from within, not from without; but it recognises that true independence for man means dependence upon God. Freedom is not a power to sin (sin being bondage), but it is a power to rise, a power for goodness, not morally neutral, but positively good and creative; a power to swim upstream against the current of the past and its forces of inertia and heredity. It is a positive faith in unlimited advance, and our power is according to our faith, i.e., our power to affirm "I can" is in proportion to our vision, to the love of God and of goodness released in us, and to our tenacity in holding to these. It is, again, the power of the creative imagination which lifts us out of the actual into the possible. Life is still made by dreams, and from the spirit and faith and dreams of freedom comes all human progress. By conceptual images of a better self, and by purposive planning thereto, the creative imagination gives our faith in progress both definite content and a specific programme, by which we rise from bondage to a continually larger and freer life. Freedom also stands for deliberate and personal self-determination, for the growth of the divine in us from the focus of the self-regarding instinct, which can develop to be the dominant factor deciding all issues in reference to itself, i.e., to its ideal or best self, which is God. Apart from the submerged rocks of unintegrated primal impulse there may also be antinomies left for our thinking, in various respects, as between determinism and freedom; but they are no greater than that between position and movement in space, both of which are reasonable interpretations of experience, however incommensurable or paradoxical.

The question of freedom, however, is no mere academic one; it is of practical importance, as one can easily find in attempting to heal the moral wounds of one's own life or of the lives of others - both system and freedom matter if we are to succeed. As a vote for evolution is today no vote against a Creator, so a vote for determinism is today no vote against freedom. The study of how mind or spirit works and chooses can help us and change us, and modern psychology has given a new meaning and life to all the fundamental doctrines of the Christian Gospel, to grace and love, to freedom as obedience and sin as bondage, to personality as ultimate and to the creative faith in a God who continually makes all things new, a God in whom we all live and move and have our being.

CHAPTER XVI

The relation of doctrine
to experience

There is a very much more definite relation between doctrine and experience than is usually recognized. Doctrine is ordered thought, defined and recorded, appearing sometimes in the more authoritative group form of dogma and sometimes in the more personal form of theological statements made by individuals possessing or accorded a greater or less degree of prestige and approbation in large or small groups. Even the teaching or opinions of individuals, which have gained no group approval at all, might be spoken of as doctrine; but such doctrine has little value for our discussion since it registers nothing beyond the point of view of one person, uncorroborated and possibly fantastic. But, either as dogma or as a group-approved doctrine, religious statements of belief have a definite bearing on experience, for they are the crystallisation of certain interpretations of experience which have commended themselves, not only to individuals, but to groups. One may indeed, I think, hold that any doctrine which has gained a group, or a community has in it some experimental truth and value however small. And what is true of doctrine is also in measure true of institutions, and rites and forms of religious life or devotion; they are group crystallisations of experience which have approved themselves for a greater or less space of time to a larger or smaller community. There is a soul in a doctrine and in religious form generally as well as a body, a spirit or essence or experimental reality in addition to the temporary and limited forms in which it expresses itself (cf. the Barthian phrase, "True in the order of grace and revelation"), and group approval cannot well be gained apart from this element of basic reality corroborated by present experience. Once this basis of experimental reality is lost the form loses it hold; even if it once stood for experimental truth, as soon as it ceases to have an experience value for those who by inheritance profess it, it begins to die.

But it may be argued that some common doctrines can have no experimental meaning or verification that, for example, the belief in a transcendent God beyond our senses is but a guess, beyond the power of experience to corroborate; or again, that the belief in a future life can, except for convinced spiritualists, have no experimental verification whatever. But doctrines mean little or nothing apart from their value in experience and one might point out that God stands for many elements in experience or with experimental associations, as already argued; for the felt unity, coherence and sanity of our cosmos as we seek by a seeming necessity of our nature to integrate it in thought; for the value and worthwhileness of life; for the satisfaction of our minds in a rational, coherent explanation of our lives which makes us at home in the universe; for the recognition of creative tensions, so obvious in life, as present in life's ultimate basis according to the doctrine of the Trinity; and so forth. This God satisfies our mind as an interpretation of experience which includes unity, kinship, value, coherence, and complexity; as a concise statement of the facts of the One and the All, and of the meaning of moral conflict and growth. Again, immortality stands in part for a justification of the ways of God to man i.e., a satisfaction of our emotional and intellectual cravings and activities regarding the meaning and end of life; and in part for our clear conviction of the value of personality and the urgency of human destiny; and as an answer to the hungers for more life and fuller, and for continuity of consciousness. Thus no one can very well deny that both the doctrine of God and that of immortality, whether justified or not, have their roots in experimental urges and cravings; and it is more probable that these cravings have some meaning and some fulfilment than that they have none, for nature's hungers bear some relation to nature's needs. I am not now concerned with the actual logical forms of our doctrines, but with their vital relationship to experimental factors at every point. Nothing even in thought lives on except in virtue of life and reality within it.

From the beginning of human religious development there has been experimental meaning in the crystallised teaching of religion in taboos and customs and religious formulae; and today Christian doctrines and rites and institutions and moral codes are but the more civilised and sublimated products of the same religious activity or crystallising, into formulae and institutions, the human interpretations of our experience of the universe and its parts in their action and reaction upon us. The experimental urge towards doctrine is universal in time and place for power and peace, as is the scientific urge towards definition and formula for factual truth and progress. But forms of statement easily pass out of date, as the interpretation, and power of interpretation, of experience change and improve; hence earlier doctrines need translation into the speech of today as surely as the Greek classics, for most people, need such translation in the sphere of literature. But at every point there is a direct relation between a man's experience and his attempt to state his religion; and all collective forms, such as dogma and doctrine and institution, have some clear relation, of a corporate or corroborated kind, in man's life. Social approval stamps upon a doctrine the seal of practical meaning and value; and it is for us today to seek and find the true soul of doctrine hidden behind forms often very repugnant or absurd or irrelevant to our own age. It is not well to throw away the words and formulae of the past which have represented life, till at least we can offer better; the redemption of the great words of religion is more important than the critical activity which demonstrates their unfortunate abuse. It may be necessary to get rid of them, but each great religious term is an achievement of ages and ought to be treated with respect and, where possible, used either in an improved sense or as a bridge to a better formulation.

In pursuing this subject I wish for the purpose of illustration to confine myself to the familiar words and doctrines of the Christian faith, and to take up in order the six great divisions of Christian theology: God, man, the person of Christ, the work of Christ, the Church, and the last things, in order to show how, in each division, the important Christian doctrines, universal or sectional, have their experimental basis and value, and that what they need is translation, in order that their true experimental meaning may be made clear and conserved. Only a few cases can be taken out of many, but I hope the cases will be sufficiently clear and numerous to establish my claim that all group-approved doctrine at least has a direct relation to experience and, when translated, a definite value for life.

In relation to the doctrine of God I do not intend to recapitulate what I have said in chapters I, II, VIII, IX and elsewhere, beyond re-emphasising the meaning of the doctrine of the unity of God as standing for the experimental factors, intellectual and aesthetic, which crave and recognise unity, coherence, kinship in life, as in nature; for the need of integration, the reality and unity of our values for organic living; and for the experiences of mystical consciousness, which come in so many diverse form. The standard conception of evil and the doctrine of a devil in like manner stand for the moral dualism of experience, operating between two poles of desire, impulsive and conceptual; that is, the devil is the crystallisation of the sense of a moral conflict between ideals and desire.

The doctrine of the Trinity, or Tri-unity of God, expresses experience, as a standing for a complex source for our complex world, and as representing the experiential truth of creative tensions between elements, recognised as good in themselves, yet according to our measures, incommensurable. All life is the proceeding of a third from two elements which are in experiential opposition. In man there is a creative element of desire or craving, a limiting and directing element of individual discrimination and a practical or final element of integration and action - spirit, mind and body; Thus in God we believe in a Creator Father, in an incarnate (or limited) Son who in Logos or Mind - the characteristic of individual man - and in an integrating activity of social life which flows from them, seen in the Church and spoken of as the Holy Spirit, the one Spirit which proceeded from eternity and from history, from Father and from Son, and which integrates individuals into a church or body or organism, so that, through the many, unity returns in a richer unity by that Spirit "through whom we are builded together to be a habitation of God". In Gethsemane we see the opposition of the creative moral conflict - not my will but Thine - and, by the subordination of the Son to the Father, is achieved the witness of the Cross, the victory over death and the baptism of Pentecost, when all the disciples, of one mind in one place, were integrated by the Spirit of God into a militant society, destined to leaven and ultimately in some sense to assimilate the human race. And it is easy to point out the fundamental threefoldness of our life e.g., in desire, in system and in the actual resultant life which flows from them; i.e., desire begets system (as a means to its own fulfilment), and from the interactions of desire and system progressively proceed actual life and true society. But I must pass on, for I wish at this point to say that my purpose in this chapter is not to state adequately the metaphysical, or ontological, or specific and full meanings of Christian doctrines, but their general and psychological meanings for man's own life, which are real and yet not complete. For example, the divinity of Christ has both its specific or unique meaning and its general or universal meaning; it is with the latter meanings that I am concerned in this chapter.

I pass on to the doctrine of man. Here in the doctrine of the Fall we have recognised the backward pull both of heredity and of human institutions; in the doctrine of sin the moral conflict between desire and ideals and its failure; in the doctrine of the divine image in man the recognition of the importance of the self and of self-regard as the moral basis for the worth of Personality and for an independent adult ethic; and in the orthodox Augustinian view of grace and freewill a remarkable corroboration of the newer and better psychology of experience, which recognises that man is moved from within and that the power of moral freedom is positive and good, i.e., that goodness is freedom and sin a bondage. The doctrine of the election of Israel generalised is the doctrine of the cosmic significance of every people, as each has its own contribution to make to the human race and to the life or glory of God; the doctrine of the Messiah generalised is the doctrine of the cosmic significance of every human soul as a child of God, and so of the worth of the human individual. The doctrine of the person of Christ generalised is the doctrine of the ideal man, for, even though the categories here used are those of human and divine, yet *ex hypothosi* the human is in the image of the divine, and so human and divine represent but different stages of the manifestation of the life of God - the logos, the eternal Son of God, is the light that lighteth every man. In the early church the doctrine of the person of Christ was the chief controversy, lasting as it did for nearly eight centuries; but at every stage it can be generalised as an ideal doctrine of man as God sees him and purposes him to become. At Nicea,

Christ's consubstantiality with God is proclaimed, to be followed at Constantinople, Ephesus and Chalcedon by the proclamation of His consubstantiality with man; and the whole doctrine of two natures in one person, or two foci of spiritual significance in one life, is a "limit" statement of the experience of duality in every man who has in him the pull of the lower and the higher, the past human and the future divine, that which has been by heredity and that which may be or is to be by faith.

The definition of Chalcedon marks the end of the first stage of the controversy, Psychologically, that definition was and is puzzling in some respects, particularly as the tendency was - especially in the Roman or Western church to which our civilisation belongs - to treat human and divine as opposed, not as akin; though in the true Greek theology of the Logos no doubt, and even later, the human is itself in the image of the Logos, its antitype or prototype, who is Himself the image of God. At any rate, as has been well said, the victory of Athanasius at Nicea, for Christ as consubstantial with God, and the victory of Constantinople and Chalcedon, for Christ as also consubstantial with man, was "a victory for the deeper soul within every man's soul". The definition at bottom stands for the reality and meaning of moral experience as a universe process with a universe meaning, or, as Athanasius expressed the purpose of the Incarnation, (of the limitation of God in Jesus), "that man might become God". But Chalcedon was not the end of the discussion in the early church, though it marks the close of the most important phase of the dialectic. The question was almost at once raised - "if there are two natures in the divine man, Jesus Christ, are there two centres of personality in the one person - are there two personal energies, are there two wills?" And after a long and rather tedious controversy of little merit it was adopted as the orthodox view that Christ had two wills, not one only, a divine and a human though the word "will" in that age only meant a desire centre; it did not imply the acting personality in the modern sense of the word. Thus, it was orthodox to believe that in Christ were two centres of desire, a lower and higher, though these were in His case *ex hypothesi* in harmony.

But this is surely true in its measure of our own experience, if we leave the actual terms human and divine out of account; in each of us is a conflict, broadly speaking, between two centres of desire, a more animal and a more spiritual and here again we see how early church Christology is related to the problem of the ordinary nature of man; and as the Logos theology made this relation of Christ to all men an explicit one, so we are not unjustified in pointing out the broad human implications of Christological doctrine even in that day. But was the personality in question equally a possession of both centres, the lower and the higher, or did it belong to one rather than the other? The orthodox Dyothelate definition of Christ as possessing two wills was modified at this point in such a way that the final orthodox doctrine of the first millennium proclaimed that His personality belonged to the higher rather than the lower; not as excluding the lower from any part in it, yet in two clear ways; in the first place the human will is recognised as subject to the divine, and in the second place the humanity of Christ, while not regarded as impersonal, is regarded as en-personal (the word is actually "enhypostatic"), or possessing personality only *in* the divine. This point may seem very academic and unimportant, but I think it is really important, not merely as regards Christ but as regards all men; for the doctrine of Christ is the doctrine of ideal humanity, and in man personality, while it cannot be denied to the lower nature, belongs essentially to the higher, which is in the image of God, that is, to the spiritual, and to the lower only in and through the spiritual, i.e., God is Personality (cf. Lotze) and our growth in personality is our growth upwards toward God.

This is a point to which we come again in history in the orthodox Augustinian view, that the will is in itself essentially good, and that evil choice is not freedom but bondage. It is in virtue of our higher and more divine nature, which differentiates us from the other animals, that we are personal; and, while all in us is personal, through association with, and control by, the spiritual, yet our personality belongs to the higher and diviner element in us, and true freedom must mean the freedom of this better self, i.e., it consists in goodness and an approximation to God as revealed in Jesus, the ideal man of our faith. For a discussion of many similar points, as elucidating the relation of doctrine and experience, I might refer readers, who wish to go farther into my views than the present study permits, to my book, "The Changing Vesture of the Faith", in which I deal with many cases of psychological influence upon Christian forms which I shall not touch upon in this volume.

Before I pass to the doctrine of the Atonement, or work of Christ, I wish to speak of one other relevant matter bearing upon the person of Christ, viz., the unique divinity of Christ. It is common today to speak of the divinity of man; and I have myself used the phrase and it is, I think, rightly so used; but is this all there is in our doctrine of Christ's divinity? Is there no doctrine of a unique divinity of Christ or, in the more explicit phrase, of deity in Jesus of Nazareth? One must be careful to avoid negatives and exclusive statements of Christian doctrines; but there are some points of importance to be made here as justifying the unique and more exclusive form of the doctrine in its relation to Christ. I have dealt only with generalisations or universal meanings of doctrine in the preceding pages; but it often has also its particular meanings, as in the election of Israel, i.e., to be the world's teacher of religion, or in the unique Messiahship and divinity of Jesus. In the first place, Jesus came in the fullness of the times: His coming was the climax of a divine purpose and of a historical preparation; it was a critical or unique moment. In the second place his life is creative for our race as other lives are not, and creation is the work and meaning of deity; he is the beginning of a new creation, a social and integrated humanity founded on Him and foreshadowed in the early Christian church. And in the third place, His person is central or focal for our race, and, as the years pass, is becoming not less but more so, and that this person, not of a trained philosopher, or statesman, but of a "working man". Historical purposiveness, creative power and focal meaning all make the divinity of Christ a unique and particular, as well as a general human, conception. He did make sonship to God real and possible for all men; but, in a unique sense, historically and experimentally He is the Son of God, the manifestation in time of the Eternal Son as a creative historical act of God. No matter how high we may rise in our pursuit of the destiny and relationships He made possible for man, it is on His shoulders we shall have climbed; in the creative life of Christian history his place remains unique and unchallenged. I mention this point so fully as a caution against assuming that general meanings are all. As general providence cannot rule out particular providence, or strategy rule out tactics, so general meanings of doctrine do not exhaust the meanings of doctrine; in doctrine there are ontological and metaphysical meanings as well as psychological and relative.

I turn next to the Christian doctrine of Atonement and the word of Christ. Dr Dennoy in his last book on the Atonement begins with a chapter on its experimental basis, which he describes as concerned with the strain or tension between man and his environment and with the changing of that strain or discord into a harmony, and the environment into an ally instead of a foe; and this he calls reconciliation or atonement. And the most obvious meaning of Atonement for the modern psychologist in this very one, viz, integration or the making one of diverse or conflicting elements in the soul, which thus attains peace, sanity and power. This is the fundamental meaning of the Atonement, and it is experimental. Theories of the Atonement have been expressions of the ways in which men have found this reconciliation or integration, and these theories have followed the experimental interests of their age, the Greek concerned chiefly with the fear of death and the achievement of life and hope, the Latin or Roman with sin, moral obligation, punishment, and the achievement of forgiveness. The Anselmic doctrine is cast in the mould of contemporary feudalism, the Reformation doctrine in that of the new interest in legal codes which followed the abandonment of canon law. Further the three characteristic Protestant doctrines of Atonement, the Calvinistic doctrine of penal substitution, the Arminian governmental doctrine, and the Socinian emphasis on a free forgiveness upon repentance, with atonement by moral attraction, are but crystallisations in theological terms of the three theories of punishment, the retributive, the deterrent and the remedial all prime concerns of that juridical age.

All theories of the work of Christ have followed the lines of the emotional experience of deliverance and its conceptual interpretation in terms of current social theory and no theory, which has lived at all, is without its basis and meaning for human experience, whether it be for instance the doctrine of a ransom paid to Satan (for it *is* sin or evil in the hearts of men which demands a Cross, which exacts death and suffering as the price of redemption), or the doctrine of Christ as inspiration and example (for inspiration is a power which changes life and releases in man new desires after good). All living theories, even the most immoral in appearance, have their experimental meanings; and sometimes, the less ethical in form the theory, the more deeply it represents actual experience, so difficult is it to synthesise our values and the facts of life. This problem of integration is the problem of Atonement; and it is the fundamental problem of religion and of ethics. Its theories are as many as the lines of approach have been historically diverse, but all theories that have won a group-acceptance go back to an experience which is more than individual fantasy or subjective delusion, back to something in religious life which has its roots in reality.

As regards the doctrines of the Church or the divine society, here we come to the doctrine of an ideal humanity represented in a society, built upon the Old Testament development, or revelation, and the work of Christ, which is characteristically and potentially universal. The true Church is the integration of mankind, the integration of nations, classes, types and interests in the true social ideal, or home, of the Kingdom of God or of all good. Such is the meaning of the Holy Spirit, too, viz, as the soul and unifying force of this movement; this is the Spirit of social living, of love, humility, sincerity and wisdom, found historically in Jesus, but become the soul or spirit of society, which is potentially all inclusive and which has universalized in a collective self-expression, however imperfectly as yet, the personal revelation of God and of the Kingdom revealed in and through Jesus. The Church is the body of which the Holy Spirit is the soul, and it is slowly leavening and integrating all human life in and into the true universal community of God, which is ideally coterminous with the human race at least. Pentecost is the story of the first conscious social integration of the disciples of Jesus, and fellowship, with joy and power, is the characteristic note of the experience. Thus the Church is accomplishing the work of social integration by the enrichment of personality and the lowering of barriers between man and God and between man and man; it is a body with many members, different, yet each contributing its share, a body which, however imperfectly, is nevertheless entrusted with, and capable of, the mission of giving a soul to the growing modern political and economic integration of mankind, so that it shall be successful and permanent, a true kingdom of truth and beauty and goodness with the healthy ambitions of service and contribution.

Adult Baptism has the psychological values of a break, publicly made with the old life, a pledge to accept the new Christian life, its pattern and demand, and the forming of a fellowship of like minds. The rite of Infant Baptism, again, stands not only for the dedication of children to God and the acceptance of a covenant responsibility to give them in training our best, but it represents the experimental fact of the divine grace as present with us before consciousness, prevenient as well as cooperant, and as offered to us in all the experience of life. The Catholic doctrine of the Mass brings into effective moral opposition the sin of the sinner in confession and the cost to God of our salvation in the passion of God - it preaches the truths of grace and cost on God's side, and of repentance and gratitude as our normal response. The Protestant rite of Communion at bottom means what it meant for the early Christians, a communion of life with God and one another, a sharing or fellowship symbolised in the real physical food of the day *sacramentally* used, (though used *normally* in the Agape in the same early context), a fellowship which should issue in a real sharing of the wealth and opportunities and other blessings of life - though unfortunately it often does not. Experimentally, then, the so-called means of grace of the Church, in book and symbols and forms of worship, have real individual social values, if truly used and appreciated.

When we come to the doctrine of the last things we come to wide controversies of a serious kind over Heaven and Hell, Judgment, the Second Advent, Immortality and Final Destinies. But at least we may say that these doctrines stand for the values and the purposiveness of the cosmic teleological and human process. The Church has never been committed in any agreed and explicit way to a doctrine of final destinies as between eternal punishment, conditional immortality and universal restoration; but at least the doctrine of an eternal hell, however morally difficult, has always stood the dignity of the human soul and urgency of goodness, while the other beliefs, involved as alternatives were attempts to maintain an ethical doctrine of God, as an experimental necessity for a true trust in our moral values as eternal and permanent. The conceptions of rewards and punishment correspond to the moral sense and fitness of things, however imperfectly expressed; the sense that goodness must issue in blessing and evil in a curse, even if today we should prefer to say that the good man becomes better by his goodness and benefits the world thereby, while the evil man puts himself into bondage and pushes the world backwards by his evil, rather than to state the experimental facts in terms that savour of bribery and revenge. But ethical or unethical in our human statement, the fact of heaven and hell stands, both as a fact of mental states here and now, and as a statement of the ultimate tendencies of different kinds of moral life.

Immortality is a belief which springs from many roots - the craving for it which is not adequately met by denying its validity, any more than the craving for food could be, the desire to ethicise and justify our conception of God as an integration of values which we can trust, the desire to maintain still relationships or friendships of value with God and man which we have enjoyed; the urgent sense of the value of life and of the permanent or eternal existence of certain values which both in themselves and in relationships, we feel, have some innate principle of conservation such as we express in our doctrine of a future life; intimations, again, and even personal experiences, of contest with those who have been taken from us by death; and generally the finding of purpose and significance in mystical worths, in human relations, and in the powerful sense of the ego as a focus of the universe, which the new relational philosophy of Einstein has enormously enhanced as an argument. The doctrine of a Second Coming we see today as true of a process of divine development through historical crisis, whatever its value as a doctrine of final consummation; though even that may have some sort of value, too, of direction, if not of end. Judgment we see as a present activity of the mind and of society; we *are* judging ourselves, and history *is* judging the race, by a God who is immanent in the soul and in human social development. However crude and unsatisfactory our conceptions of a future life and its accompaniments may be, they have at least an experimental basis of a very strong kind in the sense of personal significance, of racial purpose, and of the permanence or conservation of value. Wells and Shaw and their like today have shown us that theology, like religion, is an essential of a thinking man, and that, if the Church does not satisfy men in this respect, then man must handle and restate the problems and their probable solutions for themselves and their age (and in "The Dream" Wells honestly realised at last the difficulty of finding purpose in life without some conception of personal immortality).

The past history of human thought has owed much to the power of reasoning the past in words and to the power of defining experience more and more correctly. And Christian theology *should* be a growingly true definition of actual experience. As the grub becomes the insect, so living thought must grow and change; but the life principle and its fundamental forces and realities remain substantially the same, however the outer form may change. Even in its earliest form as mythology, doctrine was not a mere dream of men, but, like the dream in modern theory, a precipitate of human experience. Early myths may be fairy tales, and even the orthodoxy of today may often be a fairy tale; but, as Mr Chesterton has reminded us in "Orthodoxy", in his chapter on "The Ethics of Elfland" fairy tales are in fact forms of moral teaching and embodiments of a religious faith. Columbus discovered America because he dreamt of it; but it was not the America of his dream, yet his dream helped him to his great achievement. And living religion at its worst always has in it the promise of better things; it has roots of peace and power and of individual and social integration, and so of sanity and well-being. Life at every stage has been a goodly thing relative to its epoch, but its promise has so far been always greater than its power; yet religion is the power or soul in virtue of which, by myths or dreams or faiths or revelation, and by venture, the world is becoming progressively better and life richer and more valuable.

Doctrine, like all the systematisation of formulae, has undoubtedly tended, and especially in religion, to stagnation and to its form becoming more and more out of touch with actual life; but, in its origin and basis thought, it is the expression of experimental facts and values; and therefore, if a doctrine be fairly translated into our own native idiom, it should in almost every case have a real meaning and value for our own lives. Doctrine springs out of need and it embodies in some measure results; and both need and results are actual things. Much of the earliest religion had to do with food and occupation, and even yet the primary needs and activities of life are part of its true concern. The suggestion value of doctrine, both as Scripture and as creed, is tremendous, and the same applies to the institutions of religion.

The Bible, Sunday, the Catechisms, the Prayer Book, the Sacraments, the priesthood or ministry, and, in general, the forms of religious belief and practice, have sprung out of experimental needs, and have brought in some degree power and peace with them. One might develop this subject at very considerable length, but I think I have said enough to shew the direct relation of doctrine to life, and the true and basic value of doctrine as registering religious experience both individual and collective. Our main business, then, in doctrine ought to be, not rejection, but translation into our own tongue and idiom, that so we might achieve social and universal understanding and the recognition of true religious experience as registering our kinship with one another and with God, and so promoting our personal social and ultimate integration with all that is living and all that is good.

CHAPTER XVII

Summary and Conclusion

I have reached the end of this study of the religious experience, its nature and validity and its form and problems, upon which I set out by request. I have not dealt with all possible or even all the important problems; but I feel I have taken long enough over my journey, and those who wish to go farther afield, or to go more deeply into matters dealt with in the preceding pages, will find at the end of this volume a fairly comprehensive bibliography from which they will be able to select further reading. As examples of subjects of importance not dealt with, I might mention, for example, sex; the varying historical levels of religious experience; the instinct for, and the form of, worship and the whole subject of the irrational in religion; and, again, faith, or spiritual healing. Of sex I would say a few words. There is no doubt that some persons, especially women, have found in religion a self-completion of a sexual kind, and there can be little doubt that sex is actually one root of religious feeling and of its creative achievements. Nuns have professed a kind of sex satisfaction in being brides of Christ, and the language of the founder of the cult of the Sacred Heart was quite frankly erotic in the description of her experience of ecstasy. One must here allow something in this matter for the influence of the Song of Songs, now frankly recognised as a collection of wedding songs, but interpreted so prevalently, till recently, of Jehovah and His people, or of Christ and the Church; but the impulse goes deeper, and religion has been one form in which the sex instinct has been sublimated. Among modern theologians Karl Barth seems to have recognised sex as ontologically significant, as did also many of the early Gnostics, and not necessarily in error. For further discussion of this subject vide Chouless, Crichton Miller, opera citt.

Again, one might have emphasised the levels or stages of religious experience in legalism, rationalism, mysticism, and the like. There are stages and levels in child and adolescent religious growth which are normal, but even in adult religious history one can trace similar levels, and especially these three - legalism, rationalism, and mysticism - and perhaps usually, though not always, in that order. Legalism is of course the childlike or primitive stage of obedience to external authority, with a religion of action, and it naturally comes first, the religion of the nursery. Rationalism may come second, or mysticism, the religion of thought or that of feeling, but generally I think the completion of religious experience in *feeling* comes last, as God passes from inference to immediate reality. One cannot lay this down as a rule, but in the greater creative spirits, in Hosea and Paul, in Alghasali, and Francis and Luther, the mystic stage seems to have been last and to have come to the climax and completion of effort in seeking to know and to do God's will. So, it was with Paul undoubtedly, and so it was certainly with Alghasali, the greatest of Islam's orthodox theologians. It is natural that the effort and process of the religious conflict should be finally consummated and integrated in power and assurance by an immediate emotional experience of communion with God, pursued so far in the twilight but now seen and felt as light and life and love. And, as there are different levels of development, so there is different food for these levels, and the food of one may in measure be useless or dangerous or irrelevant for another. Life in religion, or elsewhere, is relative in some degree at all stages of growth.

Evolution gives us a ladder of progress with many rungs, subhuman and human. Even in the animals there is some kind of moral evolution, as Huxley has pointed out; for example, the conflict between the giant saurians and the smaller mammals was in part decided by love, i.e., by the parental care of the mammals for their offspring. And in human life there are various stages of development in religious progress, racial and individual, as egoism passes into altruism or true social living. Legalism is based on fear and the herd instinct, which seeks to maintain order and discipline; and primitive religion in the race and the individual is such - obedience. The four stages given by Paterson as the historical ways of salvation are —

(1) the way of compulsion - magic
(2) the way of ingratiation - sacrifice and prayer
(3) the way of obedience - legalism, the ways of the child and
(4) the way of trust - the way of the adult.

There are dregs of the former two still in our religion, especially in our ideas and practice of prayer; but for most of us today religious experience has legalism as its first serious stage - the child stage of authority - while the way of trust may stand for rationalism (venture upon hypothesis), or for mysticism (venture upon feeling), or for both; i.e., I think we might list five rather than four ways of salvation. Legalism tends to dualism and a felt independence of God, and so to pride; it is moral and not ethical, if I may make the distinction. Rationalism means a dependence upon God for truth, a partial surrender in sincerity of mind but not yet of emotion. It is intellectual and cold, and may be called ethical, but not religious in the truest sense. Mysticism is the religion of absolute and conscious surrender and dependence, expressing itself in vision, or intuition or ecstasy, and felt communion with God. The great mystic is Jesus Himself; but mysticism is only truly healthy as it is built upon the foundations of obedience and sincerity as the Gospel followed the Law. It is then spontaneous, whole, integrated, independent only through the consciousness of dependence; it is then emotionally sincere and in the fullest sense religious. But a true religious life must be one of balance and proportion, in which all three elements of emotion, thought and will are at one, a harmony of spirit, mind and body. Such is the true and full Christian experience for such was the experience of Christ its original and exemplar – the author and finisher of the life of faith (Hebrews 12:2).

As regards worship and the forms of devotion, I have given little time to the new study of reverence and awe and the now common conception of the irrational which Otte popularized and which has its values for all discussion of religious experience; personally, I should prefer to speak of aesthetic or non-rational factors rather than of irrational. One must appreciate these feeling factors, yet one dare not depreciate the place of rational judgment, as the habit of some is. However, I have no time nor space to spend here on this question. Finally, of faith healing or spiritual healing I have said very little; the subject is not very relevant to my argument, but would-be students will find the works quoted later, by Hadfield, Baudouin, Jackson and Salisbury, Crichton Miller, Micklem, Barry, Pym, Weatherhead and others, of great help, and Pratt's discussion of the faith state. The literature on this subject alone of recent times, academic, practical, expert and quack, is enormous; and no one will find difficulty in getting hold of books upon it.

Let me now sum up and conclude this study of religious experience as to its nature, validity, forms, and problems. Book One deals with the nature of the religious experience itself. In the first chapter one have attempted to state the universality of religion in its primary elements, as having to do with the recognition of value or reality and the coordination of such experiences in a faith; in chapter two I state the characteristic or specific quality of religious experience, as found in a universe sense, as a finding of unity in the totality of experience; and the process of religious development, therefore, considered either in the individual or the race, as a process of progressive integration, necessary, in a moving world like ours, both for sanity of mind and for the well-being of society. In these two first chapters I also adopt the view that religion as a historical phenomenon is to be found in the consciousness and conservation and enhancing of social values; this follows logically the earlier points of the universality and integrating activity of religion, for man is by nature a member of society i.e., by the compulsion of his own genetic and instinctive life basis he must seek social values. His society may be considered as a larger or smaller group, but in actual fact, ultimately and potentially, it is the whole universe, of God; and the integration of society and of socially conditioned individuals seeking peace and sanity in their own minds, is the prime meaning and work of religion; and the term "God" is the only satisfactory symbol available for the description or interpretation of this experience. Religion thus is the finding and worship in service of God, or the unity of the totality of our experiences and relationships. In chapter three I point out the varieties of this universal religious experience - its intermittence, the diversity of the lines of development and the danger of standardization - and so prepare the way for the later discussion of religious development in the third book.

Book Two deals with the questions of the validity of the religious experience from the standpoint especially of modern psychological study and attacks. In chapters four to seven I attempt successively to meet the charges that religious experience is purely a subjective phenomenon or isolated individual fantasy, that it is the morbid product of a diseased mentality, that is a subjective delusion created by the wish that it should be true, and that it is a projection of ourselves as God, in other words, that God has no existence except as a shadow of our own minds. To these four charges I have answered in the first place that religious experience as experience is necessarily subjective in much of its content, but that it possesses as much objective meaning as we can fairly demand, and that its objective validity is proved by both the corroboration of other minds and its practical outcome in action. In the second place, that both the characteristic features and the fruits of religion show it to be not morbid but healthy in its normal meaning and effects, and that the more creative religious personalities have been the healthiest and the most effective for the health and sanity of others - in other words that religion is a statement or discovery of the laws of health of body, mind and spirit. In the third place, that the origination of an activity in part by our wishes does not condemn it, in as much as desire is the foundation of all good life, that, in fact, the relation of religious experience and beliefs to desire shews religion to be in line with the basic and creative forces of life, and that, whereas impotence is the mark of delusion, religion has the mark of power; illusion in some respect it has been, as all our interpretations of life are in some degree, but not delusion; it is relatively truer at every point of development than it is false. And in the fourth place, that, instead of religious experiences being a projection of ourselves upon the screen of our imaginations, it is much more in accordance with its facts, and their meaning and outcome to hold that through us God is projecting Himself in our experiences of meaning and value and unity and of all that is specifically religious in our lives; that a larger life than ours is working in and through us at every point, and that only such a theory of the transmission of God really accounts for human experience and ideals and progress. This leads me in chapter eight to sum up the lines of thought found in the earlier chapters as to the fact and experience of God by a fuller systematic exposition, so far as is relevant to my subject, of the specifically Christian doctrine of God, partly by recapitulation and partly by enlargement and addition. And this more theological statement of the conception of God I follow with a ninth chapter upon the experience of communion with God, or of definite felt contact of an immediate kind with the universe life, such that God passes from the stage of an inferential hypothesis to that of a matter of personal knowledge; this chapter forming a preparation for some later chapters in Book III, especially that upon mysticism.

In Book Three, on forms, I take up in successive chapters three main modes of religious experience, discussing the content of the experiences in question and the main difficulties, philosophical, psychological, and practical, which are raised therein. Thus, as regards prayer in chapter ten, I tabulate various theories or meanings of prayer, and discuss its validity and the chief difficulties it raises. In dealing with mysticism in chapter eleven I consider the two main forms, the greater and the lesser mysticism, their meaning and value, and the pathological or dangerous side of this experience or of allied experiences, especially some dangers associated with the revivalistic methods of Christian evangelism. As regards conversion, I deal in chapter twelve with the normal and abnormal forms of religious growth, with the statistical and scientific basis of the modern study; and with the main types of conversion known to us; and emphasise the supreme importance, however attained, of the vital central experience of decision and reorientation of life, and the need of a continual process of adjustment in a living religious experience. In chapter thirteen I deal with the experience or sense of the grace of God; with the usages of the term, and especially its reference to God's non-compulsive methods of enlisting our natures in His service by working in and through our desires, i.e., from within by persuasion and the release of love and joy so that we act freely and with consent or even enthusiasm; and I point out both the corollary of hope for all men and the need of a human ethic of grace. Asceticism and puritanism are also considered, the contrasts of law and grace, of faith and works; and the fundamental meaning of grace finally stressed as the self-giving of God to man, which should issue in the self-giving of men to God and their fellows.

Turning now to Book Four, the final book, on the problems of religious experience, in chapters fourteen and fifteen I discuss at some length the very complicated related questions of sin and freedom, though an adequate discussion of either would take more space than I can here afford. I attempt first to define, or at least describe, sin and guilt and some cognate terms, and to show the enormous difference produced in one's view by the newer analytical psychology of change and relativity and a genetic biology; I deal with sin as anti-social, regressive and disruptive, and with goodness as social, integrating and progressive; and in the latter part of the same chapter I attempt to analyse, account for and evaluate the experiences we group together under the term "conscience". In the chapter on freedom, I try first to exhibit its ideal meaning as unimpeded self-expression, unimpeded, that is, by virtue of an integration of individual and social values and tendencies through knowledge and submission; then I proceed to discuss the problem of freedom in relation to the moral conflict, the riddle of free will, and the value and limitations of psychical determinism. I admit here the great difficulty of synthesising the systematic and practically valuable hypothesis of an ordered and consistent analytical psychology on the one hand, and the creative experiences of freedom on the other; but, admitting both, I attempt to show how freedom works in and through system, that moral experience is systematic but not automatic, that determinism represents a system on which we can count, and freedom the power to rise above circumstances; and so together the determinism of adequately motivated action and the freedom of creative or emergent moral life offer us a gospel of hope in a knowledge of power and of the way to apply it.

In chapter sixteen I deal in a very outline way with the fundamental connection between doctrine and experience, in which chapter I attempt to show that all doctrine, which has had any measure of group approval, has had a soul as well as a body, i.e., has had, or has, a real experimental basis of facts and values, as well as a particular form of interpretation or expression, which it borrows from its age from the material then at hand for expressing the fundamental and vital faith or experience, which the doctrine in question, however inadequately, embodies; and, in this connection, I make a plea for translation rather than rejection of doctrine, i.e., for the attempt to express in our own language and ideas the facts, values and experiences, which have crystallized under the pressure of life and circumstances, into these forms, some not unattractive today, others repugnant, but all with value for the understanding of the human mind and its history, its conflicts and its problems.

Such is a brief summary of my argument. The views I have put forward may be classed by some as liberal or humanistic, as unduly optimistic, or unrealistic, or as weakly sentimental, but they represent religious truth as I see it and believe in it to-day while I am nearing the end of my official career as a theological teacher; and I leave judgment in the matter to the reader. God prosper what is true or helpful in them and overrule what is misleading or in error. And now a few words by way of farewell.

The conclusion of the whole matter is surely, in the first place, tolerance and sympathy, and recognition of the value of all genuine thought and experience for our understanding of the universe, and for our own life, individual and social, within it. Such a study should increase our sense of the solidarity of all human life and the common meaning of all human experience, and especially of all the critical divergent or valued experiences of men in the religious field. All things are relative in a real sense: what suits one man injures another; but all things have social meaning, for difference, as well as similarity, cements our social unity as members one of another and of the one body of Humanity. Another practical issue of this discussion is sincerity, that we should think honestly, that we should face frankly all our emotional urges and problems, that we should be humble enough to learn from anyone, and that we should be wise enough to keep life balanced and full, integrated or unified within our own minds, so far as we may, and integrated also within the larger whole of society so far, again, as we can effect that. We must prize all positive passion, love and value, and keep the door open to Life, which is God. We must seek to be our best, to live and let live, and to grant to others what we claim for ourselves. God made us different, and our difference is a considerable part of our value to Him and to humanity. So let us see sincerely with our own eyes, but not deny that others may see differently with theirs; and so let us grow together more and more, not by imitation, but by sincerity, humility, love and wisdom, by mutual contribution and service, giving and receiving as members of one family, striving after that one great society of mankind for which we are all in different ways looking and working, the true Kingdom of God and of all good, the social integration of all that has worth and meaning and power for a true, progressive and purposeful life, to the eternal glory of the one God, who is Love and Truth and Beauty.

FINIS.

Suggested list of books for further reading

In the compilation of the list which follows I have had the advice of colleagues. The literature available is now enormous, and the following books are chosen for the most part as bearing specifically, or in measure, upon the subject of the psychology of religion or its environs. I do not in every case stand over the views expressed by the writers, many of whom, in any case, differ among themselves, while some are professedly non-Christian.

Books of special importance are asterisked (about 20 in all).

A. The psychology of religion

Here we must mention the three pioneer books which are still worthy of careful study -

*Starbuck:	The Psychology of Religion
*Coe:	The Spiritual Life
*W. James:	The Varieties of Religious Experience

The following books are also cordially recommended -

*Ames:	The Psychology of Religious Experiences
*Pratt:	The Religious Consciousness
	The Psychology of Religious Belief
*Thouless:	An Introduction to the Psychology of Religion
*Macmurray:	The Structure of Religious Experience

Specifically Christian books are -

*Balmforth:	Is Religious Experience an Illusion?
Barry:	Christianity and Psychology
Rouse and Miller:	The Psychological Processes of Religious Experience
Pym:	Psychology and the Christian Life
	More Psychology and the Christian Life
Barry:	Christianity and the Christian Life

B. The philosophy of religion

*Wright:	A Student's Philosophy of Religion
Galloway:	The Philosophy of Religion
Martineau:	A Study of Religion
*Brightman:	A Philosophy of Religion
*Paterson:	The Nature of Religion and other works
Matthews:	Studies in Christian Philosophy
E. Brunner:	The Philosophy of Religion
Fulton:	Nature and God

C. The history of doctrine

Moore:	A History of Religion (2 vols.)
Harmack:	The History of Dogma (7 vols)
*Orr:	The Progress of Dogma
Paterson:	The Rule of Faith
Fisher:	The History of Christian Doctrine

D. Other books on topics of importance dealt with in this book

*Catskell:	Psychology and the Religious Quest
G.L. Dickinson:	Religion and Immortality; Religion - a Forecast; and other works
E. Carpenter:	Comparative Religion
N. Micklem:	Religion (HUL)
Brown:	Personality and Religion; The Idea of Immortality
Pringle Patterson:	The Idea of God.
*Sorley:	Moral Values and the Idea of God
C. J. Webb:	God and Personality
Wingfield-Stratford:	Facing Reality; and other works
*Caldecott and Mackintosh:	Selections from the Literature of Theism
Edmond Holmes:	The Creed of Christ
D. S. Cairns:	A Faith that Rebels
The Walker Trust Essays on Prayer, edited by W. P. Paterson.	
W. Temple:	The Realm of Personality; and other works
*McNeile Dixon:	The Human Situation
Oman:	Grace and Personality
	The Problem of Order and Freedom

Underhill:	The Mystic Way; and other books
Hennessey:	The Coming Phase of Religion
Inge:	Studies in Mysticism; The Future of Faith; and other books
G. B. Shaw:	Preface to "St Joan"; "The Showing up of Blanco Posnet"; "Androcles and the Lion"; and other plays
*Hadfield:	Psychology and Morals; and various articles.
Crichton Millar:	The New Psychology and the Preacher; and other works
*McDougall:	Social Psychology; and other works
Willdon Carr:	The Problem of Free Will
Holt:	The Freudian Wish
John Macmurray:	The Clue to History; Creative Freedom; and other works
Rashdell:	Conscience and Christ
G. Archibald:	The Modern Sunday School
Tennant:	The Christian Doctrine of Sin
*Otto:	The Idea of the Holy
Joad:	God and Evil: Decadence; The Recovery of Belief
Sargant:	Battle for the Mind
Hecker:	Religion (semi-Marxist)
Bethune-Baker:	The Way of Modernism
Bernard Lucas:	The Faith of a Christian
H. G. Wells:	The Undying Fire; God the Invisible King; etc

and for those who wish to know more of my own views -

J. E. Davey:	The Changing Vesture of the Faith
	Our Faith in God through Jesus Christ

E. On modern psychology generally, one may mention

McDougall:	Psychology (HUL)
*Tansley:	The New Psychology
Hobhouse:	Mind in Evolution
Harvey Robinson:	The Making of Mind
Wingfield - Stratford:	The Reconstruction of Mind; etc
Jackson and Salisbury:	Outwitting our Nerves
Adler:	Individual Psychology
Freud:	The Psychopathology of Everyday Life; The Future of an Illusion: and other works
Shand:	The Foundations of Character
Spurr:	The New Psychology and the Christian Faith
Jung:	Psychological Types
Groddeck:	The Book of the It
Karen Horney:	Psychoanalysis; etc
A.J. Neill:	The Problem Child; and many other books
Baudouin:	Suggestion and Auto-suggestion; Psychoanalysis
Munn:	Psychology
Thouless:	General and Social Psychology

Lightning Source UK Ltd.
Milton Keynes UK
UKHW011101011021
391459UK00003B/24/J